Portraits of Power

Ohio Politics

SERIES ON OHIO POLITICS

Abe Zaidan, with John C. Green, *Portraits of Power: Ohio and National Politics, 1964–2004*

Portraits of Power

Ohio and National Politics, 1964–2004

Abe Zaidan, with John C. Green

The University of Akron Press
Akron, Ohio

First edition 2007
Manufactured in the United States of America
11 10 09 08 07 5 4 3 2 1

All inquiries and permissions requests should be addressed to the publisher,
The University of Akron Press, Akron, OH 44325–1703

LIBRARY OF CONGRESS CATALOGING-IN-PUBLICATION DATA
Zaidan, Abe.
Portraits of power : Ohio and national politics, 1964-2004 / Abe Zaidan, with John C. Green. —1st ed.
p. cm. — (Series on law, politics, and society)
Includes bibliographical references and index.
ISBN 978-1-931968-45-4 (cloth : alk. paper) — ISBN 978-1-931968-46-1 (pbk. : alk. paper)
1. Ohio—Politics and government—1951- 2. United States—Politics and government—1945-1989. 3. United States—Politics and government—1989- 4. Politicians—Ohio—Biography—Miscellanea. 5. Politicians—United States—Biography—Miscellanea. I. Green, John Clifford, 1953- II. Title.
F496.2.Z35 2007
977.1'043—dc22

2006100764

The paper used in this publication meets the minimum requirements of American National Standard for Information Sciences—Permanence of Paper for Printed Library Materials, ANSI Z39.48—1984. ∞

Table of Contents

III. The Politics of Transition, 1977–1980

IV. Turn to the Right, 1981–2004

Foreword

For more than forty years, Abe Zaidan has fished the waters of Ohio politics, from the swirling eddies of Cleveland and Cincinnati to the quiet backwaters of small communities along the great stream that gives the state its name. It is no exaggeration to say that hardly any of the state's biggest political fish have eluded his net or dodged the sting of his barbed gaff.

Most of his trophies are suitably mounted in the collection of columns, news stories, and profiles contained in this anthology of his works, the life record not only of a skilled journalist but also of a social critic and commentator whose values infuse his writing. As a newspaperman myself, whose own career paralleled in time and often place that of Zaidan's, I can say without hesitation that he is the envy of his contemporaries both in terms of his reportorial talent and of his elegant and incisive way of making words that touch the mind and the viscera of readers.

Perhaps most remarkable, as one samples the writings in this collection, is the professional detachment he brings to the treatment of his subjects. He writes about politics, that most partisan of human activities, with balance and a sense of fair play that belies his own deeply felt ideological preferences. At his core, he is liberal-minded, a devout believer in the power of democratic government to arrange public priorities in ways, as the legendary journalist H. L. Mencken put it, that "comfort the afflicted and afflict the comfortable." He is an internationalist, not an isolationist. He believes in diplomacy rather than war; in spreading wealth rather than concentrating it; in preserving the environment rather than mindlessly exploiting it. Yet, though these values underlie his assumptions about proper political behavior, Zaidan largely remains faithful to the journalist's creed of examining all sides of disputes and of keeping an ear tuned to all pleas and advocates.

For him, politics, as he wrote in 1964 in a column for *The Commentator*, a muckraking reformist magazine in Columbus, is an endless continuum, with "no beginning, middle or end." The political process "is continuous because government is continuous." And one might add, as one looks back on his career as a columnist and reporter for the *Akron Beacon Journal* and the *Cleveland Plain Dealer,* that his accounts of the adventures and hijinks of prominent Ohio politicians provided an ample store of snapshots for future historians to sift.

Over the years, Zaidan's readers were treated not only to his perceptive analyses of political trends and events. (His capacity for predicting the outcome of close races was spooky.) Also threading through his works was a wry sense of humor that signaled to readers his private view that what a politician says is probably hokum, no matter how authentic it sounds at the moment. In writing about the fractured English spoken by the popular Governor James A. Rhodes, Zaidan amusedly observed: "Although Jim Rhodes's syntax would come off second best in a showdown with Professor Backwards, he was in fact a skillful orator. Often what he said didn't make much sense, but the believers found it reassuring nonetheless precisely because of the beguilingly primitive way he said it."

The idiosyncratic Rhodes was one of Zaidan's favorite targets, but his arrows did not spare Democrats. The late Senator Frank Lausche, for instance, after a postspeech encounter with Zaidan, who asked why the senator was ducking the press during a reelection campaign, threatened to sic the sheriff on him.

Of all the political figures that Zaidan covered over four decades, one of his favorites was former Ohio and National Republican chairman Ray C. Bliss. There is a poignant interview with Bliss, which appeared in the *Beacon Journal*, in this collection. And it demonstrates why Zaidan, though miles away philosophically from Bliss, respected the Akron native as a down-to-earth, straight-shooting, honorable practitioner of the world's second oldest profession.

In reprising a political writer's works over a long period, there is a tendency to bog down in nostalgia, in fond and humorous recollections of the larger-than-life characters, especially the occasional rascals, who seek or hold public office. Zaidan's contributions to this book reach beyond the nostalgic. As a chain of history, they are understandably missing some links. But as a collection of perceptive vignettes, as images of particular times and places and principal players, as the penetrating insights of an intelligent witness and adept correspondent, his writings cast a clarifying light on what Irish-American novelist Thomas Flanagan called "the tenants of time."

David Hess
Washington, D.C.

Preface

When John Green sat down at lunch with me in June 2003 to propose a book containing some of my earlier newspaper and magazine political columns, the idea was high flattery from one who has established national prominence as the widely quoted director of the Bliss Institute of Applied Politics at the University of Akron. John saw this project as the first book in a series of books on Ohio politics, aimed at explaining the political process in the Buckeye State.

Inasmuch as the columns were already written and sort of filed in boxes in the basement, there didn't appear to be much more involvement in the project on my part. But despite the fact that I have written four previous books, I am a newspaperman accustomed to deadlines and have a journalist's expectation of seeing his work published within a reasonable delay—say, no more than a day or two.

John patiently explained that it would take longer than that, perhaps even years. Well, here we are, several revisions later. Thanks to John's studied patience, we arrived at this point as friends with the project finally realized.

This book could not have been assembled without the help of the staff and students of the Bliss Institute. Of particular importance was the careful work and good cheer of Janet Bolois, who typed the columns into the computer and prepared the manuscript for publication. Important, too, was the cooperation of the staff of the *Akron Beacon Journal,* particularly Susan Kirkman, managing editor of multimedia and special projects, who sorted out some of the photos that appear in the book.

Special thanks is due to Elton Glaser, the interim director of the University of Akron Press, who quickly overcame the many delays when he moved into the job and presided over the book's birth, and to Amy Freels of the University of Akron Press, who supervised the book's production. The comments of two anonymous reviewers helped improve the manuscript; their time and comments were much appreciated.

Finally, a nod to my wife Nancy, who patiently put up with my scowls over delays and my appropriation of the computer for long hours. She recently was given her own laptop, so there will be far more domestic tranquility for the next book.

Abe Zaidan
Fairlawn, OH

About Abe Zaidan

Abe Zaidan was born in Johnstown, Pennsylvania, and grew up in the Western Pennsylvania coal-mining town of Mt. Pleasant. Following graduation in 1953 from the University of Illinois School of Journalism, he worked briefly as a newsman for WILL Radio in Champaign-Urbana, then entered the Air Force as a communications officer.

His first newspaper job upon his release from the Air Force was with the *LaPorte (Indiana) Herald-Argus*, where he was a reporter and arts columnist. He later worked for the *Columbus (Ohio) Citizen* and *Citizen-Journal*, as a reporter and theater/music critic before moving on as editor of a new public affairs magazine in Columbus, *The Commentator,* which won several awards, including the top magazine award from the National Conference of Christians and Jews for its progressive coverage of the civil rights movement in the 1960s.

He joined the *Akron Beacon Journal* in 1968 as a general assignment reporter with a strong focus on state and national politics. That led to his promotion; as the *Beacon Journal*'s political editor, he was a political columnist and supervising editor of staff coverage of presidential campaigns in Ohio, as well as at seven national conventions.

He was appointed metropolitan editor of the *Beacon Journal* in 1980 and then became a member of the paper's editorial board and columnist. In 1991, he joined the *Cleveland Plain Dealer* as a general assignment reporter and columnist, and resigned in 1998 to become an independent freelance writer.

During his newspaper years, he also worked as the Ohio correspondent for the *Washington Post*, which published more than two hundred of his articles over a fifteen-year span. He also was the political columnist for *Ohio Magazine* and later a columnist for *Northern Ohio Live* magazine. He has written numerous articles for magazines, and his columns, which were carried by the Knight-Ridder News Service, have appeared in many newspapers throughout the United States.

He has also authored five books, including a history of the Akron region. Among his awards is the John S. Knight Award for distinguished journalism from the Buckeye Chapter of the Society of Professional Journalists.

Abe Zaidan and his wife Nancy live in Fairlawn, Ohio. They have two sons.

An Age of Giants: Ohio Politics, 1964–2004

Abe Zaidan's forty-year journalism career spanned what might be called "an age of giants": a tumultuous era dominated by larger-than-life politicians. Among Zaidan's best writings are portraits of these giants. Ohio politicians and politics were the focus of Zaidan's work, and to understand Ohio politics is to understand American politics—a fact once again underscored by the results of the 2004 presidential election.

This book is a selection of Abe Zaidan's writings drawn from more than three thousand news stories, analyses, columns, and features written between 1964 and 2004. These specific essays were chosen because of the light they shed on this political era. They are literally the "first draft of history." Readers who lived through the age of giants will be transported back to critical junctures in their lives, while those who did not will have a better understanding of the forces that shaped their world.

On this last point, these portraits of power help explain the 2004 presidential election, when Ohio once again played a crucial role in electing the president. For those who were surprised that George W. Bush carried the Buckeye State, Zaidan shows that Republicans have long been a force in Ohio; moreover, conservatives of various kinds have been plentiful. And John Kerry's nearly successful campaign had roots in Ohio's fractious Democrats, including labor unions, liberal activists, and urban ethnics—all of whom Zaidan describes in vivid detail.

Evidence of the keenness of Zaidan's observations is that they affirm and complement the work of political scientists who have studied Ohio politics. A good example is the insight of John Fenton, who wrote about the "issueless" politics in Ohio in the mid-1960s, and Thomas Flinn, who explained the basis for the close, two-party competition that is a crucial feature of Buckeye politics. And more recently, Alexander Lamis and his colleagues have showed how the politics of the Buckeye State have become deeply polarized.[1] The corpus of Zaidan's work shows how fierce party competition transformed Ohio politics from issueless contests of personalities toward ideological warfare.

The basic organization of the book is chronological, with just a few exceptions for ease of presentation. What follows is a brief overview of the book, designed to sketch the big picture behind this gallery of specific portraits.

The 1960s Watershed, 1964–1970

The 1960s are widely recognized as a watershed decade in American politics, and this development in Ohio is described in some of Zaidan's earliest political writings. These essays chart the transformation of the Democratic Party and the conflicts among the varieties of liberalism at the center of this change. And they also cover the parallel change of the Republicans and conservatives.

Some of the political giants portrayed in this section were from the old order and some were about to create the new one. For instance, the reader will meet James A. Rhodes, a four-time governor of Ohio, a figure who stood tall even among giants, while a new collection of liberals and conservatives enter the fray. Carl Stokes, the first elected African American mayor of a major city (Cleveland), will stride across the political stage, while U.S. Senator Frank Lausche, a representative of the old order, takes a final bow. John Glenn and Howard Metzenbaum begin a long-running contest to represent the Buckeye State in the United States Senate.

The Politics of Turmoil, 1970–1976

The post-1964 political order suffered a mortal blow in the early 1970s with the combination of racial unrest, generational change, and the increasingly unpopular Vietnam War. The event that most symbolizes this turmoil was the shootings at Kent State University on May 4, 1970. Zaidan was part of the *Akron Beacon Journal*'s team that covered the event and its aftermath, for which the paper won a Pulitzer Prize in 1971.

One direct result of this turmoil was the nomination of Senator George McGovern, one of the "new liberals" of the era, as the Democratic presidential candidate in 1972. McGovern was defeated by the incumbent Richard Nixon in one of the largest landslides in American history. But misbehavior by the overzealous Nixon campaign produced the Watergate scandal, the resignation of President Nixon, a first in American history—and then the presidency of the first unelected occupant of the White House, President Gerald R. Ford. Ford, in turn, was replaced by Democrat Jimmy Carter, who (briefly) reassembled the Democratic coalition. In Ohio, this period saw the return of Rhodes to the governor's mansion, the revival of ethnic politics in Cleveland, and the renewal of the contest between Glenn and Metzenbaum for a seat in the U.S. Senate.

The Politics of Transition, 1977–1980

After the 1976 election, Ohio politics entered a period of transition as politicians began to adjust to the turmoil unleashed in the 1960s. The net result was the slow fading of the 1964 traditional Democratic coalition and the capture of the GOP by a vigorous conservative coalition.

Ethnic politics in the city of Cleveland were part of this transition with the rise of two new political giants, Dennis Kucinich and George Voinovich. A Democrat with a fierce populist streak, the diminutive "boy mayor" Kucinich presided over the decline of Cleveland, including its fiscal default, and only narrowly avoided being recalled by the voters. In many ways, the status of Cleveland symbolized the displacement of the old industrial cities from the center of national life. Kucinich has continued his maverick ways, most recently with his 2004 campaign for the Democratic presidential nomination. George Voinovich, an ethnic Republican with close ties to the city's corporate boardrooms, presided over Cleveland's slow financial recovery and its adjustment to the new world of suburban dominance. Such success would eventually make him governor of Ohio and a U.S. Senator. This era of transition ended with Ronald Reagan's election to the presidency.

Turn to the Right, 1981–2004

Beginning with the 1980 election, national politics took a sharp turn to the right as a vigorous conservative coalition took control of the GOP. The election of Ronald Reagan to the presidency twice, followed by the election of his vice president, George H.W. Bush, provided twelve years of Republican rule. The Democratic coalition was in disarray at the national level but continued to show considerable strength at the state level. Indeed, Democrats did remarkably well in Ohio, dominating state government and the Buckeye congressional delegation. The Democrats' success was led by Richard Celeste, who was elected governor in 1982 and 1986, finally ending the career of James A. Rhodes.

The rightward turn of national politics stabilized in the 1990s, and it became the Republicans' turn to have trouble. President George H.W. Bush faced fierce opposition from the conservatives in his party, led by pundit Pat Buchanan, and accompanied by a significant independent revolt led by Ross Perot. These troubles gave the Democrats an opening, allowing another Southern governor, Bill Clinton of Arkansas, to win the presidency. In a reversal of the 1980s, the Republicans did well at the state and congressional levels, capturing control of both Houses of Congress in 1994 for the first time in forty years. GOP fortunes also revived in Ohio, led by Voinovich, who was elected governor in 1990 and 1994. Republicans continued to do well in Ohio, controlling state government into the twenty-first century. And the Buckeye State played a crucial role in the 2000 and 2004 elections, when the Republicans gained and maintained control of the White House with George W. Bush.

Afterword

In his conclusion, Zaidan takes a look back at his forty years in journalism, noting how the news media and the political system have changed since 1964. Here he offers some potent insights into the current era of parity between the major party coalitions and the resulting highly polarized politics.

I have had the privilege of reading most of Zaidan's work, so it would be fair to ask about my favorite piece. Of course, this is a tough question to answer, but if I had to choose just one, it would be the penultimate essay in the fourth section, "Zero Gravitas," published in *Northern Ohio Live* in 2000. This is not because I am quoted (I have been frequently quoted in Zaidan's stories), but rather because it combines excellent writing with a playful put-down of pretension. A lifetime of journalism lies behind this marvelous essay.

John C. Green
Bliss Institute
Akron, Ohio

Part I

The 1960s Watershed, 1964–1970

The 1960s Watershed, 1964–1970

Introduction

The 1960s were a watershed in American politics, and Abe Zaidan's writings reveal what this watershed looked like on the ground in Ohio.

The first essay in this section reports on the 1964 election and Democrat Lyndon Johnson's landslide victory over Republican Barry Goldwater, two political giants of their time. This story was actually written in 1973 (on the occasion of President Johnson's death) but provides a vivid picture of the impact of the 1964 election on the Buckeye State. In electoral terms, the 1964 campaign was the center of the 1960s watershed. Indeed, the seeds of the polarization that characterized the 2004 election were planted in 1964. And both the Democratic and Republican parties were hothouses germinating those seeds.

For the Democrats, the election represented the fullest expression of Franklin Roosevelt's New Deal coalition. Like all governing coalitions, the Democrats of 1964 included disparate forces: urban machines and white ethnic communities, labor unions, rural and Appalachian working class voters, soon-to-be enfranchised African Americans, college-educated professionals, and a host of new ideological interests: environmentalists, feminists, peace activists, and the counterculture. In Ohio, this disparate coalition had been competitive but not always successful prior to 1964. And over the next forty years, the tensions among its constituencies steadily undermined the Democratic coalition.

For the Republicans, the 1964 election unleashed new conservative forces that disrupted a pragmatic alliance of business interests, the white middle class, farmers, and traditional conservatives. In Ohio, this alliance had been especially successful at the polls before 1964. Over the next forty years, it was laboriously reconstructed.

But unlike the nation as a whole, the major parties were evenly balanced in the Buckeye State, so that even small tensions within either could produce defeat at the polls. Zaidan's columns capture this competitive balance despite the 1964 landslide, noting the Republicans' difficulties in "Afterlash" and the Democrats' problems in the "Democrats' Dilemma." These essays were written for *The Commentator,* an opinion magazine Zaidan edited in Columbus in the mid-1960s. *The Commentator* won several awards, including one from the National Conference of Christians and Jews for its coverage of the civil rights movement. In a sense, *The Commentator* noted many of 1964's new liberal voices.

At the state level, the Republican pragmatic alliance was still alive in Ohio, and it had no better practitioner than Governor James A. Rhodes. Surely the giant of Ohio politics during this age, Rhodes served as Ohio governor four terms (1963–1966; 1967–1970; 1975–1978; and 1979–1982), beginning his career as the mayor of Columbus and then serving as state auditor.

Zaidan picks up the Rhodes story in 1966 with an in-depth profile on the eve of his first reelection (having been first elected in 1962). "The Wonderful World of Governor Rhodes" is still one of the best portraits of Ohio's legendary Republican governor, describing the essence of Rhodes's approach to politics. He navigated the tricky shoals of the state's political waters with a mix of economic populism ("jobs and progress" was one of his mantras), temperamental conservatism (hostility to taxes, suspicion of government workers, and a fear of disorder), a folksy touch (his fractured syntax was a source of popular appeal), and unabashed hucksterism (he endlessly praised the "wonderful world of Ohio"). Pragmatic with conservative tendencies, Rhodes had an uneasy relationship with the new right-wing forces embodied in the Goldwater campaign.

The greatest practitioner of GOP pragmatism, however, was Ray C. Bliss, the legendary Republican Party leader from Akron. Here Zaidan offers a vivid picture of Bliss near the end of his career, right after he returned from his service as Chairman of the Republican National Committee ("Ray Bliss: The 'Retired' Mr. GOP Will Still Keep a Hand in Politics"). A gifted political organizer with extraordinary personal integrity, Bliss rebuilt the GOP after the 1964 debacle, repeating at the national level a feat he had achieved at the state level in 1949 and 1959. His achievements included the election of Rhodes as governor and Richard M. Nixon as president. Although he had rocky personal relationships with both Rhodes and Nixon, he distrusted the newly aroused conservative forces.

Zaidan painted fine miniatures of these right-wing forces. One example is his satirical *Commentator* column, "Col. Umbus (Ret.)." The main character's name is a reference to Columbus, the easternmost city to vote for Barry Goldwater in 1964. A more serious tone is struck elsewhere: a challenge by a member of the anticommunist John Birch Society to Congressman Robert Taft Jr. ("A Birchite Challenges Robert Taft in Ohio"), the heir of the Ohio Taft dynasty; a small-town promotion of General Curtis LeMay, an Ohio native who became Alabama Governor George Wallace's vice-presidential running mate in 1968 ("LeMay-for-President Drive Under Way in Ohio City"); and an account of George Wallace's 1968 independent campaign's headquarters in industrial Akron ("Faded Akron Inn Blooms for Wallace Drive"). The successors of these conservative forces played major roles in national politics in the four decades that followed.

Not all the conservatives were in the Republican alliance, a fact especially noticeable in the politics of race. Zaidan covered this issue in his accounts of another giant of the era, Cleveland Mayor Carl B. Stokes. Stokes was the first African American to be elected mayor of a major American city, an achievement he had narrowly missed in 1965. No stranger to trailblazing, Stokes was also the first African American to be elected to the Ohio state legislature in 1962 (the same year James Rhodes was first elected governor).

Three of Zaidan's stories cover Stokes's second mayoral run against incumbent Democrat Ralph Locher, an old-style machine politician. Stokes prevailed in a close primary contest and then went on to defeat Republican Seth Taft, another scion of Ohio's Taft dynasty, by about twenty-five hundred votes in the general election. Stokes's victory in the face of bitter racial divisions marked a new direction in Cleveland and Democratic politics, announcing the end of the local party machine and the dominance of white ethnic politics.

Zaidan also covered Stokes's "second first": his reelection as mayor of Cleveland. In this tough campaign, Stokes won the primary and in the general election defeated Ralph Perk, himself something of an oddity at the time: a white ethnic Republican. But Perk was a harbinger, and soon many ethnic politicians appeared in the GOP. Carl Stokes's career links the old urban politics to a new politics of turmoil and transition. Indeed, no major American city experienced the results of the 1960s watershed more fully than Cleveland, as illustrated throughout this collection.

The Democratic success of 1964 was short-lived, and its disparate elements went to war with one another as the 1968 presidential election approached. Five of Zaidan's essays illustrate these divisions in the Democratic camp. The first is a snapshot of an Ohio campaign trip by a man who embodied New Deal liberalism, Vice President Hubert Humphrey ("Locked Up Most Ohio Delegates: Pros Think Humphrey Made Hay on Trip"), who lost the presidency to Richard Nixon in a three-way race with George Wallace.

The second of these pieces is a meditation on the career of another giant, Frank Lausche, a Democratic version of James Rhodes. An ethnic Slovenian with conservative views, he had dominated Ohio politics since the 1940s, serving as Cleveland's mayor, Ohio's governor, and as a U.S. senator. He unsuccessfully opposed Carl Stokes's election as Cleveland mayor in 1967 and then lost his own Senate primary in 1968—the occasion for the essay here ("Lausche: Party's Snub 'Revived' Him"). Lausche was defeated by a young liberal congressman from Cincinnati, John Gilligan, an exemplar of the new Democratic liberals ("The Man Who Beat Lausche: A New Look at John Gilligan"). Although Gilligan lost the 1968 senate race to moderate Republican William Saxbe, this campaign set the stage for his election as governor in 1970.

Zaidan had a special love of presidential politics, especially the process of selecting party delegates and their ensuing politicking at the national conventions. In this regard, the 1968 campaign represented a last hurrah for traditional party politics, a theme of many of Zaidan's essays in this collection. The 1968 primary campaign involved a bitter clash between the old and new liberals, which forced President Johnson to decide not to seek reelection, and culminated in the disastrous Democratic convention in Chicago. Zaidan's sharp, satirical column on Chicago Mayor Richard Daley's heavy-handed response to the antiwar demonstrations at the convention captures the contemporary impact of that event ("Bomb the X-ways, General Daley").

The new liberals lost the presidential nomination in 1968, but they forged a new presidential primary system that operated for the rest of the century. A key opponent to the new liberal forces and the "reformed" nominating system was organized labor, which had been a major force in the old Democratic coalition. Zaidan penned a solemn illustration of the views of Ohio's labor leaders in "Labor's Liberal Love Lost?"

As a consequence of dissension on the right and the left, Republican Richard Nixon was elected president in 1968 with 43 percent of the vote, handily carrying Ohio. Just four years after the 1964 watershed election, the political waters appeared to be running the other way.

The final pieces in this section chronicle Ohio's 1970 U.S. Senate contest. Among the Republicans, term-limited Governor James Rhodes squared off against Congressman Robert Taft Jr. And among the Democrats, two new political giants stirred, astronaut John Glenn and businessman Howard Metzenbaum, giants who would dominate Ohio politics for decades, both eventually representing Ohio in the U.S. Senate. These essays powerfully illustrate the competitive nature of Ohio politics as well as the crises of the times.

Zaidan's final essay in this section, written for the *Washington Post* ("Aura of Invincibility Dies: Glenn, Rhodes Lose"), is a model of political reporting. Painted on a large canvas but filled with rich detail, it reports an apparent return to the political status quo infused with a prescient foreboding. Ohio politics was about to explode.

~

LBJ's '64 Landslide Swept Ohio Democrats into Office
Akron Beacon Journal, January 23, 1973

The spin-off from Lyndon Baines Johnson's 1964 landslide election was devastating to Ohio Republicans. It sent then U.S. Representative Robert Taft back to private life. After trailing most of election night and beyond the dawn of the following day, U.S. Senator Stephen Young, the Democrat, nipped Taft's senatorial ambitions.

A young Cincinnati Democrat, John J. Gilligan, rode the Johnson wave to the U.S. House of Representatives by ousting Republican incumbent Carl W. Rich in the first Congressional District. Two other Republican congressmen, Paul F. Schenck, of Dayton, and Homer E. Abele, of Wellston, also lost. And when Bay Village Democrat Robert E. Sweeney defeated Oliver P. Bolton of Mentor for the at-large congressional seat, it meant that the Johnson landslide had cut Ohio's lopsided eighteen-to-six GOP margin in the U.S. House to fourteen-to-ten.

In the Ohio House, Republicans lost twelve seats, their margin dropping to seventy-six-to-sixty-one. In the Ohio Senate, the GOP saw a nineteen-to-thirteen majority fall to a sixteen-to-sixteen tie.

Preelection forecasts predicted a Johnson victory, but nothing on the scale of the final returns. How much of the high costs paid by the once-proud Ohio Republican Party could be attributed to LBJ's personal popularity, and how much to the people's fear of Senator Goldwater's outspoken, hawkish stands is beyond safe analysis. But throughout the Ohio campaign, as elsewhere, Goldwater remained the overriding issue; extremism, the code word.

Republican moderates, such as Congressman Robert Taft and Governor James Rhodes, caught between party loyalty and personal survival, gave Goldwater perfunctory endorsements and ducked out. Rhodes, then in his second year as governor, at first appeared to be favorably impressed by the noisy clamor of the Goldwaterites. According to some observers, Rhodes may have believed that the Republican nominee was headed for the White House. To everybody's surprise, including that of State Republican Chairman Ray Bliss, Rhodes announced he would release the state GOP delegation to the convention to vote for Goldwater, and then ran for cover during the remainder of the campaign.

Sensing a sizable victory, President Johnson made only a few visits to Ohio. On those trips, he sometimes laid the stick to his opponent, to the delight of large, enthusiastic crowds. Oftentimes, the imposing Texas rancher merely drawled that he was just a plain fellow countryman out to do some good for all Americans, rich or poor, black or white. As he put it in a speech to Democrats in Cleveland a month before election day: "I just want to talk to you tonight like home folks, just us."

A Republican truth squad trailed him around Akron, accusing his administration of "moral rot." The diatribes from the radical right charged him with embracing communism. Right-wing pamphleteers vilified him as a merchant of corruption. Johnson, sometimes pounding his fist, sometimes forcing a faint, benign smile, responded with a promise for peace in his time and a Great Society.

Nearly two out of three Ohio voters opted for the Johnson style. They helped return him to the White House with the heaviest majority in the history of Ohio presidential elections. Not even President Nixon's landslide victory over Senator McGovern last fall [1972] in Ohio (by more than 780,000 votes) outshone LBJ's million-vote triumph over Senator Goldwater among Buckeye voters.

Master politician, a Texan for whom no social promise was too great, a fighter, a cajoler, a swashbuckling campaigner who could not resist the temptation to press the flesh, Johnson made his presence dramatically felt wherever he went. When the police in Cleveland tried to hold back the crowds, the President roared: "Let them through, let them through. Let them come to me or I'm going to them." And he did.

Afterlash

The Commentator, November 19, 1964

The American Political Year of 1964 didn't end last November 3 because in politics there is no beginning, middle, or end. Only high and low pressure areas. The winners must now go back and reread their campaign oratory to see what it is the electorate expects of them. The losers must go back and reread their oratory to see what *more* it was that the electorate had expected of them.

Once both sides have found their answers, the next campaign cycle begins. But the political process itself is continuous because government is continuous.

For the public at least, or so the saying goes, we've now reached the pause that refreshes. This is the period of calm after the storm when, for example, neighbors can again blithely talk of stereo and crabgrass with far less chance of the conversation stumbling into a neighborhood political brawl.

What a minister says on Sunday morning will not be screened as carefully now for hints of political bias, and whether the Little League manager is a Democrat or a Republican won't seem as important to the father of the boy who's trying to make the team. There will be a sizable drop—both in number and intensity—in letters to editors, and editors themselves can relax to the extent that they will be less in demand for sidewalk and telephone cross-examination.

The politically-blitzed reader will again be able to give time to newspaper articles with such headlines as "Postage Stamp Brings $15,500—Upside Down" and "What Makes You So Certain You're No Snob?"

What's most important is that the public will return to whatever level of sanity possible on the American scene. This isn't true of everyone, of course, but nothing ever is. For instance, when most people were desperately trying to remove bumper stickers without removing the bumper, new warnings were being posted by others, who feared that the last election was, in fact, the *last* one. These people either don't understand democratic process, which seems likely, or they take unusual delight in just being different.

Still other remnants of the 1964 campaign have fallen into the postelection void. Someone has called it "afterlash"—a semantic phenomenon which Webster may someday define as what's left when you pit frontlash against backlash. "Afterlash" refers to the talkathon going on among beleaguered Republican leaders whom the Goldwaterites claim didn't talk nearly enough during the campaign.

Polls Still Active

But if the great debate within the Republican Party doesn't settle anything else, it is already giving the pollsters something to poll about. One of pollster Louis Harris's first surveys to appear after the election asked what rank-and-file Republicans considered to be an ideal candidate. (Consensus: a figure with Eisenhower's personality and steeped in "traditional conservatism.") Based on recent successes, the poll shouldn't be taken too lightly since what the GOP needs most of all now is a "winlash."

And while we're on the subject of polls, a chief source of irritation among some people before the election was the fact they not only weren't polled during the campaign, but that they have never been polled. What they, and millions like them, need is an organization. As a starter, I suggest The Society for the Recognition of Americans Who Have Never Been Polled—with particular emphasis on the "Never."

One of their first orders of business would be to form their own polling group and poll themselves. Because of this group's enormous size—clearly representing the majority of Americans—a campaign could stop the day the poll was published. Everybody wants shorter campaigns anyway.

Col. Umbus (Ret.)

The Commentator, January 30, 1964

My dear friend, Col. Umbus (Ret.), leaned against our back fence, shook a persuasive finger at my nose and snapped: "I don't like it! I just don't like it!"

Coming from Col. Umbus (Ret.), this could mean a number of things. But he seemed to be especially unhappy on this day, like the time when dampness forced him out of his new fallout shelter after a two-hour-and-fourteen-minute test run.

"It's not doing the American image any good overseas by President Johnson making it a point to insist that we have a lot of poor people around," observed the retired colonel. "What's he trying to do to this country anyway?"

"Well," I replied hesitantly, "there's nothing. . . ."

"Let me finish," he persisted, forgetting for the moment that I was his very dear friend. "Why, back in my day, we went out and did a hard day's labor—or we starved! Young man [he calls every male acquaintance 'young man'], we didn't know what the words 'government handout' meant. Everybody worked or they starved."

"Well, that's life."

"All that poverty the President is talking about is an untrue fact!"

"Truly a lie."

"What's more," he cackled, in another flash of wisdom, "nobody's going to help anybody who won't help himself. It's up to each man to put his shoulder—"

"—to the wheel."

This intrusion momentarily startled the retired colonel.

"How did you know what I was going to say?" he inquired, a hint of suspicion in his voice.

"Just lucky—I guess." (I prayed that I had not been disrespectful to my dear friend.)

To his credit, Col. Umbus (Ret.) didn't press the matter. Rather, he continued his soliloquy: "Where's our rugged individualism? We need to go back to the Monroe Doctrine!"

"I beg your pardon, sir?" (He had shifted gears too quickly for me.)

"They just don't make 'em like old Jim Monroe anymore. He knew what to do when he was in a tough ball game."

"Babe Ruth was much the same kind of guy," I rejoined, finding it hard to keep up with the retired colonel's racing thoughts.

"And Babe Ruth was an orphan," retorted Col. Umbus (Ret.).

"He had to learn how to play ball in the streets. That didn't hurt his fiber."

"And to think that the Little League is trying to change all that."

"I tell you the government is taking away more freedoms every day," he pressed onward. "If the Supreme Court really wanted to do this country a favor, it'd rule itself unconstitutional." The thought obviously delighted the retired colonel, for he gave me a friendly nudge and remarked: "Come to think of it, I ought to enter that in my diary!"

"Thank goodness, we still have the states to protect us," I added, trying to keep the retired colonel's mood up.

"What we need today are a few more *forefathers,*" he insisted.

"An Abraham Lincoln would be handy today."

"Eh, yes. . . ," he replied, but his words didn't carry their usual authority. "Actually, I was thinking of . . . eh, a few of the people who came a little earlier in our great history."

"Of course." There was no sense ruffling the retired colonel further.

Democrats' Dilemma

The Commentator, November 26, 1965

The Ohio Democratic Party has a family-sized Christmas stocking to fill this year. It will belong to the man, as yet unnamed, who must face Governor Rhodes in next year's gubernatorial race. With a task like this confronting them, the Democratic chieftains can be excused if they don't quite accept the month of December as the season to be jolly.

Though a number of names of potential candidates have been tossed about in the political off-season, the painful truth in Democratic quarters is that the party doesn't have a clear choice in mind. The quandary was intensified by Ralph Locher's tight squeeze in getting reelected as Cleveland mayor. In the four-way Cleveland race, Locher's strongest opponent, State Representative Carl B. Stokes, polled 87 percent of the vote from the city's Negro areas. Locher could only draw about 7.5 percent.[1]

Until his near disaster in Cleveland, Locher was considered to be high on the list of Democratic prospects. But now party leaders are taking a second look at him. State Democratic Chairman William Coleman claims Locher is still in contention. But he adds: "We have to admit that after a person has had a squeaker like that, he certainly doesn't have the luster that he would have had if he had won by fifty thousand votes."

Two men have already announced their candidacies: State Representative Harry McIlwain, of Cincinnati, and Ohio House Minority Leader A. G. Lancione, of Bellaire. Others who have been mentioned prominently as possible candidates are U.S. Representative Robert Sweeney, space hero John Glenn, and former Ohio Governor Michael V. DiSalle. At this point, however, Sweeney seems at least as interested in either the new congressional seat in Franklin County or the Ohio attorney generalship, and Glenn reportedly shows no interest in party overtures for the Democratic nomination.

Another possibility is Ohio Senate Democratic leader Frank King, who is also president of the Ohio AFL-CIO. Some political observers believe King could give Governor Rhodes the strongest test since he could tap labor for both money and organizational machinery, two requisites not readily available through the Democratic Party.

No matter who ultimately gets the Democratic nod, the party must still deal with its internal poverty and the external abundance of Rhodes's popularity. The problem of party finances has become so acute that Coleman recently threatened to close State Democratic Headquarters in Columbus unless county chairmen put out more effort to help pay the bills. He warned the chairmen that party headquarters is "destitute."

An even greater obstacle to party fortunes, however, is Rhodes himself. The governor has built his "no new taxes" theme—with plenty of support from the state's publishers and the good health of the national economy—into a state shrine. It will take a Democratic miracle to desecrate it.

The governor may expect to lose some support from education and welfare interests. And staunch Goldwaterites aren't likely to forgive him for his aloofness to Barry Goldwater in the 1964 presidential campaign. But the latter aren't likely to vote for the Democratic nominee either, choosing instead to just stay home election day.

Whatever chinks may be detected in Rhodes's armor, they don't appear to be serious enough to cause the governor much concern at this stage. And before Ohio's Democrats can solidify their assault on the governor, they've got to first find an attractive candidate—a doctor in their own house who can heal some old wounds and present a healthy public image before next year's wars begin.

A Birchite Challenges Robert Taft in Ohio
Washington Post, May 1, 1966

Maybe it's his youthful zeal. Maybe it's simply a matter of political naiveté. Whatever the case, William Flax, thirty-one, lawyer and avowed member of the John Birch Society,[2] is trying to crash into Republican politics by taking on one of the best-known names in Ohio: Taft.

Armed with the copybook maxims of the ultraconservatives, Flax has pitted himself against former Congressman Robert Taft Jr. in the GOP primary for the First Congressional District (covering the eastern half of populous Hamilton County).

Although the word from the Taft camp is that Flax must be kidding, he is deadly serious. He claims plenty of support in traditionally conservative Hamilton County and has directed much of his ammunition against what he laments as Taft's "moderate influence" on hardcore Midwest conservatism.

The Taft Dilemma

Even if Taft should win the primary next Tuesday, which is likely, he may find himself in another ticklish situation with his radical right. Flax claims that if he loses he will support Taft because the latter is less liberal than Democratic Representative John Gilligan. Such support could be embarrassing to Taft and give Gilligan campaign fodder in the general election campaign now regarded as a neck-and-neck race.

In some respects, Flax's candidacy has put Taft right back in the middle of the dilemma he faced in the Goldwater-Johnson race, when his bid for the United States Senate was nipped by Senator Stephen Young in a Democratic landslide in Ohio. Taft kept the

Goldwater issue at arm's length while donning a mantle of moderate Republicanism.

Now, as he sets sail for a Congressional seat in what is widely regarded as the decisive fight for his political life, Taft faces Gilligan on the left and the John Birch types on the right.

A "States' Rightist"

Flax, who has no political experience other than volunteer work for Goldwater in 1964, has zeroed in on the whole gamut of right-wing disenchantment with modern America. He has assailed "welfare-stateism," socialism, communism, social breakdown, the civil rights movement, and the anti-poverty program.

Proclaiming himself as a "states' rightist," he complains that "Eastern-style politics" is sullying the proud conservatism of Buckeye politics and singles out Taft as one of the culprits. He has attacked Taft's endorsement of the Ohio fair housing bill and Taft's opposition to a rule barring communist speakers on the Ohio State University campus.

None of this has surprised Taft's supporters. They note Flax has a history of right-wing activities. (In 1962, for example, Flax promoted a drive to place cards in retail stores to identify "Iron Curtain" merchandise. He once picketed a Cincinnati appearance of New York Governor Nelson Rockefeller, describing him as a "dangerous socialist.") To get his message across in the primary fight, Flax has bought some radio spots and half-hour time periods on local television for monologues. He's also done some newspaper advertising to announce his personal appearances.

Taft's response has been to ignore him.

The "Wonderful World" Of Governor Rhodes

The Reporter[3], October 6, 1966

When Governor James A. Rhodes revealed his plans last January to seek reelection this fall [1966], reporters and other onlookers who keep a close watch on the career of Ohio's chief executive were not the least bit surprised that he had chosen to run for what appears to be a certain second term. It was only *how* he broke the news that they might not have anticipated.

First, the governor phoned the fifteen-year-old son of a Teamsters boss in Toledo to announce his candidacy. Next, his office released a perfunctory one-paragraph statement that made it official. Then he declined to talk to newsmen about it. It was pure Rhodesiana—the sort of thing that people have come to expect from the fifty-seven-year-old Republican governor since he swept into office in 1962 with the biggest majority ever amassed by an Ohio gubernatorial candidate.

But why the son of a Teamsters official? Well, according to the startled lad, he had written to the governor to inquire about his intentions. But it also might be noted that just a few weeks earlier, the Toledo local had been the first group to endorse the governor's reelection at a dinner honoring Rhodes.

The *Wall Street Journal*, after sending a man out to size up Rhodes, appraised him as "one of the nation's most unorthodox political figures." That he is. Probably no other politician is more of an enigma to his own party, more exasperating to his Democratic foes, more disliked by Goldwaterites, more simplistic in his approach to state government, more cocksure of the rightness of his administrative techniques—and more awkward in explicating the varieties of state responsibility.

Having arrived at the top of the state ladder after serving as mayor of Columbus and state auditor, he has taken pains to reshape the state Republican Party in his image while convincing the public that there is no better alternative to his kind of leadership. Welfare groups may protest low relief grants; union publications may denounce his cosseting of big business; civil rights demonstrators may charge him with ignoring their rallies. Yet he manages to turn up with an occasional citation from an admiring NAACP chapter here and a local union there. One way or another, he contrives to cover almost all bases. Soon after his election, he shrewdly named the publisher of a large Negro newspaper chain in Ohio to his cabinet as industrial-relations director and put a number of other Negroes on the state payroll. Such moves tended to blunt charges by angry civil rights leaders that he ducked out of town the weekend of a protest march in Columbus. Although he is hardly one of organized labor's favorite politicians, Rhodes nevertheless is on good terms with building trade unionists because of his campaign for construction projects around the state.

Dark Horse or Chameleon?

Partly because of his popularity at home and partly because of Ohio's big bloc of electoral votes (which went to Johnson in 1964 but to Nixon in 1960), Rhodes has been touted as a dark horse for the Republican national ticket in 1968. Barry Goldwater sees him as a "sleeper." But Rhodes repeatedly denies such ambitions. Each time he does, the talk dies down for a while, only to revive when off-season political speculators get together down at the press club.

For the moment at least, Rhodes seems content enough to maintain his image as an "Ohioan for Ohioans." At the Midwestern Governors' Conference in Cincinnati in late June, where he was named chairman, Rhodes chose the occasion to have his finance director announce a $28-million surplus in the state treasury—a gambit designed to show his out-of-state peers, as well as Ohio's citizens, how well things were going back at the Statehouse.

Later at the National Governors' Conference in Los Angeles, where interest in GOP prospects quickened in the presence of Ronald Reagan and [Michigan] Governor George Romney, Rhodes kept himself in the background and let his finance director issue still another glowing statement on Ohio's finances. Indeed, Rhodes was one of two Republican governors who failed to show up at a Reagan breakfast, his aides explaining only that the governor had a tight schedule. (The other absentee was Governor William Scranton of Pennsylvania, who was committed to a meeting arranged a month earlier.) The Ohio press corps later reported that Rhodes was on the golf course or was preoccupied with collaring industrial prospects in Ohio, or both. Reagan said he was "sorry Jim wasn't at the breakfast. He's done a lot of good things in Ohio."

When the conference ended, Rhodes had still given no hint about his preference for a 1968 GOP presidential nominee. Rhodes's customary standoffishness toward national Republican affairs has marked him as a loner in his own political family—a position Republicans can ill afford to maintain in their unity drive against President Johnson. He turns down most invitations to appear at out-of-state party functions, preferring the image of a hard-working governor who is just trying to help his state become Number One in everything from tomato-juice production to state fair attendance. (The estimated cost of this year's state fair entertainers alone was upwards of $300,000—providing an extravaganza that Ohio's have-nots viewed somewhat more grimly than did the farmers for whose delectation it was staged.)

Any attempt to place Rhodes ideologically in the political spectrum is fruitless: he abounds in contradictions. For those who see him as a political moderate, it is sufficient to recall that it was Rhodes who, to the chagrin of Ray Bliss, then Ohio Republican chairman, freed the state's delegation to vote its conscience at the Republican national convention in 1964. Rhodes's unilateral action served to hand over the delegation to Goldwater, even though Bliss had urged the governor to hold out as a favorite son. Others who see Rhodes as a conservative are troubled by the fact that, having delivered Ohio to Goldwater, he sidestepped every opportunity to be identified with the Arizona candidate during the campaign.

Although he has closely allied himself with big business in Ohio and is much given to preaching the free enterprise doctrine, he seldom hesitates to avail himself of federal aid. Just recently, he declared war on water pollution in Ohio and, having aroused public concern, insisted that the cost of pollution control was a federal responsibility. Of the five states that got together to discuss pollution control of Lake Erie last summer, Ohio was the only one that had no program for financial aid to municipalities to combat pollution problems. But this did not discourage the state from publishing a booklet that boasted, "Ohio Takes Lead in Pollution Fight."

Rhodes's vision of his role as a political leader became clear the day he assumed office. The state's finances, he then declared, were on the verge of bankruptcy. He contended he had inherited an $83-million deficit from his predecessor (Governor Michael V. DiSalle, a Democrat)—a claim open to doubt because the financial audit by a private firm was never made public.

Rhodes pledged austerity in government and vowed he would never increase taxes. To show he meant what he said, he refused carpeting for his office—a gesture that failed to impress critics who contend he doesn't spend much time in his office anyway. The chief function of state government, he seems to believe, is not very different from that of an employment agency. All of mankind's ills can be traced to unemployment—racism, neuroses, crime, and whatever. When Rhodes appears before a mental health group clamoring for more state aid, he recites statistics that show a correlation between mental illness and unemployment. His task as governor, he tells them, is to assure a "healthy economic climate" that will produce jobs for everyone.

No one can minimize his zeal. Most of the time Rhodes can be found at an "industrial appreciation" dinner in one Ohio town or another, patting the local merchants on the back and urging the chamber of commerce to go out and find more business. At one point, he rounded up some sixty Ohio businessmen and took them off to Europe to ballyhoo the state's export business. Once abroad, he followed his instincts to Rome to visit the pope, then went on to Israel in a typical exhibition of political equipoise.

The governor's Department of Development has opened offices in Washington and New York, and he repeatedly has dispatched teams of state officials and businessmen—they're called "Rhodes's Raiders"—to other states to drum up trade. To encourage tourism in the state, he has led newsmen on tours of Ohio's historical sites and state parks. He has ice-fished on Lake Erie with shivering reporters in an effort to make his point that sport-fishing is a $20-million business.

This sort of thing may enhance the image of a state-on the-go under a governor-on-the-go, but Rhodes's critics charge that he is making a lark of the governorship, doing what he likes to do most while the big problems pile up on his desk. Rhodes attempts to refute such criticism by describing his role primarily as that of a salesman.

A Policy of Silence

Rhodes has never been much good in direct confrontations with his critics. One of his first moves after taking office was to eliminate the regularly scheduled news conference, an institution under his predecessor. After a few press sessions, which turned out to be highly unsatisfactory for reporters seeking fresh copy, Rhodes resorted to canned press releases. The few press conferences he has held in the past three years have been staged on his terms and have usually served to flatter his administration. But Rhodes replies that he is always accessible to the press. Such sessions, however, are on a private consultation basis and lack the hazards of spontaneity in a large gathering. His awkwardness in parrying incisive or hostile questions could be devastating if he should try for national office and be subjected to the probing of the national press corps.

Rhodes seems to sense his deficiencies as a polemicist and has scrupulously followed his prepared script for public utterances. When in doubt, he says little or nothing, particularly on sensitive issues that could drag him into controversy. What, for instance, are his private convictions about capital punishment, a topic that former Governor DiSalle fashioned into a personal crusade? Rhodes replies only that so long as the death penalty is sanctioned by Ohio law, he will abide by it. Did he plan to ask for the resignation of one of his appointees to the Ohio State University Board of Trustees who had been suspended from law practice by the Ohio Supreme Court for violation of professional ethics? The governor insisted he couldn't comment because the case was being appealed to the U.S. Supreme Court. (The high court refused to hear the appeal, the trustee resigned, and the case passed quietly into history with Rhodes unscathed.)

Consider, too, the race riots that ripped Cleveland's Hough section last summer. After sending in the National Guard on Mayor Ralph Locher's request, Rhodes was discreetly unavailable for comment. The governor's indispensable administrative assistant, John McElroy—an able factotum who keeps the executive machinery whirring at the Statehouse while the governor bounds around the state—explained Rhodes's silence by averring that "Any statement by the governor regarding the riots would automatically supersede the role of the city." Cynics noted, however, that the governor did not hesitate to show up in Ohio communities at times of natural disasters, such as floods.

It was in Hough that the welfare march from Cleveland to Columbus originated to protest substandard state relief grants last

June. Rhodes refused to accede to the marchers' request for a special legislative session to free additional welfare funds, but the state Welfare Department has said it will seek more money from the 1967 General Assembly to cover higher grants.

The official state reaction to the welfare march and the riots, as voiced by McElroy, is to construe them as two unrelated events. "To do otherwise," said McElroy, "would be to construct a connection that isn't there."

Later in the summer, when rioting erupted in Dayton, Rhodes was at the state fair, where he had to be contacted by an aide before guardsmen could be called in.

Although Rhodes has tried hard to create an image of an economic paradise in Ohio, his critics are hammering away at the darker side of the picture. Thus, while Ohio has gained more than three hundred thousand jobs under the Rhodes administration, it still has one of the largest groups of welfare recipients in the nation. Besides, it can be argued that Ohio has merely shared a booming national economy—and it could also share a recession.

Perhaps even more informative is the plight of state services. Ohio is the sixth wealthiest state in the Union. Yet it ranks near the bottom on what it spends for mental health, and its facilities for mental treatment are rated among the nation's poorest. The *Columbus Citizen-Journal*, a newspaper that only last January acclaimed Rhodes as the man of the year, recently itemized some less flattering facts: Ohio ranks forty-third in state support for public education, forty-fifth in per capita state funds for higher education (Ohio's students pay more tuition at state universities than students in any other state), fiftieth in state support for child-welfare services (indeed, the state government contributes nothing for child welfare), thirtieth in family relief allowance, and forty-eighth in per capita state funds for aid to the handicapped.

Characteristically, Rhodes largely ignores such criticism, trumpeting instead a long list of capital-improvement expenditures made possible by three bond issues under his administration, totaling $1.4 billion. Even this achievement is vulnerable in the long run because, while Ohio may be spending, for example, $320 million on college building construction, not a single cent is available for staffing those buildings, nor is there any certainty about where such funds will come from.

Rhodes's penchant for floating bonds instead of seeking new taxes has been the topic of more than one hot discussion among state economists, some of whom claim that without tax reform in Ohio the state treasury is headed for a day of reckoning. As early as 1962, a thorough study of the state's tax system, sponsored by the Ohio AFL-CIO, Ohio Education Association, Ohio State Council of Retail Merchants, and Ohio Farm Bureau Federation, warned that the state was living on borrowed time with an antiquated tax structure. Last May, the *Wall Street Journal* pointed out that although Ohio has a 3 percent sales tax, it is "porous with exemptions," while Indiana, with a 2 percent sales tax, raises more revenue per capita.

What exasperates Rhodes's critics is that they are unable to establish a dialogue with him. No matter how they approach critical state problems, he parries their thrusts with his "Look, I'm simply trying to find everybody a job" theme. The trouble with this line is that it doesn't account for the many thousands of Ohioans—the aged, the disabled, the mentally ill, the children of problem families—who can't work but need help.

The Democrats' Predicament

That Rhodes has built such a huge following with so simple a formula must be viewed in the light of two other factors: Ohio's intrinsic conservatism, flavored with ruralistic self-reliance as the solution to man's worst social ills; and a fragmented state Democratic Party, which former Governor DiSalle once described as a "loose confederation of local organizations."

The Ohio Democrats, with a new party chairman and a strikingly handsome young Toledo lawyer—Frazier Reams Jr.—running against Rhodes this year, show new signs of life. Reams, a state senator with a liberal voting record who is portrayed as being "in the Kennedy image," is wooing the support of statewide interest groups who grumble that they have been shortchanged by the Rhodes administration. He has been working to develop a strong Democratic-labor coalition, which has subsisted on nothing more than a nominal relationship in the past.

Reams, however, is confronted with a fundamental predicament. To pay for the many lagging state services, he must necessarily call for new taxes, which isn't the easiest way to win votes from the great mass of Ohioans. At best, it's a precarious political road for Reams in the "Wonderful World of Ohio," where, as Rhodes's slogans remind us, "there are no new or increased taxes" and where "profit is not a dirty word." In fact, most people believe Reams will be sidetracked.

Negro Carl Stokes Is Underdog Again

Washington Post, August 20, 1967

In the corridors of the Ohio Statehouse, his fellow lawmakers are starting to greet him teasingly as "Mayor Stokes." But State Representative Carl B. Stokes, a trim, stylishly-tailored Negro lawyer who is making his second bid to become the mayor of Cleveland, has been in the political caldron long enough to know that such banter has little to do with the gritty realities of his present campaign. Although he nearly wrested the mayor's job away from incumbent Ralph S. Locher in 1965, losing by only 2,144 votes, Stokes is generally regarded as a decided underdog in a three-way Democratic primary field.

And despite widespread dissatisfaction with the Locher administration in Cleveland, Locher is expected to emerge the victor in the October 3 primary. The third Democratic candidate, Frank Celeste, former mayor of suburban Lakewood, could, however, cut deeply enough into the white votes to narrow the gap between Locher and Stokes.

The Democratic nominee will run against Republican Seth C. Taft, a Cleveland lawyer. In heavily Democratic Cleveland, however, the winner of the Democratic Primary usually winds up the mayor.

Stokes knows he is an underdog in a city where the color lines are clearly drawn, but he bristles with indignation when he acknowledges the fact that it is his color that has mounted the odds against him.

"I'm not solely interested in being a Negro mayor of Cleveland—I'm interested in being a progressive mayor who will start getting things done for all the people. And all you have to do is to look around Cleveland to know that the city desperately needs leadership," Stokes asserts for openers. "But how the hell do you run against your own party, the incumbent, organized labor, the ethnic groups and the power structure, particularly when the press in Cleveland keeps reminding everyone that Carl Stokes is a Negro?"

The Cuyahoga County Democratic Party has endorsed Locher. So whatever organized support Stokes will be able to muster for his primary drive will have to come from a loose confederation of Stokes loyalists among Cleveland's three hundred thousand Negroes and their allies.

"At this point," Stokes says, "you won't find a single Stokes-for-Mayor committee in the whole state of Ohio. Yet I'm confident that the job somehow is getting done."

At forty and in his third term as a state representative (he is the first Negro Democrat to sit in the state legislature), Stokes has reached another embattled phase of a life that spans a childhood on welfare and young manhood as a state liquor agent, the latter marked, back in his early twenties, by gun battles with and intimidation by freewheeling saloon operators.

Stokes recalls those days when he flirted with death to make a point: "I don't scare easily—I'm ready to take whatever they dish out in the campaign."

But, in fact, Stokes is fearful of one thing that could destroy all chances of his winning the Democratic nomination—a preelection riot similar to the one that tore up Hough last summer. He repeatedly accused the Locher administration of hankering for trouble in the ghetto to assure his defeat.

"Maybe this Carl Stokes won't win," he muses, "but someday a Carl Stokes will win—and someday all those who are working against me now simply because I'm a Negro are going to understand that."

Negro Nominated in Cleveland Race
Washington Post, October 4, 1967

Negro state legislator Carl Stokes won a dramatic victory tonight over incumbent Ralph Locher in a bid to become mayor of the nation's eighth largest city. Locher conceded late tonight and wished Stokes well.

When 850 of the city's 901 polling places reported, Stokes closed the gap and passed Locher with fifty precincts still out. The only other candidate, Frank Celeste, former mayor of suburban Lakewood, ran a poor third. With all but one of the 901 precincts reporting, Stokes had 110,354 votes to 92,029 for Locher and 8,543 for Celeste.

The winner will face Republican Seth Taft in the November general election. The Democratic nomination in Cleveland is normally tantamount to election, but some observers believed that Locher's supporters may switch to Taft in November.

In a victory statement tonight, Stokes said: "They [the voters] have vindicated my faith in American democracy. I will feel obligated to keep the faith and wage a vigorous campaign in order to move forward and recover the city's reputation."

Stokes had campaigned heavily in the predominantly white wards, and he won more votes than expected in these areas. In Locher's own ward on the South Side, which is integrated, Stokes won by a four-to-three margin. Two years ago, when Stokes ran as an independent, he lost to Locher by a mere 2,144 votes in a four-way race.

Despite favorable weather and the high feeling that had run through the bitter campaign, the total voter turnout appeared to have fallen behind preelection expectations. The total was not expected to go much over two hundred thousand.

Through the campaign, Stokes described himself as a man of moderation seeking to build a city from which both Negroes and whites could derive benefits. Negroes comprise about 34 percent of the population. "Don't vote for a Negro; vote for the man," Stokes had repeated endlessly in the campaign.

Locher had also stressed that he did not consider race an issue. He had run on his record as mayor with the backing of the Cuyahoga County Democratic organization and the Cleveland AFL-CIO. But the Democratic Executive Committee's newsletter had openly fired up the race question by accusing Stokes of being a "Republican racist" and had urged white voters to show up at the polls to offset a heavy Negro registration. It has charged that Stokes's election would set up the Reverend Dr. Martin Luther King Jr. for a "dictatorship" of Cleveland.

Locher's primary support came from the regular party organization, organized labor, and nationality groups such as Polish-Americans Incorporated and Slovak Democratic League. Locher also got the support of U. S. Senator Frank Lausche, former Ohio governor and mayor of Cleveland.

Stokes, meanwhile, was supported by civil rights groups, some businessmen who are critical of Locher's administration, and Dr. King, who came out for Stokes on election eve. Stokes received about 10 percent of the white vote in tonight's election. He received 2.2 percent of the white vote in his unsuccessful campaign against Locher in 1965.

If Stokes is elected in November, he will become the first Negro elected mayor in a major U.S. city.

Stokes Victory Foreshadows New Direction in Politics
Akron Beacon Journal, November 8, 1967

Negro State Representative Carl B. Stokes's incredible come-from-behind victory over Republican Seth Taft in this city's mayoral election Tuesday augurs a new direction for Cleveland and national politics. Stokes squeaked in by 2,501 votes.

That he hurdled every obstacle to become mayor of a major American city attested to the rising power of the Negro vote in urban politics. His victory, despite powerful opposition in his own party, marked the end of a political dynasty that had handpicked the city's chief executives for twenty-six years. Stokes's emergence as the Democratic Party's top man in Cleveland stunned not only veteran party hacks but also venerated elder statesman U. S. Senator Frank Lausche. Lausche, who had guided Democrat after Democrat to city hall simply by blessing them with his approval, chose to ignore Stokes. In the primary, the senator endorsed Mayor Ralph Locher over Stokes. For Lausche, it was his last hurrah at city hall.

For most of election night, it appeared that Stokes, a forty-year-old lawyer who grew up in the slums and was the great-grandson of a slave, was overmatched. As a heavy West Side white vote piled up a commanding lead for Taft, political observers sat back and waited for a concession from Stokes. The massive number of voters who turned out in the bleak November weather indicated that a white backlash was in the making from the white West Side to the ethnic enclaves on the East Side.

It was not until 2:30 A.M. today, with only a handful of precincts remaining to be tallied, that Stokes surged ahead on the strength of Negro votes. The final unofficial tally was 129,829 for Stokes, 127,328 for Taft. Although there was immediate speculation that Taft would demand a recount, the Republican nominee insisted his decision would await the final official tally.

Meantime, jubilant and beaming, Stokes pressed through the packed throng of supporters at his Rockefeller Building headquarters to plead for unity among Clevelanders. His attractive wife at his side, Stokes declared in his victory statement that "Carl Stokes must have help and support of all kinds. . . . We want everybody to help us." As he had done frequently during his campaign, Stokes called upon all nationality groups to close ranks behind him to build a great city.

"This is not a victory for Carl Stokes," he said. "It is a privilege accorded me." How did he come by that "privilege"?

Although Stokes chose to laud all Clevelanders for his astonishing victory, the raw fact is that he had to overcome a defection of more than eighty thousand white Democrats to Taft. But by the same token, the more than twenty-five thousand white votes he added to the Negro bloc were crucial to his victory.

Taft, a well-meaning political novice who tried in vain to suppress the race issue, also appealed for unity in his brief concession statement. Reflecting on the bitterly contested campaign, Taft urged the city: "Forget the words spoken in heat and think now of things that can be done to make ours a great city."

In trying to make good his pledge of an urban renaissance for Cleveland, Stokes will have to reckon with the inherent distrust of many white Clevelanders and Negro militants alike. For the next two years, beyond his programs to remedy unemployment, decaying neighborhoods, and the score of other problems plaguing great urban centers, Stokes may find that achieving unity will present his strongest problem.

LeMay-for-President Drive Under Way in Ohio City

Akron Beacon Journal, June 17, 1967

This week's featured film at the Vernon Theater on the town square in Mount Vernon, Ohio, is *Those Magnificent Men in Their Flying Machines*. Just up the block there's a small but zealous group of fledgling campaigners who will tell you that one is so magnificent he ought to be our next president.

With little more than "sweat, muscle, and blind faith" to pilot their man to the White House, the group has staked out some space in the lobby of the postbellum Hotel Curtis, hauled in a desk, some colorful signs, and the usual paraphernalia of a political campaign—and has hopefully labeled it all the "National Headquarters of LeMay for President."

The grand gesture is, of course, for retired Air Force General Curtis E. LeMay,[4] one of Ohio's notable native sons (he was born in Columbus) and an old campaigner himself, with a medal-studded military career. And what is encouraging the grassroots committee to work all the harder is that the general has not ordered it to retreat.

In a letter to the committee's founder, the hawkish, cigar-chewing former Strategic Air Command (SAC) chief wrote from his California home: "While I have never been interested in politics I, along with a lot of other people I guess, am very dissatisfied with many things that are happening in our government, and I think these should be corrected. I think it probably very remote that I will enter politics, however, if some of these people, who have been sending me letters, become organized, and I thought there was a popular demand, then, of course, I would have to give it very serious consideration."

The letter's recipient, Mrs. Shirley Fletcher, a portrait- and sign-painter, is satisfied that the general is prepared to accept an idea whose time has come. "The nation needs a military man in Washington," she insists with a note of urgency.

Dr. W. E. Steffan Jr., an optometrist who, along with Fletcher, serves as co-chairman of the citizens' committee, adds enthusiastically: "General LeMay is a qualified candidate and a dedicated American, a man of action who can get the job done."

Despite the fact that both Steffan and Fletcher are political novices, they have had some early success. The committee has picked up about $4,000 from well-wishers. It now has more than thirty volunteer workers and incipient LeMay-for-President cadres in other states.

Even the headquarters' hotel name—Curtis—is a publicity windfall of sorts for the general.

The committee has been busy in other ways, passing out more than four thousand handbills and "*All the Way With LeMay*" bumper stickers. (It seems only right that hundreds of these were dropped from a plane flying over the nearby Knox Lake Fishing Derby recently.)

Fletcher, a pleasantly intense mother of four, says her interest in a LeMay boom developed through a friendship with the general's parents in Mount Vernon. The older LeMay died several months ago. The general's mother celebrated her eightieth birthday this week.

"I heard and read a lot about General LeMay and decided that he was the man that could best lead this nation," Fletcher says.

Although Fletcher disdains labels, the committee's philosophy seems pitched at ending the war in Vietnam and many of the federal programs at home.

"The Vietnam War has dragged on three years too long," Fletcher says, "and I'm sure General LeMay would know how to handle it."

By the same token, Steffan has nothing good to say about Medicare and Social Security.

Both say they are "basically Democrats" and care not if the sixty-year-old LeMay is a Republican. "Our appeal is to Democrats and Republicans," they explain. "LeMay is our man because neither the Republican nor the Democratic Party has the kind of candidates we can accept."

Though they claim they will win widespread support from "Jews, mothers, and veterans," the two committee leaders have only a vague idea of how this might be accomplished. "We're playing it pretty much by ear now," says Fletcher. "Our main job now is to get out the word, find a national chairman, and then work on the Republican Party to nominate General LeMay."

The committee has been in touch with such political luminaries as Governor Rhodes, State Republican Chairman John Andrews, U.S. Senator Lausche, and U.S. Representative John Ashbrook (whose district includes Mt. Vernon), all of whom have chosen to remain politely aloof.

"I know these people," Ashbrook said from his Washington office. "And they are fine people. But really my heart is with Nixon or Reagan."

"Anybody has the right to promote the candidacy of the person of his choice," Andrews said in Columbus. "But the prevailing mood at this time seems to be one of sending Governor Rhodes to the convention as a favorite son."

The committee failed to enlist Arthur Godfrey, LeMay's longtime pal, or Captain Eddie Rickenbacker, another flying notable, as the committee's national chairman. But it is trying for somebody of equal prominence, encouraged all along that things will work out because history is on its side. "Remember that we've had eight presidents from Ohio and six were generals," Steffan says.

Even the hometown newspaper, the *Mount Vernon News*, isn't overlooking historical precedent, editorially ruminating: ". . . let's not forget there is legend that the actual grassroots work which started Abraham Lincoln on the way to the White House originated in Green's Drug Store in Mount Vernon. Admittedly, LeMay for President is a long, long shot at this stage of the 1968 campaign. It is not an impossibility."

Locked Up Most Ohio Delegates: Pros Think Humphrey Made Hay on Trip

Washington Post, May 4, 1968

Vice President Hubert H. Humphrey, for whom happiness is a way of politicking in his bid for the presidency, had ample reason to be smiling after his first foray into Ohio for precious delegate votes. By the best estimates of Democratic professionals, Humphrey appears to have locked up a majority of Ohio's 115 delegate votes.

There were no firm commitments made during his eleven-hour stay in Akron Friday, and some party leaders such as Cuyahoga County chairman Bert Porter were professing neutrality. But sources inside the delegation acknowledged that Humphrey was running at high tide in Ohio. One source, admittedly a supporter of Senator Robert Kennedy, summed up the delegates' mood this way: "There is a strong feeling for Humphrey because they think he's the man who has the best chance of winning."

State Democratic chairman Morton Neipp said little to indicate a change in the party's official position of supporting favorite son U. S. Senator Stephen Young on the first ballot at the Democratic convention. But he reportedly confided to a group of delegates that "there is a real groundswell for the Vice President." Summit County Democratic chairman Robert Blakemore echoed these sentiments: "The vice president made a distinct impression on our delegates and it will be felt in the coming weeks."

The Franklin County (Columbus) delegation is already waving Humphrey's banner. Columbus's Mayor Jack Sensenbrenner was among the first to endorse the vice president moments after President Johnson had announced he would not seek another term. "We're all in Humphrey's camp," said a Columbus delegate Friday night, "and that's official."

Frazier Reams, chairman of Humphrey's Ohio campaign, had estimated the vice president's Ohio delegate strength at between sixty and eighty, but at the end of Humphrey's busy stay in Akron, some sources were putting the tally even higher.

Some observers believed that, although U.S. Senators Robert Kennedy and Eugene McCarthy had impressed the Ohio delegation in earlier huddles with it, Humphrey had gone a step further by winning it over.

The vice president had come into Ohio with the strong backing of AFL-CIO President George Meany, and local unionists were falling into line without much added persuasion. On hand for Humphrey's visit here, in addition to Ohio labor leaders, was Alexander Barkan, national director of COPE, the political arm of the AFL-CIO. "We're committed to Humphrey all the way in November," Barkan said without hesitation.

Humphrey's major obstacle in sweeping the Ohio delegation lies in the strength that Kennedy or McCarthy, or both, show in Indiana Tuesday and in the primaries elsewhere. If the "Kennedy Express" gains significant speed, the vice president could find himself in a different ballgame in the weeks ahead.

But, his spirits swelled for his reception here, Humphrey seemed little concerned that he might be sidetracked. In his appearances at Kent State University, Elizabeth Park, and Friday night at the Jefferson-Jackson Day dinner, he overflowed with the familiar Humphrey enthusiasm. "When I think of the great potential in the American people—Wow!" he effervesced Friday night.

And he concluded his long and meandering speech to the Democratic professionals with the Pledge of Allegiance. Patriotism, honor, unity, brotherhood, good humor, the promise of America and the potential for fulfillment—all these marked the vice president's rallying call here Friday, and this is how he plans to win the presidency.

After a morning of overcast skies, the sun shone as the vice president stepped out of his plane. "The power of happy politics," somebody explained.

Lausche: Party's Snub "Revived" Him
Akron Beacon Journal, May 5, 1968

It is much like a religious ceremony: they come to give and receive blessings, joined in spiritual communion, exalted by a generation of true believing.

They offer up faded postcards and brown newspaper clippings and old political buttons. They ask only in return that each gift revive the memory of a happily shared moment in history. The postcards tell of political meetings long past. They are typed in English and translated into Polish. And that, too, is part of the history.

Whether the service is held in a school cafeteria in Mantua or at the Elks Club in Delaware, the ritual is the same because the high priest is the same: U.S. Senator Frank J. Lausche, a politician by choice but a cultist by nature, first elected to the senate in 1956. As such, he has transfixed Ohioans for three decades, having served as governor 1945–1947 and 1949–1957. But at seventy-two, and with a young, traditionless, and restless generation beating down upon him, the senator has been forced to fall back and regroup his loyalists in his toughest campaign for a Democratic nomination for a Senate seat he's held for a dozen years.

It has been a strange campaign indeed. Though he is the incumbent, he has found himself on the far side of the Rubicon. For years, he had traveled his own political course while the party professionals back home grumbled about his self-willed absence from the fold.

This year, with Lausche casually tuning up for a third term in the U. S. Senate, the state Democratic Executive Committee, locking arms with the Ohio AFL-CIO, decided the time was ripe for a coup and endorsed former U.S. Representative John J. Gilligan, forty-seven, as its choice for the Senate. Lausche was twenty-six when Gilligan was born, and this factor has worked itself into the campaign as a clash of generations; it would be hard to find another race where political style and philosophy so sharply defined and divided the candidates.

Lausche has been alternately tearful and caustic over the unprecedented snub by his party. But, all emotion aside, the former five-term Ohio governor, as a practical matter, could not ignore the challenge with pronouncements from his Washington office (he has none in Ohio). He came home to campaign.

And his old friends, people who worked for him back in the 1940s and 1950s, ward heelers and Statehouse typists, heads of ethnic groups and Old Guard sympathizers, all came out to greet him. His return brought out an added measure of fraternal reunion: some of the old gang hadn't shaken his hand in years. Some had never met him.

Lausche patterned his campaign to reinforce past loyalties rather than to encourage new ones, and he invoked the broad Lauschesque style that has brought him this far: the sweeping gestures, the hand aside the beaming face as he confides a joke on himself, the fist-pounding and the finger-counting as he ticks off points to support his attacks on wild spending, immorality, disloyalty to flag and country.

Thus the spiritual crusade surfaced and swept over the politics of it all.

While his lesser-known opponent tramped the streets of the big cities searching out new faces, Lausche saved himself for carefully handpicked audiences that were largely conservative, friendly, middle-aged-and-over, and, more often than not, Republican.

The Republican thing wasn't by chance. Friends around the senator, including a co-chairman of his campaign, openly called for Republican crossovers in Tuesday's primary. The Ohio Information Committee (OIC), which waves a nonpartisan flag but is in fact a heavily Republican registration and education outfit, has been flooding the state with advice on how Republican voters might vote for Lausche. That some of the advice was misleading, if one pays any attention to election laws, seemed not to cool the OIC's enthusiasm.

Lausche's romance with Republicans surprises no one. Although he insists he is an independent, his conservatism has been anathema to organized labor and moderate-to-liberal Ohio Democrats. His critics contend that he votes so regularly with the GOP in the Senate that it would be more accurate to describe him as a "dependent Republican" than an "independent Democrat."

Of late, Lausche has gone on television and described himself as a "liberal"—but his heart didn't seem to be in it, nor is his record.

He was the lone Democrat to vote for a cutback in Teacher Corps funds; he has supported right-to-work legislation, opposed the nuclear test ban treaty, poverty programs, Medicare, and urban transit aid. He was against creating the Housing and Urban Development (HUD) and joined Senator Everett Dirksen (R-IL) in Dirksen's attempt to undercut the Supreme Court's one-man, one-vote decision. In 1966, he voted against closing off a filibuster against the Civil Rights Act. In 1964, he voted for an earlier rights bill but also supported an amendment by Georgia's Senator Richard Russell Jr. to delay enactment of the bill until it was sent to a national referendum.

Another measure of the Lausche record is the so-called party unity vote, which counts up how often a man votes with his party. In 1966, Lausche agreed with the Democrats only 7 percent of the time, disagreed 74 percent. In this respect, he topped the list of all Democratic dissent. Next is Virginia's Senator [Harry] Byrd, with 63 percent disagreement.

Lausche has made shibboleths of "political independence" and "fiscal responsibility." And when the people come up and pump his hand at rallies, they never fail to thank him for this. In turn, he rakes his fingers through his medium-cropped gray hair and says with an expression of deep hurt: "They've got their biggest guns aimed at me." "They" are his critics, or "that gang of bosses down in Columbus." Translation: Democratic and labor leaders.

Against this "conspiracy," as he defines his opposition, "I've got no contact man, no advance man, no speaker's bureau, no organization." He says this over and over at his informal meetings around the state, and the underdog sympathy pours out from his admirers. "All I've got are a few postcards that people are sending out in my behalf," he muses.

His image of taxpayer watchdoggery and personal penury was in evidence at a meeting of the Area Mayors Association (of Summit, Portage, and Medina counties) a few weeks ago in Mantua, where he attacked inflation and the gravity of America's financial condition.

An oldtime Lausche committee worker produced twenty-four-year-old Lausche-for-governor buttons partly painted over to bring them up to date.

The smalltown mayors loved him that night. Mantua Mayor Robert Thomas, introducing his guest, enthused, "I now present to you Mr. Integrity, the one, the only, the inimitable Frank J. Lausche." Standing ovation. Cuyahoga Falls Mayor Del Ackerman clutched Lausche's hand and glowed, "God bless you, Senator. I'm a Republican, but I'm in your corner!"

Lausche took it from there with a tub-thumping call for renewed patriotism. "I don't believe that any time in my whole life have I felt so abysmally low as I do now in contemplating the disunity in our country and the willingness to condemn our own land. . . . But if we remain strong and sturdy as our forefathers did, our country will survive."

In Delaware, he lashed the critics of American foreign policy and charged that some American officials were spreading "dastardly lies" about our behavior in Vietnam. Long a hawk and political enemy of Senator William Fulbright, Lausche has lately moderated his stand on Vietnam to an expressed willingness to send the matter to the United Nations for disposal.

Despite the informality of his politicking and the enthusiasm of his admiring audiences, Lausche grew testier as the campaign wore on. On successive nights in Lancaster and Delaware, he flared up with reporters. He stalked out of the Delaware Elks Club after refusing to answer any questions about his speech.

Observers suggested that perhaps the demands of the campaign and the daily blasts from his opponents were starting to bug him, and he was wearying from it all. But no one would bet it would cost him Tuesday's election.

The Man Who Beat Lausche: A New Look at John Gilligan

Akron Beacon Journal, May 21, 1968

Throughout his successful challenge to dethrone U. S. Senator Frank J. Lausche, in the Democratic primary, John Joyce Gilligan[5] repeatedly startled his followers with daredevil rhetoric.

Though feeling was running high after rioting shook his hometown, Cincinnati, Gilligan condemned the city courts' heavy-handed treatment of alleged curfew violators and thrust himself into the eye of public controversy.

In Akron, the home of four of the world's biggest rubber companies, he lashed big business for engaging in "economic colonialism" abroad.

In Columbus, he lectured uneasy blue-collar workers who showed up at a union fund-raising dinner that organized labor must forget its "fears and prejudices" and stand up for Negro rights.

At another labor dinner in Akron, he declared his campaign, spearheaded by a new alliance of the state Democratic Party and the Ohio AFL-CIO, had made "labor take a good look at itself as a political vehicle—and it ain't there."

Though the more orthodox politicians considered his oratory brash, Gilligan seemed always to enjoy his mission of taking the big issues to the people. "The day for apple-pie campaigning," he said, "is over."

In conservative Ohio, and against a champion conservative vote-getter like Lausche, Gilligan was clearly asking for trouble. But what he got was a landslide victory. It started a new course for Buckeye politics.

At forty-seven, tall (six foot, one inch), trim (180 pounds), red-haired ("banana-nosed", he adds breezily), Jack Gilligan is now regarded as the top man in his party's renaissance. "He is the hottest prospect in America," exclaimed Eugene P. O'Grady, the party's executive secretary, moments after it had become evident that Gilligan had trounced Lausche.

Gilligan has been running against the odds throughout his political career. A biting liberal in a conservative state, he managed to win a congressional seat in 1964 with the help of a Democratic landslide across the state. In 1966, he was ousted by U.S. Representative Robert Taft by seven thousand votes after a GOP legislature dumped an additional ten thousand Republican voters into Ohio's first congressional district.

Last year, he was elected as the only Democrat to the nine-member Cincinnati City Council, where he had served from 1953 until he went to Congress. A Silver Star winner in World War II and an English professor at Xavier University from 1948 to 1953 (he lacks only his dissertation for a Ph.D.), Gilligan relied on the same spirit and scholarship to topple the seventy-two-year-old Lausche.

He attracted young people with his own youthful bearing and turned them on by bestowing upon them the "keys" to America's destiny. "The greatest thing about this generation," he told a campus audience, "is that it is finally asking questions that should have been asked a long time ago."

The college crowds shouted their support. But Gilligan got his biggest boost from organized labor and an effective television campaign featuring half-hour documentaries of his life.

Labor had never been happy with Lausche's disdain for social welfare programs and his support of right-to-work legislation. It promptly echoed the state Democratic organization's unprecedented endorsement of Gilligan against an incumbent. The Democrat-labor alliance, which further alienated the party conservatives, staged a meticulously planned campaign for money and votes and came up with a war chest of $250,000. With computers and data processing, labor checked out voters, down to their telephone numbers, and prodded them into the fold. The results testify to their diligence; Gilligan won all of the major urban areas in Ohio while Lausche carried the rural counties.

Actually Gilligan set his caravan moving last spring when he stumped the state to oppose Governor James A. Rhodes's Ohio Bond Commission proposal, a measure that was expected to win handily with powerful support from the Statehouse and the press. Lausche favored it. But it lost in a landslide, and Gilligan stood tall at state Democratic headquarters for putting his personal reputation on the line against what had appeared to be a popular state development.

Despite his decisive victory last week, Gilligan must now face stiff opposition from the Republican nominee, three-term Attorney General William Saxbe, fifty-one. Though he lacks Gilligan's colorful style, Saxbe is a seasoned campaigner who can rely on a strong party organization in a state that has been good to GOP candidates.

A political moderate, Saxbe had been moving to the left in anticipation of a clash with Lausche. But now the spectrum has been narrowed, and personalities and sheer party numbers are expected to play a bigger role from now to November.

One thing is certain. Gilligan's astonishing upset has firmly secured the party control in the hands of the Democrat-labor alliance. The Lausche wing that threatened a housecleaning at state headquarters once Gilligan was put down has been disfranchised.

Bomb the X-Ways, General Daley!

Akron Beacon Journal, August 29, 1968

Something must be said in defense of General Richard Daley's controversial tactics in thwarting the desperate August Offensive against Chicago this week.[6] For all the barbed wire, the teargas, and the bopping of newsmen, hippies, yippies, and other minor revolutionaries, there is a growing feeling that history will prove Daley to be on the side of the doves. More significantly, it will show that even doves can win bloody military victories.

Consider the wily old commander's dilemma: intelligence reports had it that the enemy's assault force would perhaps exceed one hundred thousand seasoned veterans of the Columbia and Berkeley campaigns. Included among these were the twenty-eighth McCarthy Battalion that did so well in New Hampshire, Wisconsin, and Oregon, and some scattered volunteer outfits like the crack thirty-second Public Park Brigade and the fifteen, eighteenth, and nineteenth Press Club Platoons.

Daley was faced with other problems, too. The enemy already had succumbed to paralyzing telephone communications and crippling transportation with cab and bus strikes.

With this ominous information in hand, the General met with his advisory staff in an all-night session at city hall last month. Reports leaking from that meeting indicate the talk among Daley's advisers was largely hawkish. Among suggestions advanced by aides but finally rejected by Daley:

•BLOCKADE Lake Michigan to prevent the shipment of supplies to enemy troops dug in on the beaches.

•BOMB the major expressways leading into the city to reduce enemy infiltration of men and supplies.

•DEFOLIATE Lincoln Park.

"Lincoln Park?" Daley was heard to gasp incredulously when an adviser pressed the point. "That would be senseless and immoral. It's a damned showplace for the city. My God, that's a bankrupt way to sell democracy!"

He reminded his staff that one cannot save institutions by destroying them and besides, bombing and blockades would seriously impair the peace talks underway at the Democratic Convention.

He would have nothing to do with the old rhetoric. Instead, he said, wisdom and restraint must prevail. He went on to explain that he would deceptively allow the enemy to mass under the city's big "Welcome" signs, encircle the invaders, and, in his words, "when nobody's looking, we'll just bop 'em on the heads."

A Republican alderman from the West Side later huffed that General Daley had adopted a "no-win" policy and issued a "start the bombing" ultimatum—without any preconditions.

Unlike the general, he had no sense of history.

~

Labor's Liberal Love Lost? Bosses Fret

Akron Beacon Journal, September 8, 1968

The American labor movement, once a radical infant born of a bloody class struggle, is shifting to the political right with such force that continuous cracks are beginning to appear in the liberal platform upon which tattered unionists once stood and sang "Solidarity Forever."

Labor's age-old commitment to higher wages, broader benefits, and a general uplifting of the workingman's lot is still very real. So it is indeed ironic that labor's success in rewarding its people may now be contributing to the new erosion within the rank-and-file.

The economic rise of the unionist, who in this century has been belted with billy clubs and besieged by federal troops, has left a vacuum filled by the Negro, who is now making his own push toward the top. The unionist, of course, now fears that his job and neighborhood is threatened by the black movement, and a reaction has set in from the assembly line to the construction site.

National and Ohio polls indicate that as many as 20 percent of blue-collar workers favor the "law and order" presidential candidacy of George C. Wallace. With Wallace, the medium is the message, all oratory to the side. The union leaders are clearly worried. But they are carrying their concern beyond Wallace's racial views. They fear him as an enemy of labor and in the weeks ahead will concentrate heavily on bringing this message to the straying working class.

The August issue of *Focus,* an Ohio AFL-CIO newsletter, scorned the low level of union benefits in "Wallace's Alabama" and charged the former governor with being an "enemy of the little man." "Wallace and his right-wing cohorts, like the super-patriots of yesterday, hate the labor movement," the article bristled.

But the leadership also is making some concessions to the angry mood running through many unionists. Last week, President P.L. (Roy) Siemiller of the International Association of Machinists warned an IAM convention in Chicago that the nation could "end up with a government that is not only racist but anti-union"—a reference probably not only to Wallace but to Richard Nixon. Still, he said he was "pretty sick of rioters, looters, peaceniks, beatniks, and all the rest of the nuts who are trying to destroy" the nation.

Such words turn dramatically away from the labor movement's own violent past, when, for example, the Molly Maguires emerged during the railroad strikes of 1877 to terrorize employers and strikebreakers. A strike at the Carnegie Steel Company plant in Homestead, Pennsylvania, in 1892, was broken by two thousand strikebreakers protected by the state militia. The Chicago Haymarket riot brought death to one policeman and four strikers.

Not far from the site of this year's Democratic Convention on Chicago's South Side, ten people were left dead and more than eighty were wounded in 1937 in a Memorial Day clash between police and members of the Steel Workers Organizing Committee at the Republic Steel Company.

Bloody events are now being repeated, but times are changing—and so is the union movement, which is pulling apart from its own history.

Faded Akron Inn Blooms for Wallace Drive

Washington Post, October 13, 1968

It has been a long time since anybody has had to call the cops to put down a Saturday night brawl at the old abandoned tavern that had been left for dead among the tacky storefronts of South Main Street.

But now the cops are coming back. Leaving their motorcycles running at the curbside, they poke their happy faces inside the faded tavern with its walls lately papered over with posters of George C. Wallace.[7] "How are things going?" they ask, and a round-chested man named Sam Huba smiles from under a bushy moustache and replies, "Fine, boys, fine."

Huba is delighted to avail himself of these brief "progress" reports. The word is getting around that at least 90 percent of Akron's 398-man police force is going for Wallace. When the officers leave, Huba squashes down into a chair behind a wooden table cluttered with Wallace trinkets and lectures reporters on the evils of the local press. "The only bigger liars," he fumes, "are the Republicans and Democrats. They are the biggest ones they ever was."

Sam's helper—a thin, elderly man who left Virginia a half-century ago for a job with the rubber industry here—coaxed his visitors to read the campaign literature: "It's all there. The facts. Just read them and see for yourself." The packet included copies of *The Councilor*, the Citizens' Council newspaper out of Shreveport, Louisiana, which bannered "FRIGHTENED NATION TURNS TO GEORGE C. WALLACE".

A lot of people who had never heard of *The Councilor* are seeing it in Akron these days. Copies are stacked in neat piles at the Wallace headquarters here, which is close by the big Firestone Rubber Company plant where many of the blue collars are going for Wallace, too. *The Councilor* is given out free; bumper stickers and pins sell for a quarter over the counter of authorized dealers only, meaning Wallace people.

The people who have been gearing up the Wallace campaign in Ohio are mostly amateurs like Huba and Truman Webb, an Akron cab driver who presides over the Summit County operation and pays for bumper stickers out of his own pocket. "We haven't gotten a cent out of Montgomery," says Webb, a small owlish man who wears a Wallace tie bar. He confides this matter-of-factly without a trace of pique over having to pony up all the money himself.

In Cleveland, the self-appointed Wallace man is Louis Molnar, who says he is a chemist and a former Hungarian freedom fighter. Molnar once had a plan to repatriate all Negroes to Africa. Molnar lists among his organizational ties the Liberty Lobby and the National Association for the Advancement of White People. He's also worked closely with Robert Annable, of Cleveland, an outspoken segregationist who has assumed the role of Wallace coordinator for northern Ohio.

In Columbus, Richard Kochensparger, a sheet metal worker, is the chairman of the Ohio Committee for George C. Wallace, an outfit that has been competing with Molnar's organization. The months-old feud has featured charges by Molnar that Kochensparger is fronting for the John Birch Society, which, according to Molnar is using the Wallace candidacy to establish its own political base after the election.

Oblivious to the warring between the Cleveland and the Columbus Wallace factions, Shirley Fletcher, a Mount Vernon, Ohio, sign-painter and mother of four, is frantically resurrecting the remnants of her LeMay-for-President campaign now that the general is Wallace's running-mate.

It was Fletcher, the wife of the Knox County dog warden, who along with Dr. W.E. Steffan, started a boomlet for LeMay in 1967, setting up national headquarters in LeMay's hometown of Mount Vernon. When the general finally backed off, the drive collapsed. Until LeMay was named to the Wallace ticket, Fletcher had decided to stay home on election day. Now she says she's on a round-the-clock campaign schedule.

But for all the confusion and backbiting and amateurishness, Wallace seems to be doing well. Secretary of State Ted Brown, a Republican, predicts that more than four million Ohioans will vote in November and that Wallace will get a fourth of it if the Supreme Court orders his name on the ballot, which seems a likelihood.

~

Ray Bliss: The "Retired" Mr. GOP Will Still Keep a Hand in Politics

Akron Beacon Journal, April 20, 1969

In the staged and starry world of national politics, where men are events and events often seem bigger than life, let alone men,

Raymond Charles Bliss was easily mistaken for a misfit. Uncommonly shy, and self-conscious about an image that added up to little more than a pudgy, round-faced man with a fleshy nose and slicked-back hair, Bliss had to be content to make political history offstage while the headliners took the bows.

That was all right with him. And after a generation of quietly stage-managing winners—the last four years as Republican National Chairman—Bliss just as quietly slipped out of the theater and came home to Akron, satisfied that he had done his best, earned his pay, and, most of all, helped restore the two-party system after the GOP had been crushed in 1964.

In a rare and exclusive interview with the *Akron Beacon Journal* upon his return from Washington this week, Bliss, still the chain-smoker with the crackly dry voice, rambled over the Bliss years as party chairman in a political recital that may have marked a shift in his customary self-imposed reticence.

In a span of thirty minutes, an eternity compared with past Bliss interviews, he declared: He did not leave the $40,000-a-year party chairmanship under duress from the Nixon Administration but had chosen "my own time and place to resign."

He had declined offers for "a top ambassador's post in Europe—and a good one" and the chairmanship of a federal commission because he was tiring of public life.

He also has turned down offers to write a column for a national publication.

From now on, he will treat politics as "an avocation and not a vocation" but will speak out on political issues when he feels moved to do so.

Bliss, sixty-one, resigned amid widespread speculation that the young Turks around Nixon had demanded that he be replaced by a younger man with a more attractive public image. He was succeeded by U.S. Representative Rogers C. B. Morton, a fifty-four-year-old Maryland congressman.

If he was squeezed out of the job, Bliss gave no outward hint that he is brooding about it. Indeed, he insists that he had been considering retirement since the Republican National Convention last summer.

"I had intended leaving after the convention," he said. "I never went to Washington with any ambition of staying there permanently. I know everybody wants to know why I picked April to resign. Well, it rounded out a four-year term. If I had stayed on longer, there would have been the 1970 elections and then we would have 1972 coming up. So I said I couldn't stay. It was simply a choice of getting out now or staying through 1972—and I just didn't want to do that."

Bliss said that for the same reason that he resigned, he declined the invitations to serve as an ambassador or commission chairman; public life was wearing on him, and he preferred the relative privacy of his insurance business in Akron.

"If I had accepted the European ambassadorship," he said, "it would have meant my leaving the country and running around some more. I'd be right back where I started. No, I couldn't see that for me now."

Bliss's departure from the leadership of the Republican organization, and the arrival of Morton, already have contrasted the political styles of the two men. While shunning the limelight and a public identity with partisan issues, Bliss worked at rebuilding the party by tightly-disciplined organization from the bottom up.

He left the rhetoric to the politicians while he sat in his easy chair at home past midnight with a telephone, staff reports, and a bowl of popcorn—fretting over each detail in the table of organization.

Morton, on the other hand, already has given notice that he will be chief spokesman for Nixon Administration programs and will go to the people to drum up support for the president and his policies. Bliss carefully avoided a judgment on the Morton approach, saying only, "I won't speak for Morton. He's a new chairman, and he'll have problems just as I did. I'm not going to put a stone in his path."

But then Bliss recalled his own way of doing things, and the contrast became apparent. "If you believe as I do," he explained, "that our government must be built from the bottom up, then that is what has been done in the past four years.

"Since 1964, the Republicans have gone from 17 to 31 governors—the highest since 1920 [the GOP has lost one governor this year, in Maryland, although the change in reins, of course, had nothing to do with it]; we have gone from 32 to 43 Senate seats and from 140 to 192 House seats, in each case the highest since 1956; we gained control of both houses in 20 state legislatures, the highest since 1954. In 1964, the Republicans controlled only 7. We also gained 648 state legislators, 1,420 county offices, and nearly 100 mayors since 1964."

Bliss, the mathematician-technician-architect, was warming up for the kind of facts he likes best. "Remember," he said, "the state legislature is very important because it controls redistricting and affects congressional seats. And we now hold the most congressional seats since 1956." Almost as an afterthought, he added: "And we also elected a president."

Not that he didn't consider this important. It was just Bliss's way of saying that the Nixon victory depended on party organization all the way down to the precincts. The local and state elections, he believes, are "the bedrock of party strength. And without this kind of organizational effort, we couldn't have elected a president."

Reminded that Morton had stated this week that Republicans had profited in recent elections by votes from the "dissatisfied, not by the Republican enthusiast" and that much work lies ahead in generating honest enthusiasm for the party, Bliss acknowledged that a certain amount of votes are negative—cast against the other party rather than for your party.

"The record of the opposition party is bound to have an impact. You always pick up a certain amount of anti-votes. But I've never seen an election analysis in which the majority of the votes cast for the winner were anti-votes. The better the organization, the more you will be able to exploit the opportunity handed you by the opposition. And where this really counts is in close elections."

Without mentioning Morton, Bliss touched on another philosophical difference simply by addressing himself to criticism that he buried himself in the nuts and bolts of party organization to the exclusion of ideology. "I'm deeply interested in issues," he retorted. "But as a party, we're out to win—not to fight with each other over ideologies. Once a chairman starts sounding off on issues, people begin to feel that you are using your position unfairly for personal issues."

As party chairman, Morton has leaped into the ABM [Anti-Ballistic Missile] controversy in defense of the president and has indicated he will counter the ABM opponents at every turn.

During his tenure, Bliss relied heavily on the party's forty-seven position papers on foreign and domestic issues drawn up by the Republican Coordinating Committee, composed of former President Eisenhower, Nixon, congressional leaders, and other GOP spokesmen. Without taking a public position himself, Bliss could draw upon these party stances in response to questions on issues.

A major criticism of the position papers was that they were so general as to be meaningless.

Still, Bliss, the master organizer who took over the shattered party structure with $341,000 in the GOP treasury in 1965 and left it with more than $1.5 million in the bank and a Republican administration, was loathe to open any further wounds through intraparty clashes as he attempted to reassemble it precinct-by-precinct.

"I don't want to leave the impression that I rebuilt this party myself. It took a lot of hard work by a lot of people. It took good candidates. And it took financial responsibility in running the party. If we had fifty programs on the drawing boards, but couldn't afford all of them, we assigned priorities. If we were going to preach financial responsibility as a party, we had to practice it. And remember that we set out to raise money at a time when people were reading in the newspapers that the party was dead."

If all this seems defensive in the wake of the changing of the GOP guard under awkward circumstances, Bliss has earned the right to write his own epitaph. "I'll let the record speak for itself," he says.

Now, Bliss seems almost relieved that he is back rocking in his leather chair at his insurance agency up on the twenty-third floor of the First National Tower. He's been on the move since he accepted the Ohio Republican Chairmanship in 1949.

An Akron native, Bliss virtually cut his eyeteeth on politics. Even as a student at the University of Akron, he was busy trying to elect a campus May queen—Ellen Frances Palmer—who twenty-eight years later became his wife (Bliss married at fifty-one).

After working in both local and state campaigns for Republican candidates, Bliss was named to the Summit County Board of Elections in 1935. Six years later, he became chairman of the County GOP Central Committee.

In 1945, he was offered the Republican state chairmanship, but he couldn't afford to accept it. At that time, the job did not pay a salary. However, a year after he started his insurance agency in 1948, he accepted the state post and held it until he was elevated to national chairman in 1964 after the Goldwater fiasco.

"I've been up to my ears in politics for years," he reflected. "You do not control your own time under those circumstances. Events cause you to constantly move from one thing to another. You're not able to plan on anything. I don't know how many times I had planned on taking a vacation or a trip during a theoretically [*sic*] lull period. But something always caused me not to make the arrangements. From now on, I'll be on my own time and will pick and choose what I want to do."

Bliss, of course, will not be completely out of politics. He remains a member of the National and State Republican Committees and serves on the Summit County Central Committee and Board of Elections.

"But now my insurance business will be first with me," said Bliss. "I've been living out of a suitcase for twenty years, and I just want to settle down and start living like a human being."

Stokes Seeks a Second "First"

Washington Post, April 13, 1969

Carl B. Stokes, who became the first Negro mayor of a major American city by a margin of only 1,679 votes in 1967, has now set his sights on another and perhaps even more difficult challenge: to become the first Negro mayor of a major American city to get reelected.

The forty-one-year-old Stokes gave his supporters the word shortly before midnight Wednesday to climax a nearly five-hour $100-a-plate testimonial dinner that had been billed as a "non-partisan civic tribute" to the mayor but, in fact, was a lavishly-staged nominating convention—appropriately, in the cavernous Convention Center here.

$200,000 Put in Kitty

More than two thousand loyalists—the very rich, the middle-income blacks, and white liberals, the political achievers and those who would like to—put $200,000 (gross) into Stokes's campaign kitty, and, although the advance text of his "thank you" speech denied that he was going to make any political announcement of the sort, as did his press aides, Stokes decided not to send his people home empty-handed.

Six other big-city mayors—Allen of Atlanta, D'Alesandro of Baltimore, Alioto of San Francisco, Cavanagh of Detroit, Hatcher of Gary, and Majer of Milwaukee—flew in to provide the laudatory rhetoric for Stokes's high-powered sendoff. So did U.S. Senator Edmund S. Muskie of Maine, an early campaigner himself, who declared the nation must entrust black Americans with "not only citizenship, but with leadership."

Muskie was joined at his dinner table by Ohio National Committeeman Albert S. Porter, Stokes's old political enemy, who has been for the most part relegated to the sidelines since the mayor arrived at city hall.

Porter, in fact, had blasted the whole idea of the dinner several weeks ago, but was finally persuaded by powerful Cleveland Democrats to pay his $100 for the dinner and fly back from a Florida vacation in a fragile display of party unity.

Porter, the Cuyahoga County Democratic chairman, left the big hall quickly after Stokes's announcement. When Muskie was asked by reporters about Porter's whereabouts, the senator nodded back to his table and said, "He was over there." But Porter was nowhere in sight.

Notably absent from the dinner, too, was Cleveland City Council President James V. Stanton, who also happened to be vacationing in Florida. Stanton, who had once aspired to the mayorship himself, has frequently mixed gloves with Stokes on civic issues. At the same time, Stokes has frequently berated council for dragging its feet on needed programs and just last week declared at Yale

University that if trouble erupts in Cleveland this summer, it will be council's fault.

In the explosive setting of urban politics today, political victories can be determined more by unforeseen events than by campaign rhetoric. Political observers here say Stokes must be considered the favorite against any GOP nominee, mostly because the city's big money is behind him and because the mayor has worked diligently to bring a new civic conscience and pride to bear on a city that had been paralyzed by inaction for decades.

Although Stokes's 1967 opponent, Seth Taft, has been mentioned as a possibility for a rematch, the most likely challenge will come from county auditor Ralph Perk, an old-politics campaigner who was an unsuccessful mayoral candidate in 1965.

Pleading Poverty

Whether it will be Perk or Taft or somebody else, Cleveland Republicans are already pleading poverty as they look toward the starting gate for their campaign against Stokes. In mockery of the $100-a-plate dinner for Stokes, Republicans the same night held six 98-cent-a-plate dinners for Taft and Perk, neither of whom used the occasion to announce his candidacy.

But in a less frivolous attempt to raise money, GOP leaders have been trying to persuade Republican business leaders, many of whom have overtly or tacitly allied themselves with Stokes, to return to the political fold with open wallets. But they aren't very optimistic that this will happen.

Stokes Is Reelected Mayor of Cleveland

Washington Post, November 5, 1969

Carl B. Stokes rode a late surge of black voters to reelection last night as mayor of Cleveland. Complete unofficial returns showed Stokes the winner over his white Republican challenger, Ralph J. Perk, by a margin of 7,401 votes out of 246,631 cast. This bettered his winning margin of 1,600 two years ago when he became the nation's first big-city Negro mayor, but that was another cliff-hanger.

As in 1967, Stokes, forty-two, trailed in the count all evening as the white West Side precincts reported four-to-one majorities for county auditor Perk, fifty-five. But at midnight, as the vote count passed 90 percent, the traditionally late-reporting black precincts came in. Perk's seven thousand–vote lead disappeared, and a similar winning margin for Stokes emerged.

Perk cracked fifty years of Democratic control when he was twice elected county auditor and carried the city of Cleveland in the process. But no Republican had been elected mayor in thirty years.

Stokes had the support of the white business establishment, labor unions, and the two major newspapers. His campaign was better financed than two years ago, and the city is nominally four to one Democratic. But there was some question about how strongly the party organization fought for his reelection.

A statewide vote on a constitutional amendment to lower the voting age from twenty-one to eighteen was defeated. It fared better in rural than urban areas.

On the East Side, Stokes was getting 97 percent of the vote, but the more important factor affecting his chances to overtake his opponent was the size of the Negro turnout. What had concerned Stokes's supporters was a drop of about eleven thousand Negro registrations from 1967.

The Perk camp had predicted that if the city's total turnout exceeded 240,000, the county auditor would win. Election board officials estimated this afternoon that the vote would approximate that figure.

Perk's campaign staff intensified their efforts today to turn out the vote on the West Side with a massive telephone drive. Perk reportedly reserved $100,000 for the final voter pitch by sixty-three hundred staff workers, or one worker for every twenty homes on the West Side. On Monday, they saturated the West Side with a door-to-door appeal. They followed up today with telephone calls and in some instances duplicated their efforts.

The Stokes people complained today that about four hundred off-duty plainclothes Cleveland policemen and firemen were challenging East Side voters on their qualifications to cast ballots on a state issue that would lower the voting age from twenty-one to eighteen. They charged that the challengers, who are barred by law from partisan politics, were using the voting age issue as a device to discourage votes that would obviously go to Stokes. But the mayor himself reportedly discouraged his advisers from overly dramatizing the issue in hopes that it would backfire and gain him voter sympathy.

Perk, whose Czech descent made him a folk hero in the ethnic wards, mounted his assault on Stokes with a series of charges that portrayed the mayor as either unwilling or incapable of dealing with the city's rising crime rate. He accused Stokes of playing politics by delaying the appointment of police recruits until the mayoral campaign and generally pictured the mayor as the villain in the seething hostility between the police department and city hall. Throughout his campaign, Perk also declared the crime problem could be solved by adding more police to the force—a move he said could be financed through tighter fiscal management at city hall.

Stokes, meanwhile, maintained that the city—once crushed under the weight of problems that it had accumulated under previous administrations—was finally moving on several fronts and that its national average was never better. He credited his administration with taking the initiative with programs for housing, recreation, air and water pollution control, and appealed to the voters for two more years to see these programs through.

Stokes repeatedly tried to draw Perk into a public debate and when that failed, appeared at the traditional City Club forum to denounce his opponent as "a local Spiro Agnew."

Stokes, 42, became the first black mayor of a major U.S. city two years ago when he took 98 percent of the black vote and 19 percent of the white vote to win by less than 2000 votes over Taft of the Ohio Tafts.

As mayor, Stokes helped contract $100 million in financial aid to help rebuild Cleveland but, as Stokes himself has said, the mere color of his skin could not end black unrest. Stokes had bad relationships with the city police. He opposed a pay raise for them, and police faulted his handling of a black nationalist shootout where ten persons were killed. He blocked off the area to all but black policemen and white residents.

But Stokes built a close relationship with the business establishment of the city and projected an attractive image. Perk broke a thirty-five-year tradition of public debates by mayoral candidates by refusing to take part.

Governor Rhodes Seeks Ohio Senate Seat

Washington Post, November 7, 1969

Governor James A. Rhodes today announced he will seek the Republican nomination for the U.S. Senate in 1970. Although there has been speculation over whether the sixty-year-old two-time governor would enter the race, the timing of the announcement—a one-paragraph statement released by his office this morning—caught many political observers by surprise. Rhodes, who cannot succeed himself for a third term as governor, had said earlier that he would announce some kind of decision around Thanksgiving.

Answers Charges

Last Tuesday, the governor, in a rare prepared speech for television, replied to charges by *Life* magazine that questioned his role in efforts to commute a life sentence for Toledo mobster Thomas (Yonnie) Licavoli and accused the governor of running afoul of the Internal Revenue Service by not declaring personal income allegedly converted from political funds.

In his television rebuttal—the text of which was carried in full-page newspaper ads around the state—Rhodes said the IRS had merely overruled his tax advisers on what constituted personal income during the years 1954–61. He further declared that this personal wealth today totaled only $65,000.

Cites Investigation

The governor also denied any wrongdoing in the Licavoli case and noted that an investigation by the state police had not turned up any irregularities.

The governor's sensitivity to the magazine's charges had raised speculation that he might retire from politics rather than engage in a campaign in which the *Life* article was certain to become an embarrassing issue. But the governor apparently decided that he could survive it and chose today to give himself a head start over other GOP officeholders who seek the Senate nomination. Among them are U.S. Representatives Robert Taft and Donald E. (Buz) Lukens.

Both Taft and Lukens, however, said the governor's decision was of no consequence to them. Taft's aides said their man had not yet made up his mind but that Rhodes's candidacy "will in no way affect the congressman's decision on whether to run for the Senate."

Lukens echoed Taft's statement. "After all," he said, "I always considered if I ran I'd have to face Rhodes or Taft in a primary, or both in a primary." Lukens aides had said that his decision to confront Rhodes depends largely on whether he can raise substantial money for a tough primary campaign. He is believed to be seeking much of it from conservative sources outside of Ohio.

Lukens and Rhodes have never been on friendly terms because of their conflicting ambitions. The thirty-eight-year-old Lukens, a hard-driving campaigner, has attempted to establish his power base within the state Republican Party's right wing and is known to be itching for a winner-take-all primary fight with Rhodes.

Glenn Runs for Senate from Ohio
Washington Post, December 12, 1969

Former astronaut John Glenn Jr. ended months of speculation here today by announcing that he will seek the Democratic nomination for the U.S. Senate next year. Glenn, forty-eight, a retired Marine colonel and the first astronaut to orbit the earth, in 1962, said his decision to return to politics was based on his "dedication to my country and sincerity in wanting to solve its problems." Glenn will seek the Senate seat that will be vacated through the retirement of his old political adversary, Senator Stephen Young, whom Glenn had opposed in the 1964 Democratic primary.

Forced to Quit Race

Glenn was forced to abandon that race when he fell in a bathtub and suffered an ear injury. Young went on to defeat U.S. Representative Robert Taft in the general election.

Next year's campaign could virtually duplicate the cast of the 1964 race. Taft has announced he will challenge Governor James A. Rhodes for the Republican nomination. Although Young will be on the sidelines, it is fairly certain that Glenn will be opposed in the primary by Young's close political and personal friend, Cleveland financier and lawyer Howard Metzenbaum, who is expected to declare his candidacy later this month.

A Glenn-Metzenbaum contest would put two friends of the Kennedy family into the same ring. Glenn said the Kennedys had encouraged him to run but would not comment on whether they have pledged him financial support.

A native of New Concord, Ohio, Glenn had been a vice president of Royal Crown Cola in New York City but resigned and moved to Columbus recently in preparation for his campaign.

Campaign Financing

He has repeatedly said that his decision to run again rested solely on whether he could raise the money for a campaign. He maintains that he still doesn't have much money and will have to rely heavily on news coverage for political exposure.

State Democratic leaders have considered a Democratic ticket headed by Glenn for the senate and former U.S. Representative John J. Gilligan for the governorship is the party's best hope for victory next year. Gilligan has remained noncommittal about his political future but is expected to announce his candidacy for governor later this month.

Glenn's Opponent Closing Gap in Ohio Race
Washington Post, April 30, 1970

Shortly after John Glenn Jr. had wound up a long, informal discussion of national issues in a crowded auditorium on the Kent State University campus near Akron, he was greeted outside by a college youth who pumped the former astronaut's hand and asked: "What does weightlessness feel like?"

Exit John Glenn, forty-eight, a Democratic candidate for the U.S. Senate. Enter Colonel John J. Glenn Jr., who eight years ago became the first American to orbit the earth, now talking at length about his space feat as a circle of rapt students gathered around him. The image that Glenn had quietly worked to subdue in his bid for the Senate was emerging again: a ruggedly lean, soft-spoken national hero—and only incidentally a politician.

Wherever he goes on the stump, Glenn is met with placards harking to 1962: "Glenn is A-OK." Mothers push their tots up to him to autograph bits of paper or photographs. He grins shyly, fills each request, and the kids wander away as if they had just talked to a department store Santa Claus.

Glenn's strategists have counted the hero worship as both an asset and a liability in his low-keyed attempt to win the Democratic nomination from an aggressive, liberal millionaire businessman-lawyer, Howard Metzenbaum, and two less formidable opponents next Tuesday.

The Glenn people have banked on his exotic public image to provide the lift-off for his political ambitions—which were thwarted six years ago when an injury forced him to withdraw from the Democratic senatorial primary against Senator Stephen Young. But the Glenn camp also has been concerned that, although voters admire him as a space hero, they may not take him seriously as a political candidate.

So he has crisscrossed the state reciting his generally liberal positions on Vietnam, inflation, busing, the space program, and the Nixon administration, usually in informal groups, seldom raising his voice, but always pleading his credentials as the only candidate who can win next November against the tough opposition of either U.S Representative Robert Taft Jr. or Governor James A Rhodes, the two Republican contenders in the state primary.

"We're confident but not cocky," one of Glenn's aides said this week.

But what had been at first counted on as a landslide for Glenn seems scarcely probable now. Metzenbaum, fifty-two, a former state legislator and political confidant of Senator Young, claims to have closed the gap with what some political observers say is the best campaign organization the state has seen in recent years.

Once virtually unknown outside of his native Cleveland, where he built a fortune as a developer of airport parking lots, Metzenbaum has carried the fight to Glenn with a campaign punch estimated to have cost more than $500,000. He has saturated the state's eight television markets.

He has tramped through condemned county homes for the elderly, debated college students, and insisted all the while that he is the legitimate political heir to his good friend, Senator Young, because he and the senator have shared a concern for the poor and oppressed.

Once conceded no chance of victory, Metzenbaum now elatedly refers to private polls that indicate his "recognition factor" had increased from 12 percent to 55 percent through March. He claims that 63 percent of the voters who now know him are "on my side."

With a final TV blitz this week, he figures he will have passed Glenn by election day.

Ideologically, Metzenbaum and Glenn are separated only in degree. Both, for example, oppose the Vietnam War, with Glenn calling for a quick but responsible troop withdrawal; Metzenbaum has proposed a withdrawal deadline. Metzenbaum also had urged deep slashes in space spending; Glenn has countered that space cuts should not be allowed to hinder the benefits derived from space research.

The two other Democratic candidates have posed different problems for Glenn and Metzenbaum. Dr. Kenneth Clement, a Negro and prominent Cleveland surgeon, has been accused by the Metzenbaum forces of entering the race merely to siphon black votes away from Metzenbaum, who was endorsed by Mayor Carl Stokes, a Negro.

Clement, who split with Stokes over policy matters after being one of his early campaign advisors, has repeatedly denied that he was anything but his own man in the race, declaring: "It would be presumptuous to think I know which black votes belong to Mr. Metzenbaum." The indications are that the black vote will be fairly evenly divided between Glenn and Metzenbaum.

The fourth candidate, John W. McAlarney, is a bearded Akron rubber worker who has been accusing local Democratic leaders of preordaining Glenn as the nominee simply because he is a space hero.

Taft Intensifies Campaign as Governor Rhodes Gains in Ohio

Washington Post, May 5, 1970

U.S. Representative Robert Taft Jr., his normally deadpan mien flushed, and smiling absently as though he had just startled himself, turned to a group of reporters last week and asserted: "I'll be damned if I'm going to let anybody think I'm not a fighter."

Newsmen covering Taft's hitherto gingerly campaign against Governor James A. Rhodes for the Ohio Republican senatorial nomination couldn't recall when the three-term Cincinnati congressman was more animated.

Taft had just finished an hour-long television debate with Rhodes at WAKR-TV in Akron in which he took off after his opponent's credibility as governor ("a new issue in this campaign," as Taft put it), loyalty to the Republican Party, and honesty as a candidate. Obviously satisfied with his performance, Taft then sat down for an impromptu press conference as Rhodes dashed from the studio, shrugging off reporters along the way with a hasty apology that "my wife is ill and I have to get home."

This was the third face-to-face confrontation by the two candidates, and by far Taft's most aggressive showing after taking a pounding from Rhodes in the first debate in Cincinnati.

The fourth and final match was held Saturday at the Cleveland City Club, where Rhodes, quoting extensively from Taft's earlier praise of the Rhodes administration, seemed to get the best of it. Before the confrontation, Rhodes had been slowly cutting into Taft's lead, according to the polls. His Saturday performance—telecast extensively in the state—may have given him still another boost.

Out of Character

Plagued throughout the campaign by a diffident and self-conscious style on the stump, Taft has had to step out of character to match the flamboyance and earthy combativeness of Rhodes.

Rhodes's followers have long touted him as the state's greatest "salesman"; at the Akron debate, Taft labeled his opponent's methods as "blowoff hucksterism."

After being conceded a slight edge over Rhodes, partly because of the political value of the Taft name in Ohio, and partly because Rhodes had been bruised by a *Life* magazine article that questioned his income tax returns, the fifty-three-year-old Taft appeared to falter as he droned through speeches that even an accountant couldn't find exciting.

An example from one of Taft's dissertations on inflation: "Industrial production—the aggregate measure of our total output—has trended downward for the last several months—and labor demand has begun to ease. While the monetary climate still remains relatively tight—and interest rates are still high—some relaxation has occurred."

Meantime, the sixty-year-old Rhodes, a veteran of the state's country roads and county fairs, plowed up voters by resorting to a theme that has not wavered in his eight years as governor: The answer to society's problems is jobs and more jobs through industrial and business development. He cited millions of dollars of capital improvements under his administration, cast himself as the tireless servant of all Ohioans, and contrasted all this by charging his opponent was a part-time congressman who showed up for roll call only 40 percent of the time. "The issue in this campaign," Rhodes insisted, "is a working senator."

Both Back President

Both men seemed eager to campaign from the front door of the White House. Rhodes questioned Taft's loyalty to President Nixon on key administration issues. Taft replied that he stood foursquare with the President on issues from Vietnam to inflation and recalled that it was Rhodes who held back the Ohio Republican delegation from Nixon at the Miami convention in 1968.

Aura of Invincibility Dies: Glenn, Rhodes Lose
Washington Post, May 7, 1970

Ohio voters destroyed two legends in Tuesday's primary elections: that Governor James A. Rhodes, the state's all-time champion vote-getter and master of the Republican house, couldn't lose against whatever challenge, and that a liberal Jewish millionaire—Howard Metzenbaum of Cleveland—couldn't win in a state in which many Democrats take their conservatism in large doses.

But when the final votes were counted at daybreak today, Ohio's Republicans had dramatically turned down Rhodes's bid against U.S. Representative Robert Taft Jr. for the GOP senatorial nomination, and the state's Democrats had just as dramatically lifted Metzenbaum to victory over former astronaut John Glenn, a folk hero whom they said couldn't lose—but did.

Thus the voters set the stage for what already is being touted as the "battle of millionaires"—Taft against Metzenbaum in the U.S. Senate race. It may also be a clear test of the Nixon administration's policies in Vietnam. Taft has endorsed the President's policies while Metzenbaum has taken every opportunity to denounce our widening military role in Southeast Asia.

For Rhodes, the outcome was a bitter climax to an old-school ribbon-cutting political career that began in the 1930s and peaked with two overwhelming victories over Democratic opponents in the 1962 and 1966 gubernatorial races.

With heavy support from his home county of Hamilton (Cincinnati) and from Cuyahoga County (Cleveland), Taft, despite a lackluster campaign, managed to squeeze past Rhodes by 3,165 votes. The unofficial totals gave Taft 467,866 and Rhodes 464,701.

Metzenbaum, backed by what many observers believe was the finest political organization ever mounted in Ohio Democratic politics, carried only thirteen of the state's eighty-eight counties but scored heavily in the big cities to oust Glenn by 12,466 votes.

Metzenbaum unofficially polled 427,294; Glenn, 414,848. Two other Democratic candidates were a distant third and fourth.

In view of the closeness of the Taft-Rhodes race, some observers believe that a *Life* magazine article last spring that questioned the governor's income tax returns and his motives in commuting a Toledo mobster prison sentence produced just enough impact to swing the election to Taft.

Another issue that could have played a role in the governor's defeat—although nobody is prepared to say for certain—was the tragedy at Kent State University, the day before the election, in which National Guardsmen that Rhodes had ordered to the campus shot to death four students and wounded ten others.

On the Democratic side, Metzenbaum, a political unknown when he entered the race, coupled a well financed and expertly executed media campaign to introduce him to the electorate with a hard-driving footrace around the state to overcome Glenn's familiarity in the eyes of Ohioans.

He worked to the left of Glenn's own moderate-to-liberal views, loudly denouncing the war, calling for a troop withdrawal deadline, lining up with civil libertarians, defending the U.S. Supreme Court, and arguing the cause of blacks and the poor.

On many of these issues, Glenn declared he was equally concerned—but Metzenbaum's convictions apparently were more persuasive to the Democratic voters.

"Half of our victory can be attributed to our own effective campaign," said a Metzenbaum aide. "But the other half drew from the weakness in Glenn's own organization." As the campaign wore on, it became apparent that Glenn's underfinanced organization was being finessed at every turn by the enormous staff and political savvy of Metzenbaum's forces, who are believed to have spent $500,000.

Metzenbaum will team with another liberal, John J. Gilligan of Cincinnati, who easily won the Democratic nomination for governor over two other opponents.

Taft will be paired with State Auditor Roger Cloud, a colorless but competent political moderate who won the Republican nomination for governor in a four-way race that included Rep. Donald E. (Buz) Lukens.

Part II

The Politics of Turmoil, 1970–1976

The Politics of Turmoil, 1970–1976

Introduction

The first years of the 1970s were characterized by political turmoil in Ohio, driven by tensions unleashed in the 1960s. Zaidan's writings capture this unrest, sometimes up close and personal, and sometimes from a distance.

The shootings of antiwar protestors at Kent State University on May 4, 1970, exemplifies this turmoil. The Kent State University campus is twelve miles east of the offices of the *Akron Beacon Journal,* and Zaidan was part of a team of seven journalists who covered the tragedy and its aftermath. The paper won a Pulitzer Prize for their work in 1971. Three of the articles reviewed by the Pulitzer committee are included here: the first shocking headlines, Zaidan's own crisp analysis of Governor Rhodes's controversial involvement, and the first detailed chronology of these terrible events.

There is no substitute for reading these frank portraits of a national tragedy, even more than thirty years later. However, the letter nominating these pieces for the Pulitzer Prize by journalism professor Murray Powers comes close:

> At about 12:24 P.M. on May 4, 1970, a detachment of Ohio National Guardsmen fired a volley of shots that killed four students and wounded nine on the campus of Kent State University.
>
> It was the bloodiest incident growing out of the unrest on an American campus. It was also the bitterest.

Murray goes on to note:

> Media coverage of the incident was clouded from the start, beginning with an inaccurate report that two Guardsmen were among the fatalities. Controversy quickly developed over the question of whether a sniper had fired at the Guard. . . . With the national mood quickly fragmenting, and a tendency to explain the shootings with slogans, accusations and epithets becoming dominant, the *Beacon Journal* staff responded to the mandate for thorough, accurate reporting that would reveal the truth about Kent State.
>
> What distinguishes the *Beacon Journal*'s work is that the nature of its disclosures, all under the pressure of a deadline, contributed to a common understanding of what happened on May 4.

The Pulitzer Prize committee agreed with this assessment. The nation owes Zaidan and his colleagues a debt of thanks for their coverage.

As if this turmoil were not enough, racial tensions continued in Cleveland. After two difficult terms as mayor, Carl Stokes decided not to seek reelection, but he made a strong effort to pick his successor in 1971. These efforts split the Democratic vote in Cleveland, allowing Republican Ralph Perk (who lost to Stokes in 1969) to win the general election for mayor. Perk briefly brought back a version of the old-style ethnic politics in Cleveland, which Zaidan describes in brilliant detail ("Ethnic Cleveland: Mayor Rebuilds Old Politics on Voices of Old World"). Perk served three terms as mayor in the 1970s, during which time the city rapidly deteriorated and became the laughingstock of the nation. (Not only did the Cuyahoga River catch fire, but so did Mayor Perk's hair.)

The politics of turmoil spilled over into the 1972 presidential campaign. Democratic Senator George McGovern used the fervor of the antiwar movement and the new primary rules created after the disastrous 1968 Democratic convention to secure the presidential nomination, giving the new liberals a victory over the old liberals, including the 1968 nominee, former Vice President Hubert Humphrey, and his allies in organized labor. By this time, Zaidan had begun to write regular columns for the *Akron Beacon Journal*. He incisively describes the change in the nomination process in "The 'Politics' Is Just Beginning" and "It's Farewell to Kingmakers."

In another column, he covers the less exciting Republican renomination of President Richard Nixon in "Any Glamor Left for the GOP?" Like Goldwater in 1964, McGovern was quickly tagged as outside of the political mainstream in 1972.

Two humorous columns connect the dots in the desultory fall campaign that led to President Nixon's landslide victory in 1972. Zaidan notes the failures of the McGovern campaign in "For Sale: 10,000 Peace Signs," and in "Buggers Can't Be Bunglers," he satirizes the origins of the Watergate scandal, the break-in at the offices of the Democratic National Committee by operatives from CREEP (the Committee to Re-elect the President), Nixon's campaign committee. Along with the Vietnam War protests, the Watergate burglary and the resulting cover-up by the Nixon White House are also powerful symbols of the politics of turmoil. Zaidan provides a columnist's overview of the two historic results of the Watergate scandal: the first president to resign in American history, Richard Nixon ("Both Parties Will Benefit: Ford Restores Civility to Politics"), and the first president not chosen in any fashion by the voters, Gerald Ford ("Ohio GOP Hit by Pardon of Nixon").

In 1974, the political turmoil spread to the Republican Party. Partly as a reaction to the Watergate scandal and partly due to a weak economy, the Democrats won a stunning victory in the midterm congressional elections. However, Ohio was a bright spot for the GOP because James A. Rhodes recaptured the governorship. Despite the baggage from years in office and his role in the Kent State shootings ("Old Skeletons to Rise and Haunt Rhodes"), he managed to defeat his successor, Governor John Gilligan (who had been elected in 1970 when Rhodes left office). Associated with the new liberals, Gilligan's failure to win reelection reflected in part his intellectual style, better suited for a college seminar than the campaign hustlings ("Gilligan Campaign Muscle Not There"). Zaidan provides humorous yet insightful snapshots of Ohio politicians in 1974 in "Ohio's Four Biggest Political Mouths: Who Says All Politicians Sound Alike?"

This period of turmoil witnessed the continued clash of Democratic giants: another duel between former astronaut John Glenn and businessman Howard Metzenbaum for a seat in the U. S. Senate in

1974. Metzenbaum won the first meeting with Glenn,[1] only to lose to Republican Robert Taft Jr. in the general election. Metzenbaum reached the Senate first when he was appointed to replace Senator William Saxbe, who resigned to become Attorney General under President Ford ("Metzenbaum Finally Has His Prize").

However, Metzenbaum's joy was short-lived: Glenn defeated him in the 1974 Democratic primary ("Glenn May Be Headed for a Job") and then went on to claim the Senate seat in November, defeating Cleveland mayor, Ralph Perk. Glenn quickly became a national figure in Democratic circles. But Metzenbaum took a page out of Rhodes's book and ran again in 1976 ("Metzenbaum Image Is 'Fluffier' "), defeating his old Republican nemesis, Senator Taft ("Taft Running Hard to Meet Challenge from Metzenbaum") to join his old Democratic nemesis, Senator Glenn in the Senate.

The politics of turmoil also had a major impact on the 1976 presidential election, which Zaidan covered in his columns. Among the Republicans, the simmering tensions between moderates and conservatives boiled over in the fight between President Gerald Ford and former California governor Ronald Reagan ("Ford-Reagan Battle Shows Severity of GOP Trouble"). Ford outlasted Reagan's challenge, but, as Zaidan put it, "Ford Won Party Nomination, but Reagan Stole its Heart." Meanwhile, among the Democrats, former Georgia Governor Jimmy Carter defeated a field of candidates from among the old and new liberals to secure the presidential nomination. Carter's peculiar mix of Southern charm, moderate policies, and outsider status allowed him to outlast his many rivals in the primaries and secure the nomination ("Story Scraps Were Big News"). Carter ultimately won the 1976 general election by a narrow margin, returning Ohio to the Democratic column. Zaidan offers a snapshot of the Carter campaign in Ohio in "Oh, the Games They All Play"). Both of the major parties had made significant moves to the right in 1976, entering a period of transition.

Four Dead, Eleven Wounded as Guard Fires into Rioters at KSU[2]

Akron Beacon Journal, May 4, 1970

Four persons were killed and at least eleven others shot as National Guardsmen fired into a group of rock-throwing protesters at Kent State University today.

Three of the dead were tentatively identified as: William Schneider, Jeffrey Miller, and Allison Krause. The fourth was an unidentified girl. Injured were: Dean Mahler, Thomas Grace, Joe Lewis, John Cleary, Alan Canfora, Robert Stamp, Dennis Brackenridge, Doug Wrentmore, and Bill Hersler. Two of the nine are National Guardsmen.

Six of those taken to Robinson Memorial Hospital suffered gunshot wounds. Three were in critical condition. Two of those taken to the hospital were identified as Guardsmen suffering from shock. One of the Guardsmen was released this afternoon.

(Telephone communications between Akron and Kent were severed at about 1 P.M. A call to the Ohio Bell Telephone Company in Kent brought this recorded message: "Due to the martial law in effect in Kent, the telephone company is closed.")

Gunshots rang out about 12:30 P.M., half an hour after Guardsmen fired tear gas into a crowd of five hundred on the commons, behind the university administration offices. Demonstrators hurled rocks and tear gas grenades back as they scattered.

Police are holding a man who said he used a gun he was carrying when he was attacked by demonstrators. The man reportedly had press credentials and carried a camera.

The highway patrol reported earlier they were looking for a sniper reported atop Johnson Hall, which is on the edge of the campus commons.

A newspaperman, an eyewitness to the shooting, said the gunshots rang out after one student hurled a rock as Guardsmen were turning away after clearing the Commons. "One section of the Guard turned around and fired and then all the Guardsmen turned and fired," he said. According to the witness, some of the Guardsmen were firing in the air while others were firing straight ahead.

Guardsmen and police immediately cordoned off all buildings on campus, permitting no one to enter or leave. One National Guardsman collapsed during the melee, complaining of chest pains. He was rushed by ambulance to a hospital.

The wounded were taken to Robinson Memorial Hospital in Ravenna. They were unconscious and covered with blood. At least one was shot in the leg, and two others were shot in the abdomen.

The shooting broke out after students had rallied on the commons at the center of campus in defiance of an order not to assemble. An officer in a jeep ordered them over a loudspeaker to disperse. He begged them to break up "for their own good." The protestors laughed and jeered. The troops, wearing gas masks, then began to launch canisters of tear gas.

The troops were en route back to their original positions when about twenty students, both boys and girls, ran toward them from behind Taylor Hall. Stones and sticks fell on the troops, and obscenities filled the air. Apparently without orders, the Guardsmen turned and aimed their M-1 rifles at the charging students and began firing.

Students in the emergency room at Robinson Memorial Hospital, who would not give their names, said they had wanted to get on the commons to discuss demands. As they started gathering, the Guardsmen started throwing "pepper gas" at them, and the students started throwing rocks.

Then, they said, the firing started.

One nonstudent with a guru mustache and long hair said: "They'll pay for it. It's not the radicals, it's the most conservative groups on campus who will bring the university down now." One youth said the most conservative kids are out screaming the same as the long-haired kids.

With National Guardsmen now patrolling all of Kent, schools were dismissed, stores were closed, and traffic was blocked from either entering or leaving Kent.

More than one thousand antiwar demonstrators, many of them students, clashed with Guardsmen and police Sunday night before they were driven back with bayonets and tear gas. Nine persons were reported injured in the rioting, including three Guardsmen.

More than one hundred were arrested, the majority for violations of an 8 P.M.-to-dawn curfew imposed by Kent city officials.

Militants in the three nights have burned the university's Army ROTC building, smashed fifty-six downtown store windows, and threatened Kent businessmen. National Guard Brigadier General Robert Canterbury said the Guard will remain as long as necessary.

Sunday's demonstrations began about 8 P.M. when students massed around the student union near where the ROTC building was leveled by flames the night before. Police from thirteen communities and four counties were called in. Guardsmen first fired tear gas at 9 P.M. in an abortive attempt to scatter the crowd as it marched behind Dunbar Hall, a men's dormitory. At about the same time, a door window was broken in the Music and Speech Building and a small fire set inside. The blaze was extinguished quickly and damage was slight.

Guardsmen read the Ohio Riot Act at 9:12 P.M., but it went unheard by the jeering demonstrators. The crowd then began to move toward Main Street as Guardsmen again fired tear gas volleys. Police and Guardsmen formed near the Kent Motor Inn as the crowd halted at the intersection of Main and Lincoln Streets. National Guard and State Highway Patrol helicopters hovered overhead, illuminating the area with searchlights. At least two hundred demonstrators sat down in the intersection while several hundred others stood behind them on the campus lawn.

Self-styled protest leaders attempted to open "negotiations" with the police, asking that Kent Mayor LeRoy Satrom and KSU president Robert I. White be brought to the scene. A policeman said Satrom and White would meet with them if the demonstrators returned to the campus.

Satrom said later he had authorized no one to tell the demonstrators he would talk with them. University officials said White would not meet with the protestors. The demands included abolition of the ROTC program, a decrease in tuition, amnesty for forty-seven arrested in Friday and Saturday nights' disturbances, and removal of the Guardsmen.

Guardsmen fired more tear gas at the crowd at 11 P.M., scattering the students toward campus. The crowd broke up a half-hour later. Two students were wounded when prodded by a bayonet, and a Guardsman was injured by a rock.

Damage to the ROTC building was put at $50,000, and other losses connected with the rioting were estimated at $36,000. Kent businessmen report they were flooded with telephone threats Saturday to put up antiwar signs or face burning of their stores. Several businesses damaged Friday night displayed such signs.

Governor Rhodes, on the campus Sunday to survey damage from the previous two nights' rioting, said he would ask the Ohio Legislature to make rock-throwing at police and firemen a felony and to make automatic the dismissal of any student, teacher, or administrator convicted of participating in a riot at a state university. The governor blamed the rioting on "a handful of militants who have a studied plan to destroy higher education, a band of militants who we now know have been active going from campus to campus."

The KSU Student Senate passed a resolution Sunday condemning Rhodes for using the disturbances as a campaign tool in his U.S. Senate race against Robert Taft Jr. Twenty-three faculty members issued a statement deploring the violence.

Units of the National Guard's First Battalion, 145th Infantry, and Second Squadron, 107th Armored Calvary, both based in Akron, were called to duty by Governor Rhodes. The Second Squadron moved in Sunday night. Many of the men had been on duty in the Teamsters strike. Their equipment included armored personnel carriers.

The rioting Friday night came a day after President Nixon told the nation he was sending troops into Cambodia. Friday's riots capped a day of antiwar demonstrations marked by the burning of a copy of the U.S. Constitution.

Rhodes Took Full Control at KSU, Guard Charges

Akron Beacon Journal, May 8, 1970

Governor Rhodes assumed full control of the tense Kent State University situation last Sunday morning and apparently issued orders without consulting National Guard or university officials, Guard sources told the *Beacon Journal.* Among the orders, a source said, was that Guardsmen were to break up all campus assemblies—peaceful or otherwise—and would remain on the campus twelve months a year, if necessary.

The governor spelled out his policy for handling campus demonstrators during a meeting with university, state, and local law enforcement officials at the Kent fire station. "All we knew in advance," the Guard source said, "was that the governor was going to hold a meeting, then a brief press conference before touring the campus."

At this point, the source said, the Guard had not been told it would be ordered to break up peaceful assemblies.

"Our mission," the source said, "was to protect lives and property and not to spend our time chasing kids. But Sunday's meeting was the governor's show. There were no objections by anyone there, no discussion—it wouldn't have done any good. The governor had made up his mind."

Although Rhodes himself remained unavailable to newsmen, his chief aide, John McElroy, denied that the governor had ordered the National Guard to break up peaceful assemblies. "No specific direction of that sort was ever given," McElroy said.

When asked whether the governor had threatened to investigate faculty members who agreed with the dissenters, McElroy first said "No," then added: "What happened when he [Rhodes] was up there, only the governor and those there would know."

It was at the same meeting, the *Beacon Journal* reported earlier, that the governor rejected a plea by Portage County Prosecutor Ronald Kane to close the campus immediately to avoid a possible violent confrontation with militant students. Once, Kane called Rhodes into another office for a private discussion during which he advised Rhodes to close the university and send the students home. Rhodes rejected the suggestion "because he felt it would be playing into the hands of the SDS and the Weathermen," radical student groups, Kane said.

The source said Guard officials apparently were surprised by the order to break up peaceful assemblies, which are protected by the Constitution. The source reported Rhodes also promised to investigate all faculty members who advised or agreed with student dissenters, and to see "that they would never teach again."

The source said many Guardsmen resent the anti-Guard feeling that has been apparent in some quarters "because none of us looked forward to clashing with students." "We were there," he said, "because we were ordered there as military people with military equipment thrown into a civil situation and expected to act as police auxiliary."

He described Guardsmen as just as frightened as many of the students, and said: "We wear only fatigues and helmets, no chest protectors or any other shield against rocks and bottles. Even a baseball player has a glove to catch a ball. We use World War II equipment—old-fashioned tear gas canisters that anybody can pick up and throw back at us, rather than the new tear gas bombs that go off on contact with the ground. The kind we use are like throwing a roll of toilet paper."

He also was critical of arming Guardsmen with M-1 rifles, weapons with "tremendous velocity" that are meant to kill. "These things will shoot through a tree—a slug can pass through three or four people."

Four students were killed, and ten others wounded Monday when Guardsmen fired on a rock-throwing group.

The Guard spokesmen said that when a group of students gathered Monday to call a strike, highway patrolmen tried twice to disperse the crowd. When that failed, Guardsmen moved in, and the shooting resulted.

~

Three Violent Days—Then Tragedy[3]
Akron Beacon Journal, May 10, 1970

It began on May Day—the international symbol of distress. It was one of those perfectly sunny spring days on the gentle slopes of an ordinary Midwestern college campus, but there was something about it. . . .

The night before, the president had told the nation he was sending troops into one nation to shorten a war in another. Start a war to shorten it? It was the topic of the morning at Kent State University. And it was the focal point that touched off a chain of events that rocked the world seventy-two hours later.

What happened in those seventy-two hours is a matter of record and conjecture. But why did it happen? Did supposed outsiders lose control of the mobs in three successive nights of rioting? Were city and university officials lulled into thinking the Ohio National Guard was a cure-all for all troubles? Above all, why were trained, armed soldiers called in when just a year before similar demonstrations were handled efficiently by local law enforcement personnel?

On Friday, May 1

The prelude of things to come began at noon Friday when students called a rally on the main Kent State campus to protest President Nixon's invasion of Cambodia. Groups involved in that protest were the New University Conference and the Student Religious Liberals—self-assumed successors to the Students for a Democratic Society.

About five hundred people heard graduate student Steven Sharoff say, "Nixon killed the Constitution last night by entering an undeclared war on Cambodia. It is dead, and we are going to bury it."

Three hours later, Black United Students held another demonstration that drew 350, including 47 black students. Demands for more black programs and enrollment were read.

It was quiet the rest of May Day on the campus. But just before midnight on a downtown street a mile away, a bonfire was started.

~

"From the outset the Kent Police Department realized that a potentially dangerous situation existed in the Kent area," Mayor LeRoy Satrom said. "I was called from out of town—Aurora—at the first reports of disturbances in our city."

Students spilled out of nearby bars to see what was going on in the middle of South Water Street. They saw a bonfire, and blocked traffic, and waved signs denouncing President Nixon.

It was something to do on a Friday night.

The crowd milled around, waiting for the initiative. Police also waited. "By the time I arrived, the Kent Police Department had seen fit to summon aid from the Portage County Sheriff's Department," said Satrom. "Only after arrival of the sheriff's department did the

Kent Police Department begin to take action against students and others involved in demonstrations in the downtown area."

~

By that time the crowd, numbering five hundred, had moved along Water Street to Main Street, breaking windows and tossing beer bottles. Windows of fifteen business places, many of them financial institutions, were smashed.

"It is estimated that over $50,000 damage was done," Mayor Satrom said.

Sixty-five deputies and twenty-four Kent policemen finally threw tear gas into the mass of students at 3 A.M. as they reached Lincoln Street, entrance to the main Kent State campus. The students fled onto the campus, some taking refuge in dormitories. Fourteen were arrested for disorderly conduct. The mayor and Police Chief Roy Thompson imposed an 8 P.M.-to-dawn curfew for the rest of the weekend.

"I immediately notified state officials in Columbus of the situation," Mayor Satrom said.

He talked to John McElroy, Governor Rhodes's executive assistant. "He [Satrom] was in quite an uproar," McElroy said. "He said the students had taken over the city, were breaking windows and terrorizing businessmen. He said they had been using local police and sheriff's deputies for several hours and had been unable to subdue the students. He said he needed help.

"I'm not sure, but I think I called General [Robert] Canterbury then. I do remember calling the duty officer [Colonel John Simmons] at National Guard headquarters here. I told him about the mayor's call and said a Guard liaison officer should talk to Satrom and see what the situation was. An officer did go and reported back that the violence seemed to be subsiding and that they probably wouldn't need the Guard."

On Saturday, May 2

It was quiet Saturday morning at Kent State University.

University President Robert I. White was still in Iowa at a meeting of the American College Testing Program. Administration Vice President Ronald Roskens had been away since Thursday.

Vice Presidents Robert Matson (student affairs) and Richard Dunn (finance) were in charge of the university. Matson and his assistant, Dr. David Ambler, called in twenty-eight faculty members and thirty to forty students in a "Cool-It Corps."

"We set up a rumor center, manned by faculty and students, as a sitting place for information and to give out factual information," Ambler said. "We also worked with the Inter-Residence Council. We set up hall dances in the dorms and got a couple of bands. It is my understanding these were fairly well attended. We kept the Student Union open."

The city was locked up tight, and the university planned to serve snacks while the curfew was on downtown. It also served supper in the dorms on the weekend, "something we don't often do," Ambler said.

Meanwhile, reports of impending trouble that night kept reaching Mayor Satrom.

~

"At 5 P.M., I again telephoned Columbus and this time requested National Guard troops to aid local officials in protecting the life and property of the residents of the city of Kent," the mayor said.

State Adjutant General Sylvester Del Corso was already in Kent along with General Canterbury, assistant adjutant for Army troops. "Del Corso called me from Kent and said he had some troops already mobilized to go to Cleveland on the Teamsters thing," Satrom said. "He said as a precaution we ought to get some of them into the Kent area. I said it sounded like a good idea, so he moved in some National Guard troops who had been standing by in Akron."

The First Battalion of the 145th Infantry left the Akron Rubber Bowl for Kent. Troops arrived at Walls School about 7 P.M. It was about 7:30 P.M. when the State Highway Patrol Post at Ravenna was alerted.

"When you bring in police, it's because the situation has reached a point of seriousness that you know they will be needed," Vice President Dunn said. "If you bring them in at the first sign of trouble, you only inflame the students."

The patrol began to gather its units at Ravenna while the university sent buses to pick them up.

Crowds were assembling on the campus. It was about 9 P.M. "All of a sudden," Dunn said, "these crowds began leaving where they were and gathering on the Commons. From there, they marched around the residence halls, picking up little groups. They gathered tremendous speed and came over the hill by Taylor Hall in a rush down to the ROTC building."

The front ranks of the crowd were described by Dunn as "ugly and vicious. They were not recognized by any of our security officers. These faces were strange."

Twenty-four security men at the ROTC building were unable to control the mob, numbering three hundred. The building was fired once but didn't catch. The crowd fell back. Then the building was fired again with railroad flares and gasoline-soaked rags.

There was a ten-minute period after the crowd got to the ROTC building when university officials discussed calling the Guard because the highway patrol had not arrived and campus security could not protect firemen, who were being stoned by the crowd. A fire hose was severed by students.

The call for Guard help was never made. Both the Guard and Patrol arrived before more action could be taken. "The National Guard just sort of oozed onto the campus with Del Corso because of the destruction of the ROTC building and on information supplied by the Patrol that they were dealing with a real and existing danger," McElroy said.

~

It was on April 16, 1969, that a similar demonstration erupted at the hands of the Students for a Democratic Society (SDS). Seven SDSers were to face disciplinary hearings for a confrontation with police in front of the Administration Building eight days previously.

A 4 P.M. rally in front of the Student Union led to a march to the music and speech building where the closed hearings were scheduled. "Open them up or shut them down," the SDSers screamed. The students broke into the building, storming it.

A thirty-man highway patrol platoon arrived and with the help of police and sheriff's deputies dispelled the students and arrested fifty-eight for trespassing.

The National Guard, which had been on alert, was not called. Why now?

~

"We didn't have manpower enough," said Kent Law Director Robert Hart. "The mayor called the Guard. Insufficient manpower is the only basis on which you can call the Guard."

Hart said 96 of about 130 available highway patrolmen were patrolling Ohio State University, which was rocked by riots the week before.

Said McElroy, "The moment I have any request for National Guard troops, I call the governor. However, by the time I talked with the governor, we had already moved on it. I do have that authority."

"There wasn't any sequence or any determination to be involved or not involved," said Roskens. "We didn't decide to call the Guard or phase in the Guard. The governor said Sunday they were in charge. We cooperated in their decisions, and they cooperated with us."

"Once the guard was committed to the city of Kent, it was committed to KSU," Dunn said. "When things began building up on the campus, they just came on."

The Guard was a welcome sight when troops arrived on campus about 9:30 P.M., Dunn said. "They were totally cooperative with university officials," he said. "We suggested spots that might need securing—water and radio towers and the power plants."

Several students in residence halls reported strangers on campus. One who appeared several times was identified as Andy Pyle. He is known as a radical leader, who has been observed taking pictures of military equipment at Kent and who has turned up during many controversial events, including an Asian affairs conference. He was also on the steps of the administration building on April 8, 1969, when SDS members clashed with police. Four SDS members sentenced in that incident were released from jail three days before last week's disturbances began.

National Guardsmen prevented another invasion of the downtown area following the ROTC fire by forming a line on East Main Street. The turmoil ended about 11:30 P.M. Police arrested thirty-three for curfew violation.

Last Sunday

Governor Rhodes came to Kent Sunday.

He went about 7:30 A.M. with Patrol Superintendent Robert Chiaramonte, and they met in the Kent City Building with Del Corso, Satrom, County Prosecutor Ronald Kane, and some student representatives. During that time, he also toured the city and the campus.

During that conference, it was decided that the campus would not be closed. Kane, however, wanted to shut down the university—and he went to Common Pleas Court to get an injunction. "Something had to be done," he said.

Meanwhile, President White returned from Iowa. He met briefly with Rhodes before the governor left for Columbus. "No university official had any private conference with the governor," said Roskens, who returned to the campus Saturday afternoon.

~

There was more rioting Sunday night. Persons with red armbands, headbands, handkerchiefs, and flowers were seen among those gathered outside the Student Union. The group suddenly moved by the burned ROTC building and went over the hill between Prentice and Taylor Halls.

About two hundred demonstrators sat in the intersection of Main and Lincoln Streets. At the campus entrance, they were finally driven back by Guardsmen's tear gas. Sixty-two were arrested for curfew violations.

Who were the demonstrators?

~

"There is no doubt in my mind that off-campus revolutionaries planned the gathering at the ROTC building and the timing—to hit at dusk and get away before we could mobilize," said one high-ranking official. He points to the many little gatherings on the campus that converged at the same time on the building.

There are conjectures that some of the planning may have been done during the last six months, when the four SDS leaders were in jail for their part in last spring's riots. Officials emphasized that imported, radical leadership was important to the development of events, but the Cambodian situation served as a rallying point which attracted many nonstudents. One administrator said the unfamiliar contingent around the campus seemed to disappear quickly once trouble started.

~

There is no question that the National Guard gave the orders once troops arrived. "Everything was being handled from Canterbury's command post on campus," McElroy said.

Portage County Sheriff Joseph Hegedus said he "attended a few meetings, but I wouldn't call them command affairs."

Kane was not consulted on maneuvers until the Sunday morning conference.

"We had a conference with the university people, but the Guard commander was the ultimate authority," said General Canterbury. Command was assumed Saturday night by the Second Squadron of the 107th Armored Cavalry based at Akron-Canton airport. That unit, as well as the 145th Infantry's First Battalion which arrived earlier, had been on duty protecting truck drivers in the Teamsters strike since Wednesday morning, April 29. A total troop strength of thirteen hundred was available for duty, although only about eight hundred were assigned at one time.

"There were no recruits in there," said Lieutenant Colonel Charles Fassinger, commander of the Second Squadron. "All these men have served at least six months' active duty with the regular Army. All of them are trained in riot control. We've seen duty in Hough, Glenville, Youngstown, Akron, and Geneva-on-the-Lake."

Said Lieutenant Colonel Harold M. Finley, control commander of the Second Squadron, "We're not untrained people. We've gone through this before, but we've never been as pressed as here."

~

The troops were assigned on a shift basis, Finley said. Those on duty were "pretty fresh."

They also remembered the words of General Del Corso during their Teamster duty: "Return fire with fire." Said General Canterbury: "We have a book that gives the Guardsman the rules of engagement. It says if somebody shoots at us, we shoot back."

Guardsmen went into action under terms of the Ohio Riot Act, which forbids assembly of four or more persons during proclamations of emergency. But there were no mass arrests made at any time.

Matson and Ambler said this was discussed by the patrol, campus security, and Guard, but it was decided the university and the city streets were public property. They agreed that if there were no compelling charges, arrests would only incite the crowd.

Donald L. Schwartzmiller, chief of campus security, contends, however, that if mass arrests had been made on the demonstrators at Main and Lincoln Streets Sunday night, there would have been no more incidents. "They had them all there," he said.

Monday, Day of Tragedy

Monday came. "Our sources indicated that all would be quiet in town and that the Guard had the situation under control," Mayor Satrom said.

"Anytime you get into a situation like this, it's a strain," said General Canterbury. "There's no use kidding ourselves."

"Anytime a man's away from home for so long, he's got to be under some stress," said Colonel Finley.

~

It was chilly as the sun rose over the budding trees. And at noon, the victory bell rang, summoning students to a rally on the Commons.

Ninety-eight Second Squadron Guardsmen who were nearest the area were called to the Commons, facing a crowd of five hundred. The students hurled rocks, and the Guardsmen advanced, firing tear gas. The students fled behind Taylor Hall, and the Guardsmen proceeded to a parking lot.

Ten minutes later the Guardsmen began a return sweep back to the Commons. The rocks and bricks flew again, and then the bullets. . . .

Democratic Party Split in Three in Cleveland
Washington Post, September 20, 1971

With the September 28 mayoral primary only a week away and the November 2 general election just beyond that, the Democratic Party here is split in three.

On August 30, Cuyahoga County Democratic Chairman Joseph Bartunek stood before more than 350 members of the party executive committee and called for the endorsement of Cleveland millionaire-developer James M. Carney. Moments later, the committee voted 194 to 160 to support Council President Anthony Garofoli in the mayoral primary.

The shocked Bartunek told reporters afterward, "I'm seriously thinking of resigning. I feel I've been repudiated." The next day, Bartunek, who resigned as probate judge to devote more time to the party chairmanship, reconsidered. He said he, too, would support the thirty-four-year-old Garofoli in the latter's bid to succeed the retiring Carl B. Stokes. A few days later, Bartunek thrust the whole explosive Democratic session in a positive light. He said these facts were an indication of "party interest and vitality."

Whether the Democrats can, in fact, unite behind one candidate in the relatively few weeks ahead before the November showdown remains to be seen in view of the passions that permeate Democratic politics here.

The man the party repudiated, Carney, is a powerful party angel who has contributed heavily to his favorite Democratic candidates over the years. He had garnered a number of IOUs he had hoped to collect in this year's race. It didn't work, despite the fact that he had successfully lined up Bartunek behind him for the important committee endorsement.

In the other corner, however, was Garofoli, regarded as the rising young antagonist of the party establishment, and running with U.S. Representative James Stanton, the man he succeeded as council president, as his chief ally. On the other hand, Carney had been a strong supporter of former U.S. Representative Michael Feighan, whom Stanton ousted in the 1970 Democratic primary.

To further complicate the Democratic picture, Arnold Pinkney, a black man and Cleveland's school board president, has decided to run this year as an independent and will square off in the general election against the Democratic nominee and either County Auditor Ralph Perk or State Representative George V. Voinovich, who are vying for the GOP nomination.

Democrats fear that in a three-way showdown in November, Pinkney will harvest the city's heavy black vote that twice sent Stokes to city hall, while the Democrats and Republicans split the white votes.

Perk Beats Odds in Stunning Upset

Akron Beacon Journal November 3, 1971

Democrat James Carney had a heavily financed campaign, a ten-to-one Democratic registration, and the endorsements of the Cleveland Police Patrolmen's Association, most of the labor unions, and the *Cleveland Press*.

Independent Arnold Pinkney had Mayor Carl B. Stokes, the Reverend Jesse Jackson, and the *Cleveland Plain Dealer*.

Republican Ralph Perk had only Democratic Councilman Dennis Kucinich, unkind words for Stokes, and 38 percent of the vote Tuesday—but it was all he needed to be elected mayor, thus ending, in one astonishing day at the polls, three decades of Democratic rule at city hall.

The final unofficial vote:

Perk—88,774.

Pinkney—72,785.

Carney—65,877.

Joseph Pirincin, the Socialist Labor Party candidate on the ballot, got 1,740.

The total tally of 229,176 votes was a record turnout for the city.

Perk's upset victory not only betrayed the pollsters and the predictors but delivered a serious setback to the dreams of outgoing Mayor Stokes, who had chosen this campaign to set up his model of black political power at the polls.

In first endorsing Carney in the Democratic primary, then calling upon the city's 102,000 black voters to switch to Pinkney in the general election, Stokes had hoped to impress politicians everywhere of the decisive might of black coalition politics.

It didn't work, partly because 20 percent of the black voters opted for Carney anyway, cutting away from Pinkney's strength, while Perk ran over Carney by nearly a two-to-one margin in the city's white wards.

And just as the fifty-seven-year-old Perk, the county auditor who was denied bids for the mayor's seat in 1965 and again in 1969, set up Stokes as his target in the campaign, political observers focused on Stokes in Pinkney's defeat.

Some of Carney's crestfallen workers maintained that if the mayor had been less visible in the primary and general elections, it would have stripped Perk of his main issue—that Stokes was the man behind Carney and Pinkney. Perk, who had called his two opponents the mayor's "stooges" in the campaign, argued that he alone represented the "little people's" interests, against the Stokes "machine."

In accepting victory Tuesday night in the basement of the Polish Women's Hall on the Southeast Side, Perk returned to that theme by declaring "this election belongs to the people."

He also praised Kucinich, a maverick Democrat who raised the specter of political manipulation by Stokes at the public's expense. Perk, who lost to Stokes in 1969 by about thirty-five hundred votes, asserted that Kucinich and other Democrats had "risked scorn and retribution by their party machine to stand up for principle."

When it was apparent that Perk was on his way to victory, Stokes appeared before Pinkney's supporters at the Sheraton Hotel to appeal for patient acceptance of defeat.

"The system elected Carl Stokes as your mayor and friend and who loves the man who lost tonight," Stokes said. "We must accept defeat the same way we accepted victory. . . . No fight for freedom ended tonight. But it might have to go into a short pause. . . . You must not sully the process should defeat come. I'm going to abide by the results. Mayors come and go. But the city and the needs of its people remain. Our responsibility is to uphold the system."

Ethnic Cleveland: Mayor Rebuilds Old Politics on Voices of Old World

Washington Post, August 13, 1973

Question: In what top-heavy Democratic city can a Republican mayor with no apparent affection for the refinements of public office be considered an early favorite to win reelection after:

•He unwittingly set his hair on fire with a blowtorch at a public ceremony for the American Society of Metals
•His wife snubbed a White House invitation so that she could keep a bowling date, and
•A member of his administration was caught playing a gypsy violin in New Orleans during sick leave?
Answer: Cleveland.

In his first nineteen months as mayor of this traditionally Democratic stronghold, Ralph J. Perk has presided over a dramatic revival of old politics in a city that was clearly receptive to the beguiling "Perkisms" after two tumultuous terms under black mayor Carl Stokes.

The fifty-nine-year-old Perk, the son of first-generation Czech parents, has cast himself as the chief theoretician of what he calls "Ethnic Power," and in so doing has mobilized the city's huge ethnic population (mostly Democrats) for a united Old World voice in modern big-city politics. In this respect, he has maintained an impeccable image as "the Ethnic Mayor," which is the way they like to introduce him these days.

When he showed up in a tuxedo at the Second Annual Czech and Slovak Cotillion Ball last February, he pranced to the microphone and laid it on the line: "I am proud to be a Czech. I am proud of my brother Slovaks. I am proud of the nationality movement. . . . There is a great upsurge of ethnic power, and you're part of it. I'm proud of all of you. We're going to grow, grow, grow. We must work to preserve and perpetuate our heritage. God bless you and have a good time."

He had just been hastily driven across town from an earlier appearance at St. Joseph's auditorium on the far East Side where he was the honored guest for a performance by a Croatian dance group.

There, Perk, in his familiar nasalized singsong oratory, reminded a cheering audience of two thousand: "Wherever there are Croatian churches, there are clean neighborhoods. There are good people. They're law-abiding. You don't see their children burning down properties or stepping on the American flag."

Although he would be quick to deny it, the Ethnic Mayor's message drew clear distinctions between righteous, hard-working, and heretofore unsung ethnics, and unrighteous, lazy, hell-raising everybody-elses. All of this goes over very well in Cleveland, where racial divisions run deep, albeit without the violence of those earlier days of the Hough riots and the Glenville shootouts with the police.

"Perk," says one of his city hall staffers, "is merely doing for the ethnics what Stokes did for the blacks. You can't criticize that, now, can you?"

So Perk, sucking on hard candy and bracing himself with a hand on the dashboard as his driver, Edward (Cap) Harrison, a retired fire captain, bullets along the expressway from one ethnic function to another, talks over and over about the "revival of ethnic pride."

"The thousands of immigrants who came over to this country during World War II and afterwards to escape Communist oppression revived the ethnic spirit in this country. That was the beginning of the revival. They are the ones who brought new pride to the ethnics."

He goes that way eighteen hours a day, usually seven days a week, operating city hall as if it were the League of Nations. His office is well-stocked with books titled *Hungarian Legends* or *The Ukrainians in America*. He also has an ancient Bible and another spiritual book for guidance.

"It says that life is an eternal struggle between God and man, on one hand," says the Ethnic Mayor, "and the Devil on the other. I agreed. See, I've underlined some of the passages."

On the same day, one of Perk's cabinet appointees walked into a meeting carrying a copy of a Lithuanian newspaper under his arm.

Perk's image among his staff at city hall is that of a no-nonsense, hard-driving chief executive who expects as much from his payrollers as he does from himself. To this end, he passed out copies of

Parkinson's Law to his whole staff. "I just wanted my staff to know that I know all of the secrets of the goofers-offers," he explained.

If Perk is annoyed by the snickers of his critics that he is a flat-witted bumbler at times, he doesn't show it. Indeed, after he was pictured on television and in the press with flames shooting up from the thick mesh of hair of a bewildered mayor, he smiled: "You'd be surprised how many newspapers around the world ran that picture of me with my hair burning. Boy, they sent the pictures to me from everywhere."

Nor did he seem riled when the press twittered that his wife, Lucille, had gone bowling instead of dining at the White House. Mrs. Perk, a heavy woman with quick words about everything, is nothing if she is not informal. Her version of the story was simply that she still had some Christmas shopping to get out of the way and didn't have time to get a dress for the White House invitation. "Besides," she explained to us, as she stood in floppy slippers and mixed up some tuna salad in her kitchen, "it was my bowling night."

Perk has yet to stand trial in Municipal Court on an assault and battery charged filed against him by Cleveland patrolman Arnold Hovan. Hovan, a 265-pounder, accused the 172-pound mayor last month of grabbing him by the shirt and badge after Hovan called to him, "Thank you, Mr. Mayor," after the city council failed to override Perk's veto of paid hospitalization for police and firemen, claiming the city lacked money. Perk was served an arrest warrant at his city hall office, tactfully escorted to the Central Police Station by two patrolmen, and booked. He pleaded innocent.

The Ethnic Mayor and his wife still live in an old, brown-shuttered house on East Forty-Ninth Street overlooking the Willow Expressway and Republic Steel's dismal scrapyard. It is a lower-middle-class neighborhood of proud immigrants whose homes somehow survive the ravages of expressways, steel mill pollution, and age.

Perk is proud of the fact that he has never moved out of his old neighborhood, not during his many years as county auditor, and not now that he is the city's chief executive, an office he reached in 1971 with only 38 percent of the vote in a three-way race.

In that year, he was helped by a split in the Democratic vote between Arnold Pinkney, the black president of the Cleveland Board of Education, and James M. Carney, a self-made millionaire businessman and a powerful operative in the Democratic Party here.

A change in Cleveland's charter has ruled out the possibility that more than two candidates (excluding write-ins) will meet in November. The change eliminated the partisan primary, replacing it with a nonpartisan contest on October 2.

The two top finishers will face each other November 6. Carney has announced that he will again challenge Perk, hoping to win back the blacks and other Democrats who backed Pinkney the last time out.

But Carney's campaign could be plagued by a power struggle in the black community between U.S. Representative Louis Stokes, brother of the former mayor, and the combination of Pinkney and Councilman George Forbes, city council's majority leader.

Stokes, long at odds with the Democratic establishment here to win a greater voice for blacks in the party, backed the Reverend Alfred Waller, a black minister, for mayor. But Waller, given little chance of winning one of the top spots, withdrew July 29, a move observers attributed to lack of support by the black community, expected to favor Carney.

Pinkney, meanwhile, has publicly ruled out his own candidacy for mayor this year—a move that was widely interpreted as a nod to Carney. As the campaign warms up, the split among the city's black leaders could become divisive enough to soften the route to reelection by Perk.

From his office at city hall, Perk has been getting mostly good news about his reelection chances (one private poll shows Perk clinging to his 38 percent of two years ago, with only 18 percent for Carney, who ran last in the three-way race. The undecided vote, then, is sizable.) Still, he says, "I'm always running scared."

That facet of Perk's political conscience isn't as apparent as his persistence in sustaining his image as the Ethnic Mayor. Though his critics may decry his lack of innovative programs for the city, his bland disposition, and old-fashioned ways, they are less precise in describing the kind of gallows that will hang him in November.

"The trouble this year," says one prominent Democrat, "is that although Perk hasn't done much good for the city, he hasn't done much bad either."

"Ralph," says a Republican politician, "isn't spectacular. But he gets things done, like picking up the garbage on time."

Not only that, Perk also keeps a listed number in the telephone book. His wife fields all of the calls from the constituents and has been known to call various city departments to find out why so-and-so has gotten the runaround. She also tells the people on the phone that "Perk," as she refers to the mayor, is the best mayor they've ever had.

The contrast in style from the old days, when Carl Stokes applied Madison Avenue techniques to Black Power, has not been lost on the great mass of ethnic voters in town.

The preseason speculation this summer is that the man who beats Perk will not do so with a sharply contrasting style but rather with one that "outPerks Perk." That may explain why James M. Carney reserved a table at the Statler Hilton Hotel the night the Ethnic Mayor made his grand entrance to the Second Annual Czech and Slovak Cotillion Ball.

The "Politics" Is Just Beginning

Akron Beacon Journal, June 9, 1972

U.S. Senator George McGovern's latest wave of victories in this week's primaries has raised more concern within the Democratic Party that the South Dakota senator might indeed win the party nomination in Miami Beach next month. So a lot of worried party professionals are now actively promoting a "Stop McGovern Movement," which is being interpreted by some observers as a "Start Humphrey Movement" in disguise.

This is a bizarre phenomenon, even for politics. Many of the party pros who claim that McGovern can't win in November are the same folks who contended six months ago that U.S. Senator Ed Muskie could. With Muskie sidelined by some severe poundings at the polls, the action has shifted to stopping McGovern.

~

"Why do you want to stop McGovern?" I asked a Stop McGovern coordinator the other day as he assisted his staff in blowing up Stop McGovern balloons for a big rally that night.

"Simple," he replied, his face flushed from a stiff fight with the last balloon. "He can't beat Nixon."

"Who can?"

"We won't know until we nominate somebody at the convention and see what he does in November."

"Humphrey?"

"He might do it, if McGovern's people would agree to support him."

"Why would the people who helped McGovern win the big primaries help Humphrey?"

"Party loyalty, for one thing. You obviously don't know anything about organizational politics."

"Who is the party organization?"

"The people who work for the WHOLE party, not just McGovern."

~

"And if you're unsuccessful in stopping McGovern at the convention, what are you going to do?"

"I'm not pessimistic. He will be stopped."

"How?"

"Why do you think we're spending a whole afternoon blowing up five thousand Stop McGovern balloons? Why do you think I'm giving up a golf weekend to mail out ten thousand Stop McGovern bumper stickers? Why do you think the Stop McGovern Party is sponsoring rallies from coast to coast this month?"

"Still, there is a possibility that the senator might win it on the first ballot. After all, he did win all those primaries."

~

"They don't mean a thing. McGovern wasn't very well known in the primaries, so the people voted for him. Voters are funny. When they think they like somebody, they vote for him, even if they don't know him. But party professionals aren't going to take any chances on sending a total stranger to the White House. Once the voters realize their mistake, the party will be over for McGovern."

"The party? Do you mean the Dem—?"

"Now if you'll excuse me, it's getting late, and we still have a lot of balloons. . . .

"Of course."

It's Farewell to Kingmakers

Akron Beacon Journal, July 14, 1972

The big story that emerged from the 1972 Democratic National Convention is that this is not a vintage year for kingmakers. Indeed, according to many of the pundits, Miami Beach may have provided the final resting place for the kingmaker and his retinue in the annals of American politics.

Whatever personal solemnity attended the historic occasion depended a lot on how close you sat to the throne. It is not an easy matter to dismiss royalty when you are a member of the court.

So it is that kingmakers (a misnomer because America is hung up on having presidents and justices of the peace, not kings) must find their way to exile through the subterranean passages that are always somehow available when the mob is rushing the palace gates.

Where will they set up their governments in exile to bide their royal time until the revolution has run its course? Some kingmakers say they will go fishing for awhile. Others confide they will sit on their thumbs. This is long established court jargon for saying there is nothing for a kingmaker to do.

Nobody knows when the idea of kingmaking began. There is no evidence in the history books that there was a labor minister behind George III or a main-stem duke behind Henry VIII, charting each move to the throne.

Apparently, kingmaking is purely an American phenomenon that began, oddly, sometime shortly after we decided to have presidents instead of kings. The term is probably a compromise for those Founding Fathers who distrusted the idea that a society could survive without benefit of regal trappings.

So instead of kings, the republic produced great colonies of kingmakers who offered themselves up as do-gooders for people aspiring to high places. In return for their unique services, kingmakers were able to boast that they were on a first-name basis with the throne.

They also were able to claim some small remuneration for their services—patronage, government grants, a secretarial job for an in-law, first rights on television coverage at a national convention. There were less dramatic, but no less enriching, rewards. An autographed picture of the king to hang in a bureaucratic office, an opportunity to introduce the king at political rallies, a Christmas card that wasn't presigned.

When you wanted to know what the king was thinking, it was understood that you started out by asking the kingmaker, and if the king didn't agree with that, too bad. Besides, there always was a flunky around to blame for any misunderstanding between the king and his maker.

It went along that way until Miami Beach, which may be as significant to the decline and fall of kingmakers as Chicago was to their greatest command performance. Some will say that one was necessary for the other.

At this point, kingmakers don't know what to think.

Fishing can be fun—but what mackerel is going to appoint your sister-in-law to wind the electric clocks at the courthouse?

Any Glamor Left for The GOP?

Akron Beacon Journal, August 9, 1972

The Republicans' major election year dilemma is not whether President Nixon can win but whether they can make their national convention in Miami Beach interesting and exciting for the television viewers.

So far, nobody has come up with a solution. Even the White House is worried. Some of Nixon's aides fear their man's TV ratings may have peaked during his Peking and Moscow visits and that a presidential mission to Miami Beach will attract almost no popular interest.

This kind of concern was present when the Republicans decided to cancel their San Diego engagement. At the time, a number of Nixon strategists argued that there was no advantage to transplanting the convention in Miami Beach.

~

According to insiders, there was strong sentiment in favor of holding the convention in Paris across the street from the peace talks or on the Western side of the Berlin Wall.

Other suggestions included Vatican City, Jerusalem, and Saigon. Although all these possibilities promised several evenings of viewing excitement, the plans for a foreign site for the Republican National Convention were discarded in deference to party tradition.

"It just seemed too un-American to have a Republican convention on foreign soil," said one veteran GOP operative. "Even at the expense of losing a few new ethnic votes, we felt it was wiser to stay in America. Love it, or leave it."

So Miami Beach it will be. And now the question is how to make it all seem enthralling to the public.

~

"We don't have a suspense factor—everybody loves everybody in the Republican Party," a GOP source said. "Once we go down there and say that, however, how are we going to sustain interest in the proceedings?"

One planner suggested that the Republicans sponsor a telethon during the convention. "We could have people call in their comments to the president, who would serve as a master of ceremonies. Anybody who called in with a campaign pledge would get a special invitation to the latest John Wayne film or a Johnny Cash record album. The biggest contributor would get to sit in the president's box at the Super Bowl."

Others suggested that the Republicans invite the Ohio Democratic delegation to serve as tellers in the vote count. "Even if the president is the only man nominated by the Republicans, the Ohio Democrats would certainly add some suspense to the tallies," a GOP source said.

~

Nothing is certain yet, mostly because the party strategists are still checking out reports that the networks may shift their convention coverage to a big cheesecake-eating contest at a Collins Avenue delicatessen in Miami Beach.

One contestant, who trains on pizzas, reportedly can down twenty-two cheesecakes in fifteen seconds. And if you don't think this trick will stand the nation on its head, you haven't tried any Collins Avenue cheesecake lately.

~

Buggers Can't Be Bunglers

Akron Beacon Journal, October 20, 1972

The National Association of Wiretappers thinks it is getting a bad rap from the Watergate affair. Joel Satrap, an association spokesman, called a radio talk-back show the other night to put the issue in proper perspective.

"The way the press has handled this incident," he complained, "has given all buggers a bad name. We are all now victims of guilt by association when nobody has even been convicted yet."

"I'm sure wiretapping can be a very honorable profession," the studio host assured Satrap. "I'm delighted that you called to give us your side of the story."

~

"You can't imagine what my neighbors have been saying about me since the Watergate episode was publicized," Satrap cried. "It's awful how people jump to conclusions."

"Have they called you to complain to your face?"

"Of course not. They call each other and accuse me of all sorts of things."

"How do you know what they are saying?"

"How do you think I know? I tune in on their phone calls. For practice, I've had the whole neighborhood bugged for the past three years."

~

"Are your neighbors incensed that we now live in a world in which no one is guaranteed privacy?"

"Of course not. They're as nosy as anybody else. They have nothing against bugging per se."

"I don't understand. If they approve of eavesdropping, what's your problem?"

"My problem is that Watergate made all buggers look like rank amateurs. Our profession depends on the trust and confidence of our clients. It's like any business. Any time you have a massive bungle like Watergate, it puts a cloud over the whole field of electronic surveillance. It's just not good for business."

"That's too bad. The field offers so many opportunities for people who need jobs."

~

"At the rate we've been growing, our association has projected that, by 1984, two out of three Americans will be seeking the services of an electronic surveillance specialist. It's reaching the point where we will propose at our national convention next year that the President assign a cabinet position to a Secretary of Surveillance."

"Maybe time will heal the Watergate blunder."

"It better happen soon. I haven't had much work lately. Some of my best friends are even saying, 'Joel, I was thinking of using you to check up on my wife, but how can I be sure you won't louse it up?' I can't afford the bad publicity."

~

"What do you tell them?"

"Only that we offer a twenty-year guarantee on all bugs and will appear in court on behalf of our clients in the event of any lawsuits."

"That's not enough?"

"So far, it hasn't worked. People are edgy."

"Maybe after the election people will calm down and the situation will improve."

"I hope so. Buggers got to eat, too."

~

For Sale: Ten Thousand Peace Signs

Akron Beacon Journal, November 8, 1972

With Tuesday's election out of the way, both Richard Nixon and George McGovern are now able to give some serious thought to their postelection garage sales, which are always eagerly anticipated by collectors of political memorabilia.

President Nixon is planning two clearance sales, one at the White House and the other at San Clemente, and he has named sixty-five surrogates to manage them. He plans to announce the sale in a special broadcast on all three networks next Friday night. John Connally also is expected to touch on the subject the same day at the Cleveland City Club.

McGovern, meantime, has rounded up a few friends and his immediate family to help him with his sale at his Washington home. His major fear is that it will rain and his garage roof will leak on his merchandise.

~

The president's sale, of course, will draw the most attention because he is the president. Henry Kissinger has been engaged in private talks in Moscow, Peking, Hanoi, and Saigon and has happily informed the president that he has reached a tentative agreement with those governments to send observers to the sale.

Nixon has taken over steps to assure a successful sale. Although it went largely unreported, the last time he was in Southern California, he stopped his motorcade to talk to a woman waving a garage-sale sign (with the address printed neatly underneath) in front of the TV cameras.

He reportedly promised her that so long as he is the president, he will never agree to allow hippies to hold communal garage sales. The woman was said to have taken a deep breath and exclaimed: "Thank you, Mr. President."

~

Although the president has not yet disclosed the items that will be put up for the sale, the *Washington Post* and the *New York Times* have speculated that he will be clearing out some things from old press conferences because he doesn't find much use for them now.

To spice up the sale, he also is expected to offer a football autographed by Don Shula and some monaural Sammy Davis albums at fairly competitive prices. Spiro Agnew, it is believed, has agreed to relinquish some golf balls and Frank Sinatra records.

McGovern, on the other hand, has been beside himself trying to figure out what the public will buy at his sale.

~

He has wheeled in his old school bus, tagged at $2.50, and will try to unload ten thousand peace signs at a dime apiece. He is expected to do better with a carton of McGovern-Eagleton buttons at $3 apiece. Even Republicans are collecting them.

The senator also is setting out on his tables some other campaign paraphernalia, including one item called "Moral Outrage"—priced to sell at three-for-a-penny.

Several Democrats who are thinking about running for president in 1976 said they would stop in and take a look at George's stuff on their way home from the office.

Metzenbaum Finally Has His Prize
Akron Beacon Journal, December 23, 1973

Everything about Howard Morton Metzenbaum bears the patina of success: His crisply tailored suits that bespeak both fashion and taste; his sedate, softly-lit seventeenth-floor law and business offices in downtown Cleveland where important people come and go amid a setting of cushy chairs, Swedish porcelain figures, and Oriental antiques; his swimming pool and tennis courts by his spacious home on two-and-a-half acres in Shaker Heights.

But it wasn't until 10 A.M. last Wednesday that Metzenbaum got the prize that eluded him in 1970, and the one he has been aggressively seeking ever since.

On Wednesday, Governor [John] Gilligan announced he had appointed Metzenbaum, a fifty-six-year-old liberal Democrat, to succeed Republican Senator William Saxbe when the latter takes over as U.S. Attorney General in January.

For a man who has spent much of his time buzzing around the state the last three years shoring up political alliances and building new ones, it seemed out of character for Metzenbaum that news of the governor's appointment found him at home with his family. But Metzenbaum explained his absence from the governor's side in Columbus: "I wasn't invited."

Although the governor and Metzenbaum have not been on the friendliest of terms, the latter says he is prepared to offer his last ounce of energy to prove he is the right man to be a senator. No one who has followed Metzenbaum's political and business enterprises will doubt his zest for the job.

The lean six-footer with silver-white hair, never leaves a task half-done. In 1970, when his polls showed that he had only 5 percent recognition among Ohio voters—in contrast to 95 percent for his Democratic primary opponent, former astronaut John Glenn—Metzenbaum staged a supercharged campaign that, according to political observers, "always left Glenn a couple of weeks behind." While Metzenbaum stood at plant gates pumping the hands of workers and recalling that he was a child of poverty, a TV blitz throughout the major markets in Ohio cut away at Glenn's "recognition" lead.

To everyone's surprise, except possibly Metzenbaum's, he beat the space hero by about thirteen thousand votes in a campaign that cost more than $800,000—more than half of which came from his wife, Shirley, and four daughters. Although he lost to a powerful Republican name, Robert Taft, in the general election by about seventy thousand votes, it was close enough to encourage Metzenbaum to start gearing up for another campaign.

Not unexpectedly for a man who has enjoyed both wealth and political influence, Metzenbaum has inspired a wide spectrum of opinion from his friends ("great desire to serve people," "compassionate," "a genius") and his enemies ("ruthless," "an opportunist," "manipulator"). But even Metzenbaum's critics concede that, as one Ohio politician put it: "He's extremely sharp. He's excellent at making the right moves at the right time. He has a great sense of political timing."

A Dayton political writer summed up Metzenbaum's political style in one word: "chutzpah."

Metzenbaum doesn't accept criticism easily and has admonished reporters who have referred to him as a "millionaire"—and he makes his case well: "There's a lot of other people in public life who are millionaires, including Bob Taft and John Glenn, and nobody mentions it. Why me?"

Metzenbaum's sensitivity to his wealth—which he says he will reveal, "and it is going to surprise some people who think that I have much more than I do"—may have something to do with his lean years growing up on Cleveland's East Side. "My father [Charles] had to sell his 1926 Essex to keep the bank from foreclosing on our house," he recalls.

Metzenbaum, the younger of two brothers, worked his way through law school at Ohio State University by selling mums at football games, renting bicycles for twenty-five cents an hour, hawking magazines and Fuller brushes, and playing a trombone for fifty cents an hour in a National Youth Administration orchestra.

"I did anything to make a buck."

After graduation from law school, he advertised in a Cleveland newspaper that he would "exchange legal services for office space."

He moved in with a lawyer named Sidney Moss. Later they opened a chain of income tax consultant offices in several cities ("We charged $1 for each tax form we handled") and that, according to Metzenbaum, gave him his start. "We earned $10,000 our first years—the first real money I ever made," Metzenbaum says.

In 1942, he ran for the Ohio House of Representatives, won, and subsequently spent a second term in the House and two terms in the Senate. In 1949, a year before he left the legislature, Metzenbaum, Moss, and business partner Alva T. Bonda opened a parking lot at Cleveland Hopkins Airport (though they were ridiculed by some who considered it a bad investment).

The parking franchise eventually developed into the Airport Parking Corporation of America (APCOA). In 1968, APCOA was transferred to International Telephone & Telegraph Consumer Services Corporation in exchange for preferred stock. Metzenbaum's stock share in the transaction: $6 million.

But throughout his expanding business venture, he remained close to politics—and organized labor, as general counsel to the Ohio Federation of Labor.

He managed former U.S. Senator Stephen Young's campaigns in 1958 and 1964, became a personal friend of the Kennedy family and, in 1968, served as Ohio chairman of the late Robert Kennedy's presidential campaign.

Now it's his turn in Washington. "I hope to be effective," he says, "but I certainly don't intend to come in with a loud voice. I'm not going there riding a white horse and being gung-ho. But I do hope to be effective."

Glenn May Be Headed for a Job
Akron Beacon Journal, May 12, 1974

In the hours after the polls closed last Tuesday, Howard Metzenbaum's top advisors sat behind closed doors in a small room at the Cleveland Stadium Club and gloomily witnessed the transformation of their senator into a lame duck at the hands of the electorate.

What had been widely predicted as a tossup was, on all fronts, developing into a rout. By 10 P.M., it was clear that the perfunctory insistence by the senator's aides that it was too early to throw in the towel was strictly a matter of protocol. By tradition, concession statements are left to the candidate himself.

Metzenbaum, who had run hard on time-tested Democrat bread-and-butter issues and had tried to lump his opponent, John Glenn, in the same pot with big Republican money, was kicked out of office by many of the same voters who have responded to bread-basket appeals in the past.

The gut issues this year, which Glenn pursued from the beginning, was not the price of beans and rice, as his opponent had supposed, but political honesty and all that the term implied in a day when most people no longer trust a landslide president.

The message to all candidates in the fall election is public cynicism is running more deeply than most politicians and pundits have perceived, despite all the talk about Watergate. So when Glenn started raising a lot of questions about Metzenbaum's taxes, and how the wealthy businessman-lawyer was able to get away with paying no federal income taxes in 1969, it was not enough for Metzenbaum to explain that he had suffered heavy business losses that year. Not in 1974, it wasn't.

On the tax issue alone, some of the postmortems are beginning to say, Metzenbaum was "Watergated." Recalling Nixon's tax problems, *New York News* political writer Jerry Greene opined that Ohio voters last Tuesday "exercised their collective distaste at the polls" against Metzenbaum.

But the senator may have administered his own coup de grace with a charge that Glenn, the national hero and Marine combat pilot, had "never held a job."

The senator's aides braced themselves for the worst while admitting privately that Metzenbaum had made an inexcusable blunder. Glenn waited until the final days of the campaign to deliver the knockout punch with a public challenge to the senator to repeat the charge to "Gold Star mothers" and military veterans.

By election day, Glenn was riding a strong tide of public sentiment aroused by his secure image of integrity, heroism, and political independence. So much so, it now appears, that thousands of Republicans, faced with a humdrum ballot, crossed over to sweeten his margin of victory.

In his victory speech, Glenn noted that "political experts can't define some of the tides moving this year. . . . It's the people who select the direction they want us to go."

The tides ought to be obvious in the elections later this year. Bread and butter, the old bell-ringers of the past, may have to go back to the cupboard until the political housecleaning is finished to the satisfaction of the voters.

Both Parties Will Benefit: Ford Restores Civility to Politics

Akron Beacon Journal, August 11, 1974

In a unique flash of history, Gerald Ford rose to the presidency this week in a changing of the guard that was as calming to the nation as Richard Nixon's final days were turbulent. Whatever the long-range consequences of Ford's solemn assumption of the White House, the immediate rewards were shared by Republicans and Democrats alike. For a time at least, it appears that a sense of quiet civility has been restored to our political life.

Contrary to the protests of Nixon's diehard defenders that he was driven from office by his enemies, the weight of evidence is that he was driven out by himself, betraying the trust of even his most loyal supporters on the House Judiciary Committee. Not even a president endowed with the broadest powers can do that.

His arrogance and contempt for some of his closest associates, as shown by the fatal White House tapes, told us more of the man than of the president, and in the end, it was the man who stood for an accounting of his conduct. Perfection is expected of no one, only a common decency and a respect for the public trust.

On Friday, Gerald Ford promised his countrymen to "uphold the Constitution, to do what is right as God gives me the right, and to do the very best I can for America." Throughout his brief address after taking the oath of office, Ford appealed for reconciliation, declaring:

"As we bind up the internal wounds of Watergate, more painful and more poisonous than those of foreign wars, let us restore the golden rule to our political process, and let brotherly love purge our hearts of suspicion and hate."

For his part, he promised candor and honesty. Although these two virtues have become staples in the political oratory of the day, Ford, in simple, moving terms, persuaded us that he meant what he said.

There was humility in his acknowledgement that he arrived at the top without a vote of the people, but in plain talk, he pledged he would not "shirk" his new and heavy responsibility. In his opening remarks to a nation that has grown increasingly cynical and disenchanted with its leaders, Ford has, in words with single meanings, told us that he is a decent human being first, and that is reassuring.

Two years of Watergate, and all that it implied, is enough.

Ohio GOP Hit by Pardon of Nixon
Akron Beacon Journal, August 16, 1974

Shortly after President Ford's startling pardon of Richard Nixon, an influential Ohio Republican leader groaned that Ford had all but guaranteed a disaster for the Republicans back home in the November elections. "And if he pardons the rest of the Watergate crowd, it's going to be disastrous in 1976, too," the same source predicted.

Although the president now appears to be taking a more cautious course with regard to the others, the damage to this year's Republican campaign could be irreparable.

The state GOP ticket, already in deep trouble, could ill-afford another political trauma. And that seems to be exactly what the Ford decision created for the GOP campaigners in the remaining weeks before the November balloting.

Hardly more than a week ago, Republicans were aglow in the sunlight of the new Ford regime. The cynicism of the Nixon days was washing away in a tide of accolades for the Ford style of fresh-air candor.

But the higher the expectations for the Ford Administration, the harder they fell. Out at Summit Mall, a disillusioned middle-aged woman summed up her feelings: "It was terrible. I was just beginning to like the man, too." It's that kind of talk that will hurt the Republicans this year.

Up in Cleveland, GOP party leaders quickly assessed the problem as though the *Titanic* had sprung another leak. Republican Co-Chairman Robert Hughes first supported the pardon, then admitted it had "hurt enormously," and then joined two other party officials in urging (by airmail special delivery) Ford to go no further in his clemency actions.

Hughes said the time had come for Republicans to speak out, a challenge that some of his more timid political brethren have yet to accept. "If the political leaders don't have the courage to present their views and earn their respect," Hughes declared, "they deserve the disrespect which they so often receive from the public."

Although the Ford decision cut deeply to the question of even-handed criminal justice and opened a new round of national debate, many of the Ohio Republican politicians issued meaningless comments and ran for cover. One needed no further proof that the kitchen had got hot again.

To quote from a letter on today's *Beacon Journal* editorial page: "If Harry Truman were alive today he would turn over in his grave."

Old Skeletons to Rise and Haunt Rhodes

Akron Beacon Journal, November 18, 1973

There's a distinct air of uneasiness within Republican ranks over former Governor James A. Rhodes's bid to return to the governor's office next year.

Although many party veterans still politely recall that Rhodes, as a two-term governor from 1963 through 1970, built a political dynasty as Ohio's Number One salesman, they will also confide that past allegations about Rhodes's income tax problems are certain to surface again in the campaign—and could be even more damaging in the context of the Nixon Administration's troubles the past year.

It's unlikely that Rhodes will have much patience with those who remind him of old skeletons. But from a cold political analysis, Rhodes's problem is a practical one that he will have to face up to sooner or later.

Maybe sooner. There's some evidence that Rhodes's only challenger (so far) in the GOP primary, State Representative Norman Murdock of Cincinnati, may take up the beat questioning the former governor's integrity.

Without mentioning Rhodes by name, Murdock declared in a statement released this week that the voters, conditioned by political scandals, will be paying close attention to all candidates "on a continuing basis. It is therefore incumbent that the Republican Party of Ohio offer the people its very best. . . ."

There's nothing, of course, unusual about self-serving campaign barbs. But in this instance, we at least have an advance peek at the style of the forthcoming primary campaign.

It has been eleven years since Rhodes trounced Governor Michael V. DiSalle by more than a half-million votes—the widest victory margin in the history of Ohio gubernatorial politics until Rhodes returned for a seven-hundred-thousand-vote win over Frazier Reams Jr. in 1966.

Tens of thousands of voters who will go to the polls next year were still in grade school when Rhodes clobbered DiSalle. Few will remember, or care, that he had labored hard to make Ohio the leading tomato-juice producer in the nation. Or that he dangled a lure through a hole in the ice to promote fishing in Lake Erie.

Rhodes's first public attempt to muster some troops for next year's campaign came a week ago at a $25-a-ticket fried chicken brunch in Columbus. Although Rhodes's helpers hoped to sell ten thousand tickets, apparently fewer than five thousand were bought.

Some county brunch chairmen complained of conflicts with fundraisers by the Republican State Financing Committee. "The way things are going in Washington these days, it's damn hard to go back to the same people twice for contributions," said one of Rhodes's ticket salesmen.

That may be so. But still another practical political problem for Rhodes is whether the Rhodes-watchers, both Republicans and Democrats, will choose to draw another meaning from it.

Ohio's Four Biggest Political Mouths: Who Says All Politicians Sound Alike?

Akron Beacon Journal, October 6, 1974

Between now and November 5—election day—Ohio's voters will be enticed, exhorted, implored, cajoled, jangled, buffeted, blandished, placated, and, sometimes, even informed by an avalanche of words from hundreds of political candidates with a common goal. And that is, to get elected.

The verbal exercise is loosely defined as political oratory, although, in the historical tradition, oratory may suggest something far more poetically eloquent—or irreverently abusive—than what we have come to expect around the election circuit today.

Gone, for the most part, are the thundergusting cross-of-gold orations of William Jennings Bryan, the spacious though simply-put perceptions of Lincoln, and the folksy vulgarity of Earl Long.

Who but Long, to refresh your memory, in a furious gallus-snapping, buttocks-scratching campaign for Louisiana governor thirty-four years past, would rise in frothing indignation amid a group of farmers and accuse an opponent of perfuming his armpits? With that delicate issue cutting to the deepest sensibilities, Long then demanded that the farmers go to the polls and "vote for a good old country boy that thinks and smells like you."

Earl Long, as well as his brother, Huey, went to the point in all of their orations with the kind of crackling candor that the folks seemed to understand. "Huey," Earl would say, "used to buy the legislature like a sack of potatoes. Hell, I never bought one in my life. I just rent 'em. It's cheaper that way." Unimpressed, *Time* magazine called Earl a "vaudeville baboon."

The more sophisticated campaigners over the centuries have relied on speechwriters to polish their pearls of wit and wisdom (Alexander the Great included among his scribes the nephew of

Aristotle; Lincoln's private secretary, John Hay, was an outstanding Midwestern poet; most of Franklin Delano Roosevelt's texts were laboriously produced by others. And, as historian Allan Nevins observes, FDR's "best phrases, like 'the forgotten man' and 'the new deal,' were borrowed from other men.")

But in today's context of informal, one-on-one politicking, the professional speechwriter, who carries in his literary arsenal the selected works of Lincoln and Jefferson, a dog-eared volume of Bartlett's quotations, and the latest statistics from the Department of Labor, is playing a lesser role in the quest for public office in Ohio.

Of the four major candidates for governor and senator this year, only one—Governor John J. Gilligan—has occasionally shown up with a prepared text in hand. And even he says he is happier without one.

The other three—Jim Rhodes, Gilligan's Republican opponent; John Glenn, the Democratic Senate nominee; and Cleveland Mayor Ralph Perk, Glenn's opponent—all work from the cuff with the aid of cue cards, scraps of paper bearing jotted reminders, newspaper clippings, and whatever other memory-joggers they can stuff into their inside breast pockets.

Though similar in that respect, the four have decidedly contrasting deliveries from the stump. Gilligan, a former English literature instructor, jauntily prods his opponent with a mock heroic humor that is sometimes imperious. Of his own goals and achievements in office, he is deadly serious. His speeches come amply adorned with statistics that, by the look of some of his after-dinner listeners, are, at best, only half-digested.

Still, of the four, Gilligan—despite his pedantic tendencies—offers the best-balanced command of subject and style. In contrast, Rhodes is a torrential downpour, half-evangelist, half-prosecutor, slaying a thousand dragons with two flailing arms and a blur of rhetoric that bestirs the viscera, albeit numbing the intellect.

Glenn, a former astronaut with all of the mental discipline that that implies, is sincere, logical, tidily in order, low-keyed, and rhetorically flat. More compelling and gracious in conversation than he is from the political pulpit, Glenn comes over on the stump much like the friendly insurance man explaining the policy to the next-of-kin.

Perk, on the other hand, is a good-natured rambler, the spinner of tales about his meager upbringing or stuffed grape leaves. Throughout, he is the nostalgic protector of God, Motherhood, and Country—and his record at city hall. In his first Senate campaign speech in Akron, Perk ranged over his own personal wealth ("I'm not rich, and I pay my taxes"), his achievements as mayor, patriotism, a ringing defense of Richard Nixon (who hadn't as yet resigned), revenue-sharing, Vietnam, taxation, Red China, impeachment, the military draft, Cleveland's operating budget, and still-to-be-completed Interstate 77.

In seeking reelection this year, Gilligan carries what has come to be known as the "burden of the incumbency"—which means he must be prepared to defend or explain the smallest blemish of his administration against the onslaught of his critics.

But he relishes extemporaneous combat, moreso than his aides would prefer. A stray zinger, though audience-grabbing for the moment, can sometimes backfire. (Back in the Democratic primary, U. S. Senator Howard Metzenbaum departed from his prepared text for a $100-a-plate fundraiser in Cleveland long enough to ad lib that John Glenn "never held a job." That deadly improvisation reportedly was suggested to him by a friend (some friend!) while the senator was making his way to the stage. It turned out to be a catastrophe, as Glenn, a military hero, challenged Metzenbaum to repeat the charge to Gold Star mothers and the patients in the Veterans Hospitals.)

Gilligan, too, has been the victim of his own asides, most recently this airy remark to reporters—when Gerald Ford was still the vice president—that Ford was a "walking disaster." He later amended those remarks with something more complimentary when Ford, as president, quickly soared in the public opinion polls.

The governor is the first to concede that his offhand remarks and rostrum technique are offensive to some. When a reporter reminded him that his "stage presence" was didactic and professorial, he interrupted long enough to add, "—and arrogant."

And arrogant.

"I plead guilty," Gilligan replies. "I know many people say I'm too dingdong professorial, that I don't make people weep or scream. But my job is to help people make tough decisions to bring about constructive change and improve the quality of life for everyone. And in order for me to do this, I've simply got to give them some factual material—all those statistics—to go on. I'm saying to them, 'You ought to do this, or do that, for the following overwhelming reasons.' Sometimes it works, sometimes it doesn't. So, of course, a lot of people look at you as if you're some fuzzy-headed nitwit who couldn't figure his way out of a revolving door. But it's one thing if you're in a position to win friends—it's easy to say the things that are popular. But it's another thing to influence people."

Although one of Gilligan's top aides insists that he is a "far better extemporaneous speaker than he is with a text—most people think he's best from the hip," Gilligan is going with a text (prepared by his research staff and edited by him) on the major speaking appearances. "I prefer working from notes, or just winging it," he says. "But I give a lot of people fits when I do that, so in recent years I've been trying to stick to the text."

If there is a text for Jim Rhodes, it was written in 1962 when he ran for governor on the theme of "Jobs and Progress." He has been using it ever since, and it has long been committed to memory by both the candidate and the reporters who have been covering him over the years. (It's not unusual for politicians to fall in love with their own words. Warren Harding, a master of fuzzy generalities, was so impressed with one of his speeches that he had it recorded with "Beautiful Ohio.")

Rhodes loathes formal texts. Rather he assails the ear with a series of verbal impulses ("Jobs" . . . "Programs" . . . "Jobs" . . . "Programs" . . . "Jobs" with little or no continuity in between). Indeed, he is gifted at switching thoughts in the middle of a sentence. But the technique is effective. If nothing else, his audiences go away impressed that Rhodes is foursquare behind jobs even though nobody can recall exactly how he put it.

"Jim works by and large with key words," says Dean Jauchius, a Rhodes administration public relations man who has come back to handle press relations in this year's campaign. Jauchius says Rhodes is "not a good reader." So his aides have provided him with about one hundred three-by-five cards that, says Jauchius, "contain very few words—except the key words. He'll shuffle those cards around a lot, depending upon the audience. And that's it. I don't ever recall him making a formal presentation."

John Glenn's campaign appearances also have been informal; his speeches brief, usually touching on the several issues that are out front in his Senate drive. For the most part, however, you'll find him in the middle of an admiring group, signing autographs, answering questions about his space feat, or telling people, "I'll need all the help I can get and would appreciate your support."

"I'd much rather talk directly with people, the dialogue type of thing with some give and take," Glenn says. "I don't have a professional speechwriter, although there have been a lot of people who have tried to write a speech for me. But I don't like texts. About 95 percent of my speeches are from memory or notes."

In one of the rare instances that he used a text, he caused a small earthquake in Democrat-land. That was in September, 1973, when Glenn, fuming with indignation, rose before the State Democratic Executive Committee with an eleven-page assault on Democratic leaders who, he complained, were trying to maneuver him out of the senate race.

Glenn says he wrote every word himself, although now that the party is getting back together again, he'd just as soon not say much more about it.

Glenn's opponent, Ralph Perk, is strictly informal (although he is one of the few politicians who uses his title rather than his first name when signing autographs, a minor ego-trip that nobody seems to mind). In the Cleveland area, at least, he is a virtuoso of ethnic politics who speaks five or six languages and will not hesitate to use them to superb effect in the right crowd. It sometimes baffles monolingual reporters, but there is always some spectator nearby who can translate it.

For all the talk in this year's campaign, in whatever language, it is at best only marginally of lasting value. There are not crosses of gold, no blood, sweat, and tears, not even a chicken in every other pot.

And if in the current outpouring of words it becomes immediately evident to the listener that he or she won't be able to go home humming the rhetoric, then the advice to a commencement audience by the late Adlai Stevenson is worth repeating: "It is my job today as speaker to talk. It's your job as the audience to listen. If you get finished before I do, please feel free to get up and leave."

'Nuff said?

Gilligan Campaign Muscle Not There
Akron Beacon Journal, November 10, 1974

Jack Gilligan, the ex-college teacher and apparently an ex-governor, had a theory—and only a theory—that if you gave the people enough facts, they would eventually arrive at the right decisions on the tough questions facing society. He supposed that to be true to the extent that it became an obsession that drove out the traditional political ideas of how to win friends and influence people. Being human, he had nothing against being popular; but being possessed by his theory of self-government, if popularity suffered, so be it.

Many of the political pros shuddered at his conception of his livelihood. They accused him of being arrogant and aloof, words they could have picked up from his description of himself. He was not at all what they had in mind for a governor who wanted to remain a governor.

But some of the national political writers who dropped in on the recent gubernatorial campaign that caved in on Gilligan last Tuesday were fascinated by his quick wit and his disdain for the old politics of hand-pumping and tell-'em-what-they-want-to-hear rhetoric. The word got around that Gilligan was an "antipolitician," who, by dint of intellect and honesty, might someday qualify to run for the presidency.

But that was a long time off, and he still had to get by a tough, old-school campaigner like Jim Rhodes—a problem that Gilligan didn't quite solve. Quite clearly, Gilligan had expected his theory to prevail and, to the end, neither he nor his advisors could take Rhodes that seriously.

In this instance, Rhodes proved to be the teacher. In the last crucial week of the campaign, it seemed that everybody except the governor, and those closest to him, suspected that he was in deep trouble. And if anybody needed more convincing, they needed only to tune in on the spate of Rhodes's hard-hitting radio and television commercials that impressively carried the attack to Gilligan over the last weekend.

Typically, the Gilligan people shrugged it off. They blithely predicted he would win by at least 10 percentage points, maybe even 13. In their eagerness to look beyond the election to a possible national role for Gilligan, it's generally agreed that the governor's campaign staff, directed by his top aide, Jack Hansan, blew it. "We snatched defeat from the jowls of victory," one campaign staffer groaned the morning after.

Even if a recount should determine Gilligan to be the winner—at best, a long shot—such a victory would have a hollow sound to many of his faithful who were convinced that Gilligan would not only carry the day, but overwhelmingly so against Jim Rhodes.

He didn't.

Political theory will take you only so far. From that point on, you have to rely on some old-fashioned political muscle. Rhodes had it; Gilligan's people didn't think they needed it. Essentially, the outcome of Tuesday's election comes down to that.

~

Metzenbaum Image Is "Fluffier"

Akron Beacon Journal, January 18, 1976

Howard Metzenbaum, his silver hair now muted and fluffed in the "dry look," is back for a third and possibly final campaign for the Senate. He will be trying to reverse years of political frustration that have prompted even some of his closest associates to question the wisdom of still one more campaign. But they also confess that once Howard had made up his mind there was nothing they could say to talk him out of it.

"I do believe I was a good senator," Metzenbaum told a group of potential backers in Akron last week. "I do believe that I have the capacity to be a great senator. I do believe I can make some changes."

In spite of his earlier setbacks, Metzenbaum remains a believer that events will finally bend his way this year. But he is leaving nothing to chance. For the past year, he has been "working the tables" at political gatherings around the state, keeping in close touch with his old friends in organized labor, battling the utilities on rate increases, and patting children on the head while shaking hands with their parents.

Some people have said the fifty-eight-year-old Cleveland businessman-lawyer enjoys running more than winning, because he has twice been denied bids for the Senate and still keeps running.

On those earlier occasions, timing worked to Metzenbaum's disadvantage. In 1970, he was matched up with Robert Taft, whose name was as familiar to the average voter as the next-door-neighbor's puppy. Metzenbaum lost, but the score was closer than anyone had anticipated.

Four years later, after he had been appointed to the Senate by then-Governor Gilligan, Metzenbaum was challenged by John Glenn, who has emerged with enough popular appeal to be seriously discussed as a possible candidate for the national ticket this year. Again, Metzenbaum lost.

(Ironically, the "times" twice-blessed U.S. Senator Stephen Young—and wasn't Metzenbaum his campaign manager? Young was first elected to the Senate in 1958 when the right-to-work issue annihilated the Republican Party in Ohio; in 1964, the Goldwater massacre returned Young to the Senate.)

Metzenbaum believes that some of the questions raised about his 1974 candidacy are now behind him. One was his tax dispute with the Internal Revenue Service, which has since been resolved in his favor. Another was his disclosure that he paid no income taxes in 1969 because of heavy business losses. These became particularly sensitive campaign issues at a time when Richard Nixon was being backed to the wall on tax and Watergate-related questions.

Metzenbaum's test, if he is to survive a hard primary fight against a younger but seasoned opponent (U.S. Representative James Stanton of Cleveland) and maybe even Gilligan, will be whether he can avoid being forced to the ropes again.

Against Glenn, he simply panicked. He bought TV time to explain his position in the IRS case, but his manner was less than convincing. He repeatedly introduced the tax issue at press conferences long after reporters had tired of hearing about it.

He was taut and defensive, hardly the image for a senator who wanted people to believe that he had the savvy and aplomb to be an effective lawmaker. And when he foolishly accused Glenn late in the campaign of having never held a job, it was easy to conclude that he would be heading back to private life after the election.

Unfortunately for Metzenbaum, his avoidable campaign gaffes overshadowed the fact that as a senator he was a hard-working and aggressive operative. He's had a year now to brush up on his campaign style and tactics. Will it be the Old Howard or the New Howard this year? The "dry look" seems to be a good start.

~

Ford-Reagan Battle Shows Severity of GOP Trouble

Akron Beacon Journal, August 15, 1976

A year ago, the only suspenseful topic among thinking Republicans was whether they would meet in Cleveland, Miami, or some other place to nominate their presidential candidate. The bidding for the party convention ranged from indifference ("Not again," Miami seemed to sigh) to near-sinful coveting. (Eager to please, Cleveland's Mayor Perk even promised to rent some cruise ships to bed down the delegates who couldn't find rooms elsewhere.)

The GOP "site committee" finally chose Kansas City, which wasn't that much roomier than Cleveland, simply because it seemed to be a nice place to show off Gerald Ford—comfortably distant from Washington and San Clemente, as the *New York Times* has noted. The right geographical setting, it was called, even if its mayor was a rabid Democrat.

Now, with the convention's grand opening only a day off, the president can only pray that this upbeat city of new buildings and happier images (no longer a cowtown, the people here say) will not be his Waterloo.

In itself, the idea that an incumbent president—a Republican thoroughbred—is fighting for his life in his own family is pretty hard to grasp. Still, the script is on the table for anyone to read, and it ranks with the best of political cliffhangers.

After months of campaigning and millions spent, Ford appears to be in worse shape today than when he started out on his mission to persuade people that he was something more than an accidental leader. (During that same period, Jimmy Carter, in contrast, rose from political oblivion to a full-scale coronation by his party in New York.)

Some Ford supporters are appalled that the race has come this far without a clear verdict for the president. But with the proven insight of hindsight, it was possible to reconstruct some of the damaging evidence.

In spite of the ominous sign that Ronald Reagan might make a race of it, Ford's own campaign was organized rather casually and clumsily with Bo Calloway (one of a series of concessions to the party's right wing) at the reins. When that situation finally became intolerable, Calloway was waylaid and replaced by savvier political guns who managed to get the president through some early primaries—including the important Florida contest—before Reagan bounced off the ropes in North Carolina.

The battle has seesawed ever since. It is now down to a handful of delegates, some of whom probably still don't honestly know how they are going to vote. Clearly, Ford underestimated the tenacity of the party's right wing, which somehow managed to portray him as something he is not—a liberal. The party's moderates ran afoul of the same challenge in 1964 and, based on the current evidence, have yet to develop a reliable response.

With the party's overall decline, and the increasing strength of the no-compromise conservatives within it, one wonders whether it can ever recover from its current agonies. Even if Ford hangs on to his slight lead over Reagan and sets out from here as the bloodied nominee, he faces a still greater task against Carter in November while his own party tries to mend itself at the seams—and in its heart.

But first things first. May we clear the aisles, please?

Ford Won Party Nomination, but Reagan Stole Its Heart
Akron Beacon Journal, August 22, 1976

Afterthoughts:

One of the big losers at the Republican Convention was Chester A. Arthur. As Ronald Reagan closed the gap in his footrace with Gerald Ford, people began to recall what happened to Arthur nearly a century ago. He was the last incumbent to be denied the nomination by his party. It was hardly the sort of thing that a president wants to leave in the record book.

Ford nearly stripped poor Chester of the dubious title. They got all the way down to West Virginia before Ford was able to light up a victory pipe. And after the reception Reagan got Thursday night at the last session, a night supposedly reserved for Ford and Dole, the wags around Kemper Arena suggested a recount might be in order. Ford managed to hang on as the head of the party, but Reagan still owns much of its heart.

And for Arthur, it means at least "four more years" in the history books.

~

The scene was of operatic proportions: Ford, Dole, John Rhodes, and the others trying to get the delegates' attention from center stage; the pit orchestra blasting out the thematic music; the story of Republican virtues sung in the slogans of "Peace and Prosperity." Up in the balcony, Reagan performed in the dual role of villain or hero, depending on one's loyalties.

When he arrived as the vanquished challenger, the hall shook with cries of encore; they wanted one more, and perhaps last, for the Gipper. Verdi, Puccini, and the others could not have put together a more melodramatic core. Reagan and his wife, Nancy, rise, wave, acknowledge the frenzy with those fixed smiles that burden most politicians. Autographs. Cheers. Delirium. It had to be distracting to the people on stage. They had to get on with the Ford show before the people went to bed back East.

~

The night before, both sides had traded their best floor demonstrations, which in spite of the confusion, are not as spontaneous as they would have you believe. On the floor, it is an eerie sight. A jungle of sweating people, placards, confetti, horns, elbows in the side of the head. Bill Scranton, the distinguished ambassador to the United Nations, is pushed along in the snake dance. The starch is out of his shirt. Seeing a reporter, he smiles shyly, wiggles his Ford sign, and is swept off by the rush of the crowd. Right behind him is Alex Arshinkoff, the young Akron Republican shouting something about how he led the stampede to the floor.

It is all mechanical combustion. Some party leaders say they feel like damn fools having to participate in the ritual. "But what are you going to do?" sighs one. "It's all part of the convention."

~

Later, Virgil Brown, the Cuyahoga County Board of Elections man, is waiting at the mike to second the nomination of Ford. He's allotted thirty seconds, and Jim Rhodes, the governor, wants him to make good use of all of it. Rhodes is beside himself, tugging on Virgil's arm. "Don't forget to mention Ohio," Rhodes shouts. The guv looks back. "Virge is the best speaker in the world. He'll do a great job," Rhodes says. "You got thirty seconds, Virge. Just get Ohio in there." Rhodes fidgets as another speaker goes beyond the thirty-second limit. "Take more time, Virge, if you need it," he booms. "The other guy went longer." Nobody can remember when the governor has had more fun at a convention.

~

The convention is over. Everybody out of the pool. Back to the real world. The cabbie is asked for a prediction because cabbies are supposed to know everything. "It will be Ford by a hair over Carter," the cabbie, a college graduate who is working on poetry, says. Why? "He always seems to luck out." If you're in the mood for soothsaying, Jeanne Dixon had other notions. Reagan, she predicted, would have demolished Carter. Ford will not. Jimmy the Greek thinks it will be close. But at this point, Chester A. Arthur couldn't care less.

Story Scraps Were Big News
Akron Beacon Journal, July 18, 1976

This was supposed to have been the city with a million stories. But for a few desperate days last week, most of the several thousand journalists who were trying to justify their expense accounts would have been delighted to have found just one.

It got so bad that Jack Germond, the veteran political writer of the *Washington Star*, wrote a "Dear Mom" column in which he confessed that "we've been fooling the public again."

Like everybody else, Germond was lamenting that in spite of all the important-looking, pin-striped people strutting around at the Democratic National Convention with reporters on their tails, there was little to add to what everyone already knew: Jimmy Carter would leave town with the presidential nomination on his sleeve.

Jimmy helped the reporters a bit by sitting on his choice of a running mate until Thursday morning. That enabled the press to build up the suspense each day by reporting in meticulous detail that it didn't know any more than it did yesterday.

One seasoned Washington correspondent resorted to a yarn about what the delegates were wearing. And over lunch, a couple of Ohio reporters hung on every word as Toots Shor reminisced with Mike DiSalle, the ex-Ohio governor, about Eleanor Roosevelt. ("A great woman," Toots testified.)

All of this presented some risks to the out-of-town reporters. Should they subject themselves to ridicule as provincials from Akron, Topeka, and Nashville by dwelling on the death-defying cab rides from their hotels to the convention hall? Did anyone really care that an old derelict had stretched out on a smelly pile of stuffed garbage bags downtown and fallen into a stupor? (The police didn't care.)

Was there a human interest story in the man who roamed around the streets in an angel's robe with aluminum foil wings and a harp? Or the fellow who dared anybody to run him down as he sat in traffic and beat on the pavement with drumsticks? What about the folks who were passing out the "Jews for Jesus" literature? Or the guy who put on a grotesque papier-mâché hood resembling Jerry Ford and hawked "pardons" for a buck apiece?

Hell, none of us wanted to come away from here sounding like hicks.

So maybe the readers back home might wonder instead about all those people on the floor of the convention pushing through the aisle night after night. From the gallery, it looked like a human mudslide. If you are curious about where they were all going, the truth is they weren't going anywhere. Many just pushed twenty or thirty feet in one direction and then reversed their field. They made up one of the great milling-around movements of our time. It is worth a paragraph on a dull day.

No rumor was too trivial to check out. John Glenn had left his hotel. Where was he going? Was it a rendezvous with Jimmy Carter? No, his aides say, he is merely going shopping. Shopping, huh? What is he going to buy? Ask him when he gets back, an aide says. He is indeed asked. Shirts. How many shirts? Four or five. "Four or five shirts," the reporters eagerly record in their empty notebooks.

There's John Gilligan on the escalator after Carter has been crowned. Hello, John. What happened to your mustache? The public has a right to know. "My family took a vote," explained the former governor. "The mustache had to be come off."

Gilligan says his party's appearance has changed, too. "I don't recognize the Democratic Party anymore. All this peace and harmony and concord," muses Gilligan, the man who frequently observed that Democrats were good at throwing dead cats at each other.

But Gilligan, one of the chief architects of party reform a couple of years ago, is revving up to the story of the evening. "Without the reforms," he says, "there [would] be no Jimmy Carter here tonight."

Carter, he says, is the beneficiary of the party's new openness: "The idea that delegates had to be picked the year of the convention (rather than slated by the party bosses before the candidates even had gleams in their eyes); proportional representation, the end to unit voting."

"It is fair to say," Gilligan notes, "that Governor Carter could not have been nominated under the old system."

Who would have been? "Oh, I don't know," Gilligan says. "Probably Hubert Humphrey." Poor Hubert. The politician of enormous joy to the end, reminding the crowd that America is "great because it is good. And when it ceases to be good, it will cease to be great." As one writer put it, Humphrey is probably tired of trying not to be a sore loser.

"Are you guys going home tomorrow?" The waiter at the delicatessen interviews the press after they had interviewed each other the night of Carter's triumphant speech. Most say they are.

"I don't blame you," he says. "I'm getting out of town the first thing in the morning myself."

Come on, waiter, we weren't that bad. We had a job to do, and we did it. Whatever it was.

Oh, the Games They All Play

Akron Beacon Journal, September 12, 1976

Jimmy Carter kicked off his campaign for Ohio votes in Cleveland last week with—as it is called in the trade—a "media hit" in a Slovenian neighborhood and a brief pep talk at a downtown reception attended by many old-line Democratic pols who show up at these things to see and be seen.

The logistics for bringing together the party VIPs in the most populous Democratic county in the state would surpass those of the Normandy invasion inasmuch as there are few Democrats in Cleveland who consider themselves anything less than a full colonel or one-star general.

But protocol for a touring presidential candidate demands that homage be paid to the Cuyahoga County Democratic Party even though it's not always certain which of the several Democratic Parties one is paying homage to.

That will be a problem for Carter in the days ahead. And if not a problem, at least a nuisance.

On one hand, a Democrat cannot carry the state without a flood of votes from Cleveland, a heavily Democratic city that, among other things, has got into the habit of electing a Republican mayor. On the other hand, it is a tricky business in Cleveland to enlist the support of one party leader without offending a dozen others.

So it was not unusual that Carter's first visit to the city for the fall campaign was greeted by a front-page story in the *Plain Dealer* about a party "spat" over the propriety of the candidate checking in with this ward councilman, or that one. ("Everyone up here," sighed one labor leader, "wants his day in the sun.")

There were other scheduling snags that bruised egos. Some Cleveland pols munching on peanuts at a Carter reception dropped little hints in reporters' ears that Carter's campaign organization was a "disaster."

If so, that also describes the state of affairs of the Cuyahoga County party and, for that matter, many other big-city Democratic organizations.

Not since Cleveland Mayor Ralph Locher's days, for example, has the party elected its own mayor; Jack Gilligan's bid for reelection against Jim Rhodes in 1974 was destroyed by lukewarm support in a county he needed to win by two-one. The party went for U.S. Representative James Stanton in the Democratic senatorial primary, and, to his great surprise, Howard Metzenbaum won the county.

It's unlikely that the Carter people can improve the internal situation in the few months before the election. The best they can hope for is that they will not make it worse.

That will require some delicate tightrope balancing by Carter's Ohio campaign chief, Dan Horgan. Horgan, an aggressive ex-Marine imported for the Ohio campaign from New Jersey, is faced with keeping the peace in Cleveland while at the same time, in his words, developing a statewide Carter effort in "businesslike" fashion.

Some of the natives who worked for Carter in the primary are restlessly wondering when the action will begin, and Horgan has been trying to explain that federal spending restrictions are imposing an austerity program that leaves no room for one unnecessary long-distance phone call.

In the early going, Horgan has won an important supporter in Warren Smith, Ohio AFL-CIO secretary-treasurer. Smith, a methodical operative himself who leaves nothing to chance, said in the corridor of the Bond Court Hotel after Carter's visit that he had heard "too damn many deprecating remarks about Carter's staff. Horgan is a guy who knows the mechanics of campaign organization," Smith said. "He knows what he's doing."

~

Taft Running Hard To Meet Challenge from Metzenbaum

Washington Post, October 19, 1976

The other day, U.S. Senator Robert Taft's campaign helicopter strayed off course during a swing through eastern Ohio and, to the surprise of the small traveling party, landed near a schoolyard in Ravenswood, West Virginia.

The Republican candidate's problems in getting his campaign back on track that day with a faulty helicopter compass produced some bright newspaper accounts—and a happy reaction from one Taft aide: "It was great! We need some color in the Taft campaign!"

The fifty-nine-year-old senator's drab political style has long concerned his advisers, who believe it detracts from his performance in Washington. Now, faced with a serious challenge from former Democratic Senator Howard Metzenbaum, Taft is being forced into a livelier pace to avoid a clearly possible upset.

His stop-action television spots project a sense of urgency in Taft's manner, whether he is fighting for a stronger navy or rushing aid to tornado-stricken Xenia, Ohio. He's even added some quips to his speeches. "Sex has been added to the campaign," he told the Republican state convention in Columbus recently. "President Ford has been interviewed by *Ladies' Home Journal* and Jimmy Carter by *Playboy. Penthouse* interviewed Bob Dole, but unfortunately the interview was too square to print."

There has been a conscious effort to enliven the Taft image on the stump, partly to dispel notions that he is physically unable to carry out a strenuous campaign. Aides are quick to say that he has fully recovered from a January 1975 heart attack.

In some respects, the campaign is a replay of the 1970 race in which Taft unseated Metzenbaum by 70,420 votes after an even tighter primary contest with Republican Governor James Rhodes. Both men are long established mainstream party loyalists, whose campaign speeches are comfortably drawn from their parties' traditional shopping lists of issues. Both are well-known ballot figures, and apparently both—despite their avowed fears to the contrary—will somehow muster enough campaign money.

If anything is different in Campaign II, it is Metzenbaum's shift from high-visibility political brawling to low-keyed diplomacy on the stump. His top campaign people say the fifty-nine-year-old Cleveland businessman has overcome troublesome issues that plagued him in previous Senate campaign—the last one in 1974, when he lost a bitterly fought primary to John Glenn. Questions about his income taxes have been resolved, and the label of "millionaire businessman" seldom appears beside his name in news stories this year.

His wealth kept him on the defensive in past campaigns, and the more he responded to that point the more he became the issue. But when U.S. Representative James V. Stanton revived questions about his finances in the final days of the Democratic senatorial primary last spring, Metzenbaum blithely ignored him and went on to a surprisingly easy victory over Stanton.

Metzenbaum has yet to win the endorsement of Glenn, who has remained cool since the 1974 Senate campaign, but he has the support of the state's big labor unions, who are again putting their muscle into his effort against Taft. The latest *Focus*, a booklet published by the Ohio AFL-CIO, carries a two-page spread praising Metzenbaum's one-year record in the Senate in 1974 (he was appointed by then-Governor John J. Gilligan after Republican William Saxbe became U.S. Attorney General).

Taft has been attacking his opponent as an "ultra-liberal" big spender. Metzenbaum's main thrust—the one that wins the loudest applause on the stump—is against the big oil companies and public utilities.

Each candidate is counting on a radio-television campaign in the final days. Metzenbaum will spend "in the neighborhood of

$300,000 for media advertising—and more, if we can raise it," an aide says. His total campaign budget is about $600,000. Taft people estimate they will spend about $490,000 on media advertising from a total budget of $1.3 million.

Although most polls give Taft a small lead, Metzenbaum says he is well within striking distance. Metzenbaum's greatest hope may lie not so much in the final bursts from the TV tube but in the sharp rise in voter registration in Democratic Cuyahoga County and other northern industrial areas.

Election officials said a special registration effort, pushed by the Ohio Democratic Party and organized labor, had added more than ninety thousand to the rolls in Cuyahoga County. Patrick Leahy, executive director of the state Democratic Party, said new registrations statewide might exceed 450,000.

Both sides agree that the registration news is better for the Democrats than the Republicans. If the newcomers turn out in large numbers on election day, it could be the decisive factor in the neck-and-neck race.[4]

Part III

The Politics of Transition, 1977–1980

The Politics of Transition, 1977–1980

Introduction

After the 1976 election, Ohio politics entered into a period of transition as politicians began to adjust to the turmoil unleashed in the 1960s. Zaidan's writings paid close attention to this transition.

During this period two new political giants who served as mayor, Dennis Kucinich and George Voinovich, were introduced in Cleveland's ongoing political saga. Each in his own way represented the displacement of the old industrial cities from the center of national life and the adjustment to new roles in an era of suburban dominance.

Dennis Kucinich is captured by Zaidan in a 1972 portrait, "Strange Political Amalgam in Ambitious Young Man," published five years before he ran for mayor. An ethnic Democrat with strong populist tendencies and a gift for confrontation, Kucinich had attracted considerable attention as he worked his way up the ladder of local offices in Cleveland. The story then picks up in the 1977 mayoral primary where Kucinich finished first, helping to oust a former ally, three-term Republican mayor Ralph Perk. Kucinich then went on to defeat the second-place candidate and endorsed Democrat in the general election by a few thousand votes, becoming the nation's youngest big-city mayor at thirty-one years of age. The brash new mayor quickly alienated nearly everyone in Cleveland, and, by the spring of 1978, a recall petition put him back on the ballot. After a bitter campaign, Kucinich survived the recall by 236 votes.

In 1978, Governor Rhodes ran for reelection, seeking his fourth term in the Ohio statehouse. Rhodes chose as his running mate an ethnic Republican from Cleveland, George Voinovich, an important event in the politics of transition ("A Study in Ethnic Politics"). Rhodes was reelected in a close race against former Governor John Gilligan's lieutenant governor, Richard Celeste, a charismatic new liberal from Cleveland, also with an ethnic background. There was much speculation that this contest would mark a transition as well, captured in "Can Celeste Stop Rhodes's Last Hurrah?" However, Rhodes postponed that particular transition, as Zaidan puts it, in "In the Knack of Time."

The situation in the city of Cleveland continued to degenerate under Mayor Kucinich, despite his surviving the recall election. It reached a low point in December, 1978, when the city defaulted on its debts—the first city to do so since the Great Depression. Cleveland and its boy mayor had become a powerful symbol of the crisis of urban America. Zaidan describes this grim reality in a feature article with the provocative title "Who Killed Cleveland?"

In 1979, Kucinich faced a stiff reelection challenge from George Voinovich, Ohio's sitting lieutenant governor and a fellow ethnic. Voinovich finished first in the primary and then handily defeated Kucinich in the general election. In many ways, Voinovich was the exact opposite of Kucinich: bland rather than colorful, stable instead of volatile. He served as mayor from 1980 to 1990 and was given credit for reviving Cleveland, an achievement he used as a springboard for successful statewide campaigns in the 1990s.

Kucinich did not fade from the limelight, however. Instead, he pursued additional offices in his quixotic style—well described in the final essay in this section. Eventually, Kucinich had some success, serving as a state senator and congressman from the Cleveland area. But the old style reappeared in his 2004 quest for the Democratic presidential nomination.

This section concludes with some of the best examples of Zaidan's political writing, features published in *Ohio Magazine* in the late 1970s. These longer pieces cover in vivid detail the political landscape of an era and are as relevant now as they were in 1979. They explain, for example, why Ohio is central to presidential politics ("Ohio's Seal of Approval") and the emergence of a new class of political operatives ("All the Candidate's Men"). Zaidan's penetrating analysis of modern presidential politics is found in "Carter in Steubenville: A Presidential Progress." What these essays have in common is a clear sense of how Ohio and national politics had changed since 1964.

The final pieces in this section are about the 1980 national conventions. Rebounding from his loss to Gerald Ford in the 1976 presidential nomination contests, former California governor Ronald Reagan defeated a leading moderate Republican, George H. W. Bush, to secure the GOP nomination. In this year, Reagan captured *both* the "head and the heart" of the Republicans ("Reagan's Fortunes Rising above His Image"), pulling together an alliance of business Republicans and conservative forces ("Can Reagan Control Leaders of GOP's 'New Crusade'?"). This reconstruction of the pragmatic Republican alliance was cemented by Reagan's choice of George H. W. Bush as his running mate.

Meanwhile, moderate President Jimmy Carter faced a fierce challenge from Massachusetts Senator Edward Kennedy, representing the new liberal wing of the Democratic Party. Carter eventually prevailed but presided over a deeply divided party. As with the Republicans in 1976, it was the loser, Kennedy, who captured the imagination of the Democratic faithful. And like Ford in 1976, Carter was unable to win reelection, losing to Reagan in a three-way race, with Illinois Republican Congressman John Anderson running as an independent. After the brief respite of the Carter years, the Democratic coalition was again in disarray.

Strange Political Amalgam in Ambitious Young Man

Akron Beacon Journal, May 1, 1972

Dennis Kucinich seldom smiles. He doesn't think there is anything very funny about what's happening in the country today.

His political opponents and critics seem genuinely alarmed, too, not so much by the condition of the world but because the ambitious young Cleveland councilman is staying up half the night plotting to go to Congress. That's only a fraction of their concern. He spends his whole day running for Congress, too.

Draped in a heavy black overcoat, and with a portfolio of campaign material flapping under one arm, Kucinich has staked out the twenty-third Congressional District to the west of this city for his midnight ride against the forces of evil in contemporary America.

Wherever he goes, the twenty-five-year-old jockey-sized (hardly 130 pounds) Kucinich clangs the tocsin against the enemy: the "wheeler-dealers" of the establishment; the "monopoly utility" companies; the "starry-eyed and mystified professional liberals"; the "fumbling class of rah-rah intellectuals"; the "mindless juggernaut" of the "corporate American state"; and "poor old Uncle Sam's political bankrupt face."

In a single day of hard campaigning in a Democratic primary he is blithely confident he will win, Kucinich emerges as a strange amalgam of Ralph Nader, George Wallace, Spiro Agnew, George McGovern, and Fiorello LaGuardia. He also is quite probably Cleveland's most televised councilman, a political benefit he derived from his frequent haranguing of the administration of former Mayor Carl Stokes.

If Kucinich is accused of returning politics to the Middle Ages by catering primarily to ethnic groups, he doesn't object. "I have a strong feeling for ethnics because I am one," says Kucinich, a Slav with a Croatian name. "America is not a melting pot, and I resent attempts by sociologists to make it one. I'm proud of my appeal to ethnics. It's about time somebody starts worrying about them." His thesis, if it can be boiled down at all, is that America's hard-working blue-collar middle class is getting a rotten deal from the fat cats.

And at Padua Franciscan High School in Parma, a high-intensity ethnic community, Kucinich laid out his line to a student assembly: "Perhaps you recall a high school teacher pointing out with shock that in Nicaragua, 98 percent of the wealth is owned by 2 percent of the people. That is not economic integration. In the U.S. of A., 95 percent of the wealth is owned by 5 percent of the people. She probably didn't tell you that. She should have, because that would make our country the greatest of the banana republics. But instead of bananas, we have corporations. Instead of oligarchy and military dictatorships, we have conglomerates and the military-industrial state. The corporate American state is a fact of our lives. The free economic system is a fiction of our past."

Although Kucinich appeared to be in friendly territory, some of his listeners winced in the face of his outrage over "irrelevant government," the "profit-hungry" manipulators, and the "amazing number of bunglers and fools holding public office." Chuck Priefer, an American government teacher, rose to remind Kucinich that this is the greatest nation on earth and there ought to be something positive to say about it.

One might react the same way to the outpouring of verbal assaults on Kucinich by his opponents. They have a hard time saying something positive about him. Their favorite words are "opportunistic," "demagogue," "double-crosser," "conniving," "irresponsible." These are not uncommon political flyswatters, but in Kucinich's case, his critics seemed moved in the viscera to flail at him.

They shudder to think that Kucinich, whose sudden rise in Cleveland politics startles even the most hardened observers of that Byzantine political arena, could now win the five-way Democratic primary in May. His opponents include Francis Witt, a Parma businessman who has the support of State Senator Ronald Mottl of Parma; the Reverend Paul Woelfl, a Catholic priest, John Carroll University political science professor, and chairman of the Cleveland Chapter of Americans for Democratic Action; Edward Batcha, a state highway department staffer; and insurance man Joseph Barrett.

Kucinich hardly mentions any of them because he doesn't think they will come close to beating him. Instead, he talks about ousting nine-term Republican William Minshall next November. Even Minshall is said to be running scared.

It is Kucinich's track record that is starting to bother his opponents. He first ran for city council from the city's old Seventh Ward against John T. Bilinski, the party-endorsed candidate then in his eighth term. Kucinich nearly won even though he didn't reach the legal age to serve in council—twenty-one—until a few weeks before the election.

But in 1969, he again ran against Bilinski and won by sixteen votes. Two years later, he ran off with a big victory to council—the largest majority in the city, he says, claiming to have "crushed" four other opponents.

In the three-way Cleveland mayoral election last fall, he jumped his party to support Republican Mayor Ralph Perk, and, when the television cameras moved in to record Perk's victory speech, Kucinich stood at his side, beaming. By that time, his congressional campaign was well underway.

The Twenty-third District is a roughly-shaped crescent bordered on the west by Lorain County, on the south by Medina County, curving to Lake Erie in the western sector of Cuyahoga County. Actually, he lives a few blocks outside the Twenty-third District, in the Twentieth District, but the law doesn't require him to move over. His sole income is his $12,500 councilman's salary, although his wife, Helen, works as a computer programmer.

When he isn't tending to city hall matters, he is running, all day and in every way. Somehow, he also is working for both an undergraduate and graduate degree in speech communication at Case Western Reserve University and expects to get both degrees in August. He maintains an A average in his field, but not at the expense of his politicking. "I watch out for courses that require attendance," he says.

Political observers think the Kucinich phenomenon will end abruptly if he should match up with Minshall in the general election. They note that U.S. Representative James Stanton, a former Cleveland city councilman, was beaten by Minshall even though Stanton was popular and spent $90,000 in defeat. (Stanton next ran in the Twentieth District and won.)

Others point out that Kucinich will run into big trouble in such hardcore Republican areas as Rocky River and Lakewood. They say, also, that the Democratic organization has already abandoned Kucinich for his support of Perk. Huh, replies Kucinich. What Democratic organization? Like the melting pot, he says, the organization is also a myth.

Glancing at his appointment schedule somewhere over in Parma, he says with some urgency, "Come on, we got to get going."

Cleveland Voters Pick Kucinich

Akron Beacon Journal, November 2, 1977

The daring young man who had come to be scorned by his critics as "Dennis the Menace" today was calling himself "Dennis the Mayor."

And in the wake of Municipal Clerk of Courts Dennis Kucinich's narrow victory over Rep. Edward Feighan in Tuesday's mayoral election, most people are saying that this city—for better or worse—will never be the same.

The thirty-one-year-old maverick Democrat, who will succeed Republican Mayor Ralph Perk at city hall on Monday, ran strongly in the West Side ethnic wards to defeat Feighan by 3,149 votes.

The final unofficial total: Kucinich, 93,172; Feighan, 90,023.

Campaigning on a theme that he was free of control by the Democratic Party and the city's establishment, Kucinich hailed his victory as an inspiration to all young people who want to rise from the "urban ghetto."

"I can hardly believe this has happened," Kucinich told his supporters at the Lakeside Holiday Inn. "For many years as a young person, I prayed to God that I'd be a somebody . . . from the urban ghetto, rising from humble circumstances. What great possibilities there are for a united effort to build a greater Cleveland." And, as the youngest mayor in the city's history, Kucinich raised his arms in triumph with Louis Stokes, the black East Side congressman who had endorsed him, as the band played "Happy Days Are Here Again."

Feighan, only thirty himself, accepted his loss as a temporary setback in his own political career. "I wouldn't have done anything differently," said Feighan. "I think this is the beginning of a bright political future." Though disappointed by the outcome, Tim Hagan, Feighan's campaign manager, was consoled by the fact that his candidate "came from only a 3 percent recognition rating with the voters to within a couple of thousand votes of winning."

Kucinich captured all but one of the city's white wards and appeared to have received more than a third of the black votes to squeeze out a victory. Some of Feighan's aides conceded afterward that City Council President George Forbes's endorsement of Feighan may have tipped the election to Kucinich.

Forbes, an outspoken black leader who had engaged in a number of battles with Kucinich when the latter was a councilman, is extremely unpopular on the West Side. In endorsing Feighan, who was drafted by the Cuyahoga County Democratic Party, Forbes had said, "If it costs Feighan votes, so be it. I'm going to tell it. I'm not going to bite my tongue." Feighan may not have been the only one to suffer from Forbes's endorsement. Three white councilmen who had been Forbes's allies also were defeated Tuesday.

The bantam-sized (five-foot-seven, 135 pounds) Kucinich talked tough throughout the campaign, saying he would "clean house" at city hall and provide many new services without raising taxes. He attacked the public utilities and charged that a tax abatement to lure industry was a "ripoff" of the taxpayers.

Feighan, meantime, campaigned as a moderate calling for gradual reforms. However, Kucinich's sharp populist appeals obviously carried more weight with the voters.

The battle since the October 4 nonpartisan primary, when Perk was eliminated, was fought on several levels, with both sides calling in reinforcements for endorsements. Senator Howard Metzenbaum (D-Ohio), out to settle a score with Democratic regulars who supported former Representative James Stanton (D-Cleveland) in last year's senatorial race, embraced Kucinich. Senator John Glenn (D-Ohio) endorsed Feighan. And other political rivals took sides for personal political reasons.

At the same time, the city's two major newspapers clashed over the candidates. The *Plain Dealer*, which had supported Perk and Feighan in the primary, surprisingly turned to Kucinich in the general election. The *Press* endorsed Feighan.

Kucinich, who had worked as a copy clerk at the *Plain Dealer* when he was eighteen years old, appeared at the paper's editorial offices Tuesday night, took off his coat and, while the cameras flashed, sent a piece of copy to the composing room.

"Well done," said Thomas Vail, the *Plain Dealer's* publisher and editor. "Well done."

Later, Vail described Kucinich's victory as a "very interesting development. He came right out of the streets. He's going to take a new look at the way things are done in the city."

Kucinich Foes Gather 47,537 Recall Petitions
Akron Beacon Journal, April 29, 1978

It may be remembered as the first modern-dress telecast of the storming of the Bastille.

Carrying children on their arms and a single box bearing 47,537 signatures, and surrounded by a horde of television, radio, and newspaper reporters, about sixty foes of Mayor Dennis Kucinich surged into city hall here Friday night to bring down the throne.

"Let's go by the mayor's door," shouted Bill Sullivan, the Ward Eight councilman who had a hand in mustering the box of recall petitions that eventually landed on the desk of City Council Clerk Mercedes Cotner. But it turned out to be only a symbolic gesture. Kucinich, who has said all along that he doesn't think he will be kicked out, was in Clintonville, near Columbus, giving a speech.

"We did it!" exclaimed Albert Ballew, a former Republican councilman and a leader of the Recall Committee to Save Cleveland, when he spotted Council President George Forbes in one of the city hall offices.

"I don't know how it's going to turn out," Ballew said. "But the city wants him recalled."

Forbes laughed without commenting. "This is their thing," the council president said moments later, then left the building to attend a wake.

The signatures exceed the 37,552 needed to put the recall issue on the ballot. But it may be several days before it will be known how many are valid. If Cotner finds that the total falls short of the minimum, the recallers will have twenty more days to make up the difference. If they accomplish that, council will then set an election from forty to sixty days after the signatures are certified.

However, most observers expect Kucinich—if forced—to challenge the petitions in court. The petitions state that the signer must have voted in the last mayoral election. But Tom Campbell, a Cleveland State University history professor and a recall leader, said his group has legal opinions that any registered voter is eligible to sign the petition, even if he or she didn't vote last November.

One of those who tagged along for the Friday night event was former Police Chief Richard Hongisto, whose firing by Kucinich set the recall in motion. Hongisto said he didn't solicit any signatures but was on hand as an observer. "This is a good indication of the public's attitude toward the mayor," he said.

In filing the petitions with Cotner, Ballew said the moment evoked "sadness and joy." He said it was "sad" because "more than forty-five thousand people had to take time to sign a petition to recall the mayor." But Ballew added there was "joy" because the campaign had "brought the city together" by getting a response from throughout the city.

"Power to the people," someone shouted. Others were content to applaud.

It's Official: Kucinich Wins by 236 Votes

Akron Beacon Journal, August 20, 1978

A vote recount upholding Mayor Dennis J. Kucinich's recall election victory came as no surprise Saturday, but the new tabulation cut the mayor's slim lead to 236 votes.

"When you consider the fact," said Kucinich, "that the major newspapers, the banks, the utilities, every important institutional power in the community lined up to try to knock me out of office and the only thing I had going for me was the poor and working people of the city of Cleveland, when you consider that, you know that it's really amazing that I was able to win."

Both sides called the recount results, announced at a meeting of the Cuyahoga County Board of Elections, fair and impartial. The recount took almost three days. The final tallies were 60,014 for recall and 60,250 against ousting the thirty-one-year-old mayor.

"There's not much to say except that the recount was conducted fairly and carefully," said Bob Weissman, Kucinich's executive secretary, who was at the elections board for the recount announcement with about twelve other Kucinich supporters. "We hope everyone will accept the results," he added. "I hope the government can get back to normal."

Kenneth Fisher, a lawyer for the Recall Committee to Save Cleveland, said the integrity of the electoral system was preserved by the recount. "With reluctance, we can see that those who voted against recalling Dennis Kucinich prevailed by the slimmest of margins," he said.

The original official vote totals, certified Wednesday, were 60,234 against the recall and 59,843 for it. The unofficial total tabulated after the election last Sunday had given Kucinich a 275-vote victory. Police guarded the ballots until the recount was finished.

Albert Ballew, a leader of the recall effort, said whether there is another effort to recall Kucinich depends on the mayor's future actions. "There's a lot of sentiment to stay together," said Ballew of the recall committee. "The Kucinich administration must be monitored for the remainder of its term, and we will see Dennis next October [during the 1979 election]. And if he doesn't behave himself, we might even see him sooner."

Ballew said a number of Clevelanders who voted against the recall were not necessarily supporting the mayor but rather didn't understand the recall concept. "But I think the aftermath [of the recall] will be that people will understand they do have a role to play," said Ballew.

The recall was held as the mayor completed his ninth month in office. Virgil Brown, director of the Cuyahoga County Board of Elections, estimated the election cost the city between $180,000 and $200,000.

It was Kucinich's March 24 televised firing of Police Chief Richard D. Hongisto that precipitated the recall. Hongisto was fired 101 days after Kucinich hired him away from his job as San Francisco sheriff. Hongisto said members of the Kucinich administration wanted him to perform unethical acts, a charged denied by Kucinich.

Kucinich at first battled the recall in court by protesting certification of signatures on recall petitions.

A Study in Ethnic Politics

Akron Beacon Journal, October 7, 1978

Governor James Rhodes and his running mate, George Voinovich, campaigned in the heart of Cleveland's Polish-Slovenian neighborhood Friday night in a crash course on ethnic purity. Voinovich, who is Serbian-Slovenian, charged Lieutenant Governor Richard Celeste, who is Italian, a Democrat, and Rhodes's opponent, with being a "Brooks Brothers ethnic," self-styled.

It happened in former Mayor Ralph Perk's bailiwick on Fleet Avenue, at the Karlin Hall, and Perk—remembered as "the Ethnic Mayor"—was host for the Rhodes-Voinovich rally, which drew more than 350 people. Some of the faces in the crowd were remembered as people who once worked for Perk.

"Celeste calls himself an ethnic, but he certainly doesn't speak [for] or understand the ethnic community," Voinovich declared, as Rhodes stood at his side. Rhodes did not attack Celeste when his turn came on the podium. Instead, he called Voinovich "the most competent person in the state"—even if his name were "George Lewis or George Jones"—and added that his running mate "has all the caliber, fiber, and fabric to be governor of this great state."

Celeste, who was in Columbus, insisted that he had "never been in a Brooks Brothers store," which might have gone without saying for the critics of his casual dress over the years of his public life.

But Steve Kovacik, a Columbus lawyer who is Celeste's ethnic voter coordinator, was a bit more combative over Voinovich's remarks. "I'm a first-generation eastern European, and my old man came over to this country to put me in a Brooks Brothers suit," said Kovacik, who dresses very well. "I'm proud of it. What the hell did they come over to this country for?"

Perk, who denied charges by Mayor Dennis Kucinich during last year's mayoral campaign that he wore $300 suits, told reporters at the rally that he doesn't wear Brooks Brothers suits. "Here," he said, pulling back his lapel. "Look for yourself at the label."

He doesn't wear Brooks Brothers suits. Case closed.

~

Can Celeste Stop Rhodes's Last Hurrah?
Ohio Magazine, May 1978

"Nothing is so uncertain as a sure thing."—James A. Rhodes

An interview with James Allen Rhodes is like trying to tow a lumbering old barge into harbor on the end of a kite string. You are usually left holding just the string.

He grunts. He rocks. He heaves. He yaws. Barnacles shake from the twisting hulk. But he never fully yields. On the few occasions when the string doesn't snap, the frustrated interviewer is reeled in, twitted, and buried in an overwhelming sea of non sequiturs, half-sentences, and strange-sounding nouns. "I do not generally," he says, "say yes or no."

It has been that way with Jim Rhodes since he first blustered into the governor's office sixteen years ago with an unfrilly pledge to put all Ohioans back to work. Veteran members of the Ohio press have come to expect nothing less in rhetorical gymnastics and nothing more in substance from their meetings with Rhodes. They are resigned to this unhappy condition like so many ulcer patients who must put up with a bland diet or bleed to death.

If there is any sport at all left in these encounters for the reporters who have covered him over the years, it is in witnessing a matchup between Rhodes and a first-time challenger. Say, for example, Jules Witcover, the syndicated columnist who is quite capable of making sense out of the singing of a whale.

In 1974, Witcover was a political writer for the *Washington Post.* He and a small group of other reporters had checked into Republican headquarters in Cleveland, where candidate Rhodes had just taken a few more whacks at his Democratic opponent, Governor John J. Gilligan, in front of a delighted platoon of GOP payrollers. Afterward, Witcover managed to get to Rhodes for a brief private interview in a room adjoining Cuyahoga County Republican Chairman Robert Hughes's memento-cluttered office. Just a few moments later, Witcover emerged from the meeting. "What did he say?" the other reporters demanded.

Witcover shrugged as though he had just seen a ghost.

Sometime early in his political career, Rhodes, a coal miner's son from Jackson County with a practiced eye for self-survival, obviously made a conscious vow to himself to deal with the press solely on his terms as the surest course to promote his own ambitions. Lacking the intellectual depth of a Michael V. DiSalle or a John Gilligan, both of whom were gifted in turning an incisive phrase, Rhodes developed a distrust of reporters.

On the other hand, he found that friendly persuasion with editors and publishers sometimes paid the highest dividends, particularly when he could go to them with a bedsheet list of capital improvements for their towns before the editorial endorsements went into print. That, and slogans: "Profit is not a dirty word in Ohio"; "Wonderful World of Ohio"; "No new or increased taxes." And maxims: "The best way to get rich is to use other people's money"; "All of the social ills among able-bodied men come from the lack of a job"; "If problems are manmade, they can be man-solved"; "We've got more things in Ohio by accident than most states have on purpose."

When a reporter asked him last year whether he planned to run for an unprecedented fourth term, Rhodes was back to his old bargelike self. "Can you tell me whether your wife is going to be pregnant next year?" he replied.

Of course, he didn't have to give a straight answer. He was running then, and now. He will be sixty-nine in September. Some of his strongest issues against Gilligan—say, education—are now dead weight on his administration. And some Republicans are grumbling that he ought to get out for a younger man.

But he is running harder than ever. There is nothing else he'd rather do.

~

Jim Rhodes is a Republican. It says so on the ballot every time he runs. But listen carefully to his utterances—he almost never mentions the Republican Party. In 1964, he made a perfunctory endorsement of Barry Goldwater, turned the Ohio delegation loose to vote any way it wanted at the convention, and vanished for the remainder of the campaign. In 1976, at no showier a GOP forum than the national convention, where Gerald Ford (the candidate Rhodes endorsed) was desperately trying to hold off an assault from the Reaganites, Rhodes seemed hopelessly bored by the action.

No, he crackled with his clippety-clip flippancy, he hadn't read the party platform—on which the conservatives had staked life and honor—didn't intend to read it and wouldn't. Shucks, he said, nobody pays any attention to those things anyway. And no, he wouldn't rap the Democrats' nominee, Jimmy Carter, because—what political instincts!—"Carter could win this thing, and I'll have some projects to talk to him about."

This is the sort of partisan impurity that outrages some Republican thoroughbreds. He is, by most assessments within the party, a "loner" whose political commitments begin and end with his own survival. He has few confidants among the party's activists. Bob Hughes, the chairman in Cleveland, keeps in touch by telephone—Rhodes is an inveterate chitchat on the phone—but regards Rhodes as a "private man" in many ways. "He goes home every night, plays a little golf. He'll play the first three holes, skip the next four, and go on that way along the course," said Hughes. "He's also closer to his family than any politician I've ever seen."

Rhodes also has a close relationship with Kent McGough, the former Republican chairman, who will be active in this year's campaign. McGough isn't sure what his title will be, if any. "You know Jim," said McGough. "He always runs his own campaigns."

Not among the governor's tiny inner circle is Earl Barnes, the Cincinnatian who succeeded McGough to the chairmanship last year with the imprimatur of being a Rhodes man. During the early months of the campaign, Barnes has kept his distance from the governor, insisting that a chairman ought not to be involved in a primary fuss. But GOP insiders say Barnes has not been comfortable around Rhodes and that the governor would be happier with a twenty-four-hour-a-day chairman. "They are not unfriendly," said one Republican, "but they live two separate lifestyles. Rhodes eats, sleeps and talks politics twenty-four hours a day, but Barnes believes there are other things in life, too."

Rhodes's strongest ties have been with the people who can help him—and be helped—the most: longtime cronies who fetched his pails back when he was state auditor in the '50s, loyalists like Roy Martin, the governor's patronage boss, and Elmer Keller, who used to be with the Public Utilities Commission. Some of those who worked for him now maintain businesses shared with Rhodes when he was out of office from 1970 to 1974. For instance, Fred Neuenschwander, the governor's development director in the '60s, teamed with Rhodes during the political off-years in Rhodes's private development company.

There are several powerful business partners, contributors, and personal friends, whose own wealth is now approached by Rhodes himself. The names Don Hilliker of Bellefontaine and Ralph J. Stolle of Lebanon—brothers-in-law who have been involved in multimillion-dollar investments with the governor—come quickly to mind. And because of their shrewd investment policies shared with Rhodes, the governor is now estimated to be worth upwards of $4 million.

Rhodes doesn't mind joking about his investments in Howard Johnson's Motor Lodges or Wendy's hamburgers. But he won't add it all up for the nosy reporter. "If I told you how much money I made in business," he said, "you would fall right off your chair. There are a lot of nuts running around, kidnappers and those types. If I would discuss my personal holdings, I would be inviting trouble. We don't need any of that."

The cross-pollination of Rhodes and the highrollers in business and industry has kept him in good standing at election time. His fundraising success largely reflects these relationships and is probably as close as Ohio will ever come to a redistribution of wealth. At the same time, however, the governor's proven ability to muster more than $1 million for a campaign—even in 1974 when he entered the race as a heavy underdog—has frustrated younger Republicans who have been hanging around years waiting for his retirement.

The grousing was particularly evident after the 1976 elections in which the GOP took a bath. Carter carried Ohio, and the Democrats swept just about everything else. "The old ideas are killing us," complained State Senator Donald E. "Buz" Lukens, who had aspired to the Republican gubernatorial nomination this year but, out of sheer pragmatism (that is, not enough money), is opting for state auditor instead.

Another young hopeful, Cuyahoga County Commissioner Seth Taft, has also been shelved. His peers regard him as decent, intelligent, and sensitive to the need for new leadership in the party. But after flirting with the idea of a gubernatorial campaign, Taft backed off. In making his rounds of the GOP brain trusts, he came away with a sense of defeat. Those highrollers were going for Rhodes. All that was left for Taft was a functionary role as master of ceremonies when Rhodes announced his bid for reelection in March at a $100-a-ticket breakfast in Cleveland.

George Voinovich is another story. Early last year, the former member of the Ohio House of Representatives had an idea that his time for a statewide race had come. But he was worried about a couple of things, not the least of which was Rhodes. "The trouble with the party," he said at the time, "is that it has been going back to the same old names and faces for years. And if Jim Rhodes runs again, he's going to be defeated."

Having said that, he still had not resolved a second problem: his name, which to Republican voters doesn't even come close to rhyming with Smith or Brown. The forty-one-year-old Voinvoich has demonstrated strong ballot appeal in Democratic Cuyahoga County, where he had been a county commissioner, and is known as a straight-ahead, competent officeholder. After announcing for state auditor, however, he was convinced that he couldn't win a state primary. It had to be considered that the name Voinovich, down there on the ballot with Lukens, would sound like Daffy Duck in the GOP auditor's race.

For weeks there were rumors that he might shift to the tandem ticket with Rhodes—rumors that grew from other Republican sources who were engaged in a kind of self-fulfilling prophecy to give Rhodes a lift in northern Ohio. The idea intrigued Voinovich—regardless of his personal reservations about the governor—but as late as a few days before Rhodes officially ordained him, Voinovich swore that the governor still had not sat down to discuss it with him.

~

On the day—Saturday, March 4—that Rhodes told everybody what they already knew (that he was running), he raised more than $100,000 in three events around Ohio. That put his March total at about $600,000, and there seemed little doubt that he could more than double it by November.

He was up in the middle of the night preparing for his grand ritual. (Rhodes does change: In 1966, he announced for a second term in a telephone call to the son of a Teamsters' boss in Toledo, then issued a one-paragraph statement confirming it.) At 4 A.M., Rhodes called his press secretary, Chan Cochran, to check out some figures in the speech he was to deliver that day. At 6:45 A.M., he was flying to Cleveland. Meanwhile, at 5 A.M., eleven members of his family boarded a bus in Columbus to meet him at the Cleveland Plaza Hotel, where the faithful supporters had gathered.

The text of his reelection speech was vintage 1962 Rhodes—recalling a day before any of his grandchildren had arrived. If there was a new twist to the old jobs theme, it was his declaration that even our earliest ancestors had come to America's shores in a "terrifying voyage to a new land. They gambled all they had for one reason. They wanted a job!" And, "The lack of jobs is manmade. Somebody passed a bad law." Occasionally, the guests politely applauded as though they had just found an old valentine in the attic.

He was to speak fifteen minutes and leave. "Just routine. Just routine," Rhodes said as he waited for his introduction. But he went on for forty-five minutes, extolling the ancient virtues of a day's wages. He could solve the problems of Cleveland's depressed black east side with a $20 million plant. (Applause.) But what plant? Who would invest? When? What the hell? Rhodes, as he is gifted in not doing, didn't elaborate. No matter.

The power of positive thinking—that's what it is. Over the years, it has made Rhodes a hit with the big contributors who are particularly impressed with his entreaties to keep government off the backs of the entrepreneurs. He works his audiences beautifully, revealing an innocent incredulity that anyone would challenge the rightness of his dedication to full employment. But who, really, is *against* a healthy economy? It's never very clear.

But to Rhodes, somebody is always getting in the way of his fulfilling his commitment; somebody is always opposed to progress. "They'll build a barn within a hundred feet of an expressway site, and the next thing you know, they're calling it a historical site," he said in the clippety-clip, down-home style that beguiles his followers.

He's for tomato juice, highways, big buildings, dormitories, state parks, sidewalks, fat cattle, and—well, as he recently exclaimed to an *Akron Beacon Journal* editor—"I'm for everything!"

~

After the Cleveland breakfast, Rhodes wandered off to a corridor and met an old friend, W. O. Walker, the black Republican newspaper publisher whom Rhodes had appointed as his director of industrial relations in 1963. Walker will doubtless work up a public relations package for Rhodes to enable him to sell himself to black East Side Democrats.

As the two chatted quietly, a Republican informant broke into the conversation. "Kurfess said in Columbus that he's not getting out of the race," the governor was told. Rhodes bit harder on his chewing gum, said nothing, and walked away. Of all things, Chuck Kurfess, a twenty-year veteran of the legislature who once, as house speaker, did much of the governor's bidding in the General Assembly, was going to challenge him in the primary.

It is one thing for Republicans to whisper their discontent with Rhodes. It is something else to openly defy him. Few have. Robert Taft Jr. did in the 1970 U.S. Senate Republican primary. And only after some prodding did Taft swing an axe in the final weeks of the campaign to salvage a hair-thin victory. Charles Fry, a pleasant former state representative from the Springfield area, tried it in 1974 and got clobbered by Rhodes in the gubernatorial primary.

Now comes Kurfess, forty-eight, a solid Republican, ambitious, a knowledgeable legislator who is restlessly waiting for Rhodes to put in for social security. Kurfess had wanted to run for governor in 1970 but talked himself out of it. The years are catching up with him, too. Like Fry, Kurfess is a pleasant man from a safe rural district. And in the early months of his campaign, he had trouble finding a killer's instinct for his invasion into the land of Rhodes. "I know the reporters won't be happy unless I attack Rhodes," he has said, apparently uncomfortable in the role of prosecutor. It is his only option, however, in a race where the odds are heavily against him. And by degrees, he has been slowly accepting the prosecutor role.

Kurfess is convinced that many Republicans, while not shouting it from the statehouse dome, are looking for an "alternative." To him, they are the party's silent majority. But it wasn't easy to prove that in campaign dollars. By March, Kurfess had raised and spent $100,000—a sixth of Rhodes's purse.

Meanwhile, he went outside the traditional GOP stable for a running mate, choosing a respected economist from Ashland College, Dr. Lucille Ford. "I would be disappointed," he said in introducing her to a small group of newsmen in Cleveland, "if having a woman on the ticket is not a political plus." Ford is the first woman in Ohio to run for the Number Two spot.

Ford obviously came aboard to help Kurfess in another way: with an academic analysis of the governor's economic and development programs. "He's holding—not going forward," was her preliminary judgment of the governor's policies. But many Republicans figured that more aptly described the Kurfess campaign as the late winter snow began to thaw in March.

~

Richard Celeste is a Democrat. Unlike Rhodes, who couldn't wait to pull out of the Republican convention (to meet with some Japanese businessmen, he explained), Celeste's gangling six-foot-four-inch figure was omnipresent at the Democratic convention in '76, as was his entire office staff, who had given up a week's vacation to be with the boss when the Democrats nominated Jimmy Carter in New York. Richard Reeves, a political writer, saw so much of Celeste that he later accused the Ohioan of shamelessly trying to hustle the delegates for his own political schemes.

Celeste, who started out as a state representative back in 1970, seldom misses an opportunity to work one more thread into his political tapestry that, for this year at least, will adorn his campaign for the governor's office. And if the race is to be against Rhodes, it could be a classic matchup of the immovable object and the irresistible force. This much is certain: Rhodes and Celeste are two of the most savvy politicians on the scene today.

Since he upset John Brown in the lieutenant governor's race in 1974, the same year the voters sent Rhodes back to the governor's office for a third term, the forty-year-old Celeste literally has had nothing to do. Some of his admirers talked half-jokingly of starting an "Ad Hoc Committee to Keep Richard Celeste Viable as Lieutenant Governor." They were dismayed for obvious reasons. The 1974 scenario backfired on Celeste when Gilligan ran a miserable campaign and lost. With a friendly Democrat as governor, Celeste would have enjoyed all the advantages of a young man on the way up to the throne.

Gilligan would have found plenty for Celeste to do while preparing himself for a possible national candidacy in 1976. Celeste was young, aggressive, and intellectually attuned to Gilligan's professorial roots. Celeste is a Phi Beta Kappa from Yale and—no pun intended—a Rhodes Scholar. But with Gilligan's loss, and Rhodes's conscious detachment from a living political threat, Celeste has been forced to live by his own wits the past three-plus years.

He's made the most of it. Last year alone, whether in sweatshirt and jeans or a blue blazer (for formal occasion), Celeste made more than four hundred personal appearances. His comparison with Gilligan ends with their scholarly backgrounds. Celeste is a gregarious, street-smart politician with a wide, rubbery smile and a supercharged fascination with anyone who shakes his hand.

He remembers names like baseball buffs remember batting averages of the 1927 Yankees. He is possessed by informality. Watch him at the Barberton Labor Day parade—the biggest annual gathering of union people and politicians in the state. He is somewhere in the middle of the sidewalk line waiting for pancakes at St. Augustine's Church while other pols slip in through a side door.

I see Dick at a state Democratic dinner in Columbus, where big-shot Democrats are a dime a dozen. I see Dick just outside the dining hall after dinner, greeting each departing guest by his or her first name, saving a kiss for the portly old matron that he met somewhere—God knows where. I see Dick at a labor picnic in Summit County, sitting cross-legged on the grass, savoring a hotdog in the wilting sun.

I see Dick hauling a bassinet with Stephen Michael Theodore Celeste, a few-months-old infant—the youngest of his six kids—into a Holiday Inn before a speech to some Stark County unionists. Could this be THE lieutenant governor? Accompanied by his wife, Dagmar, Dick works his way into the restaurant for a few words with a reporter, introduces himself to the waitresses, eases the bassinet to the floor, and digs enthusiastically into some popcorn.

I see Dick everywhere.

"He is," said a friendly Democrat, "the hungriest candidate on the stump today. And that's what you need to win these days." And that's why he is all alone as the only major Democratic candidate in the race. Others had been interested, but not that hungry. Attorney General William Brown, perhaps the most serious challenger to Celeste, had been on the trail as early as January 1977. If Celeste, as Brown contended to Ohio Democrats, was running on the party's left (which he has no intention of doing), then Brown would occupy the center and right.

Brown is feisty and has a leaky temper that, on occasion, betrays his natural good humor. In Akron one night more than a year ago, Brown and Celeste were working the crowd at a Democratic cocktail party when a reporter lit Brown's fuse. He asked Brown to pose with Celeste for a picture. The attorney general exploded. He wasn't going to appear with Celeste because of the disparity in their ideologies. "If you like Gilligan," he shouted, "you'll love Celeste." Some of the party leaders dropped their heads, muttering something about the awkwardness of Brown's outburst. It hardly won him any early points as he prepared to overtake Celeste in a bid for Democrats' love and affection.

For much of the remainder of the year, Brown geared his campaign primarily to high-visibility actions as attorney general, particularly on energy matters and consumer affairs. By November, his polls showed that he had climbed ahead of Celeste but still trailed

Rhodes. But in gambling on the polls, Brown lost the battle in the trenches. He had failed to put together a battle-ready political organization.

Celeste had. He was on the streets building an enormous volunteer army, tapping some of the veterans of Carter's Ohio campaign and Senator John Glenn's 1974 team. Marty Gold, the Columbus insurance executive who raised money for Glenn, was aboard, pledging his efforts while urging Celeste to buy a new business-type suit. So was Ace Cohn, the Toledo businessman and Glenn fundraiser, and Jim Male, the president of Parkview Savings in Cleveland. Stephen Kovacik, a Columbus lawyer who put Glenn's campaign on track in 1974 as his campaign manager, waited for Brown—his close friend—to get out, then agreed to raise money for Celeste.

Celeste raised about $255,000 last year, but spent $158,000. Even that, however, proved to be more than Brown could handle. In the end, Brown had his polls; Celeste, the commitments and money. In the nonrace, Celeste wins. Brown steps aside, saying, "I couldn't raise the money."

Two other Democrats had thought about running, too, and weren't at the finish line for the same reason. State Representative Vernal Riffe of New Boston mentioned his interest from time to time but never got his campaign off the ground. His counterpart in the senate, Majority Leader Oliver Ocasek, ran an iffy campaign for several months and matched Celeste speech for speech, if not dollar for dollar. He dropped out with about $30,000 in his treasury to show for it.

Brown, Riffe, and Ocasek each shared a liability that worked to Celeste's benefit. They held important offices, and the party people wanted them to stay put. If the Democrats had to risk an office against Rhodes, they preferred offering up the lieutenant governor.

Celeste has another thing going for him this year. In 1974, in an act of political cannibalism, many Democrats openly chewed up their own governor. They didn't like him. He wasn't your basic street Democrat. They didn't like the people around him, particularly his chief of staff, John Hansan, whom they likened to Bob Haldeman. Hansan ran the Gilligan campaign out of a secluded office in the Statehouse, devoting as much time to Gilligan's presidential strategy as he did to a no-account gubernatorial campaign. He, like Gilligan, was aloof. He didn't always answer his phone calls. Have you heard a labor leader scream when his phone call isn't answered? It's something terrible.

No great loss, many Democrats tee-heed when Gilligan went down. But, if you believe the political adage, passed down through generations, it was a betrayal of the concession that, "he may be a son of a bitch, but he's our son of a bitch." With the passing of Gilligan, the once-thriving party headquarters shriveled away. And with the arrival of Rhodes, so did the patronage and all the other little things that Rhodes could now do for fortunate Republican supplicants.

Currently, among several of the Gilligan-haters, there's a feeling that it's time to stop horsing around and elect a Democrat. The luxury of bloodletting may be over. Even Brown, Riffe, and Ocasek are finding nice things to say about Celeste these days. For all that, Celeste is generally considered to be the underdog against a clever veteran like Rhodes. Some Democrats despair that the governor is, in fact, unbeatable—an opinion that Rhodes is wise enough to reject, saying "Nothing is so uncertain as a sure thing. You can't tell when there's an election."

There's also a nagging feeling among the party's conservatives that Celeste will stumble over his past liberal tendencies, and Celeste has yet to convince them otherwise, even when he dismisses ideological labels as "deceptive." He adds, "I'm a practical politician who wants to make government work by involving people in the process." When the State Democratic Screening Committee asked him to answer the question specifically, he replied, "You can't be too liberal when you have six kids."

Rhodes went to Cleveland for Voinovich. And Celeste, a Clevelander, went to Columbus for his running mate, Mike Dorrian, a popular county commissioner who continues to get elected in the more conservative arena of Franklin County. Most observers don't figure the contenders' partners will have a significant effect on the outcome of the election, particularly in this instance, with Dorrian and Voinovich neutralizing each other's backyard appeal.

Much will depend, then, on how well Celeste develops the issues. "The real issue," Celeste is fond of saying, "is the governor's state of mind. He's been doing and saying the same things for the past twenty-five years."

Ted Celeste, the candidate's younger brother, who will be managing the campaign, insists Celeste is on the right track with his theme of "Let's take charge of the future." The variations will become evident as the campaign progresses. Government, he asserts, has grown "so big that it has become unresponsive." Celeste plans to take the message to hundreds of neighborhood house parties. And if he says that's what he's going to do, that's what he is going to do.

As for Rhodes, Ted Celeste thinks it's fair to ask why Ohio is "the laughingstock of the nation. The crisis capital. Back in 1967, Rhodes said his Number One priority was education. We are now Number One in school closings. His economic development programs were good for the '60s. But they are pure fancy now. When economic development happens now, it mostly helps Rhodes's friends."

Both sides expect a less than genteel campaign, and neither is calling it a mismatch. Neither candidate sleeps very much. Rhodes knows every street corner in the state. Celeste has been preparing for years. But the only person ready to forecast the outcome, without fear of contradiction, is Ted Celeste, who also managed Jimmy Carter's Ohio primary campaign. "People," he stated flatly, "are never going to know why we beat Jim Rhodes."

Clip and save.

In the Knack of Time

Ohio Magazine, January 1979

While some reporters were talking of retiring Jim Rhodes's number after he finished up his fourth four-year term as governor in 1982, the Guv reminded one of them that any speculation about his future was premature. After all, he'd only be seventy-three when the time comes to leave the Statehouse, he mused. That would be the political equivalent of, say, George Blanda, a graybeard athlete who went from kicking field goals for the Oakland Raiders to making hair-coloring commercials for obvious reasons.

In November, Rhodes, who regularly keeps his own hair up to date, kicked a field goal of sorts in the closing minutes of his game with Dick Celeste, his Democratic rival, to win his second cliff-hanger in a row. Inasmuch as all of his fellow Republicans on the state ticket were defeated the same day, Rhodes's triumph was all the more remarkable. But as someone once observed, "Either you have the knack, or you don't."

Except for his narrow loss to Robert Taft Jr. in the 1970 Republican senatorial primary, Rhodes has been blessed with the Knack for a generation of state politicking.

In 1962, sixteen years before the Proposition Thirteen mania,[1] he stuck the label of "Tax-hike Mike" on Governor Michael V. DiSalle and, with considerable help from a generally friendly state press, won in a landslide.

Four years later, without half trying, another landslide. Rhodes's opponent that year was Frazier Reams Jr., who was drafted by desperate Democrats and whose name appeared on the ballot as one of those remote five-letter crossword puzzle words that most people had trouble using in a complete sentence.

In 1974, en route to a successful political comeback, Rhodes pounded Jack Gilligan for "mismanaging" public education money, taking occasional vacations in Michigan, and for wanting to tax everything that "walks, crawls or flies." This past year, against Celeste, he added the notion that his opponent was preparing to double the state income tax. And even though the governor's own popularity declined—he got about 93,000 fewer votes than he did against Gilligan—the no-show voters hurt Celeste even more.

The postmortems uniformly credit Rhodes's reelection to the widespread voter drop-off in traditionally Democratic areas like Youngstown, Cleveland, Akron, and Toledo. Democratic Belmont County went for Rhodes, who mined support from the coal people by accusing the Feds of putting air quality standards ahead of miners' jobs.

But contrary to some assessments, he didn't pull off his latest victory solely on the strength of his knack of massaging the electorate with his pro-jobs, antitax appeals.

In Cleveland, for example, where it is kind to suggest that politics is played with mirrors, the governor got a windfall when a grand jury indicted six councilmen—including five blacks—on charges that they received kickbacks from carnival gambling contracts. One of the accused was Council President George Forbes, a black Democrat who has been quite friendly to Rhodes over the years. But the political effects actually worked to the governor's advantage.

The indictments brought cries of racism from blacks. And W. O. Walker, a former Rhodes cabinet member and publisher of the black-oriented *Call and Post*, fanned the outrage in all three editions (Cleveland, Cincinnati, and Columbus) of his weekly newspaper by urging blacks either to vote Republican or not vote at all. The villain in all this supposedly was the Democratic county prosecutor, John Corrigan. But the biggest loser was Celeste.

The governor also enjoyed a helping hand from the current trend toward single-issue politics, whose influence on elections is increasing in inverse proportion to the decline of voter turnout.

In this instance, it was the abortion issue that doubtless contributed to Rhodes's 49,000-vote victory. With a $7,000 contribution from the Rhodes camp, the Ohio Right to Life Political Action Committee printed and circulated more than 700,000 pieces of antiabortion literature, declaring: "If James Rhodes wins, unborn children will win. If Richard Celeste wins, unborn children will lose."

Although Celeste as a legislator had supported strong antiabortion laws and repeatedly insisted in the campaign that he personally opposed abortion, he refused to endorse the right-to-life group's "human life amendment" because it was "narrowly defined." (The amendment would prohibit all abortions except those "required to prevent the death of the mother.")

The right-to-life group obviously means business. Kay McLandrich, a Gates Mills registered nurse and chairperson of the group's political action committee, could not offhand think of circumstances in which her group would deny a political endorsement to any candidate who supported the amendment. A reporter mentioned an indicted or convicted congressman.

"I would still go with the issue," she said. McLandrich says she's now involved in politics for its "moral and religious aspects. How else can we get our amendment approved?"

Curiously, the day after the election Rhodes told reporters he had no plans to push strong antiabortion legislation through the general assembly. McLandrich expressed mild disappointment over his comments but gave him the benefit of the doubt. "I think he wants time to think about it," she said. "He wasn't prepared to give a constructive answer at that moment."

One of the elements of Jim Rhodes's knack is that he has been generally successful in getting the benefit of the doubt. If he exaggerates the unemployment figures under his predecessor, or shows up in Cleveland to dedicate a state office building that is only 60 percent completed, it is usually affectionately shrugged off as part of his old-fashioned but effective campaign mystique.

And who will argue that it isn't?

Still, in winning, Rhodes was the exception to the Ohio Republican Party's nagging problems that seems destined to worsen in the 1980s.

With State Senator Tony Celebrezze's apparent (at this writing) victory over Republican Secretary of State Ted Brown, the Democrats will be in control of the State Apportionment Board, which will redraw the legislative districts after the 1980 census. The legislature, expected to be dominated by Democrats, will then rearrange the boundaries of the congressional districts.

Ohio faces a loss of one or two congressional districts after the next census and it is easy to suppose that the Democrats will try to eliminate them from the GOP column.

The Republicans also must contend with severe recruiting problems in enticing young, attractive candidates up and down the ticket. Earl Barnes, the party's state chairman, is calling next year's local elections "crucial" to the GOP's survival and will be out beating the bushes again after New Year's Day to whip up stronger county organizations and candidates.

It will be work. In the past few years, the party has lost Republican mayors in Cleveland and Youngstown. And in Akron and Canton, Democrats will have their best opportunities in years to capture the mayors' seats in 1979.

State Auditor Roger Cloud presenting Abe Zaidan, editor of *The Commentator*, with a medallion for winning an award from the National Conference of Christians and Jews for work on civil rights. Also pictured is Richard Compton, news director of WRFD Radio, which published *The Commentator*. Photograph by Will Sheppard, copyright Nationwide Mutual Insurance Company.

Ohio Governor James A. Rhodes, 1967. Courtesy of the *Akron Beacon Journal*.

Cleveland Mayor Carl B. Stokes, 1967. Courtesy of the *Akron Beacon Journal*.

Republican supporters of Governor James A. Rhodes in Akron, 1967. Left to Right: David Eugene Waddell, Summit County GOP Chairman; Ray C. Bliss, Republican National Committee Chairman; Governor Rhodes; former Vice-President Richard Nixon; Norman Auburn, president of the University of Akron. Photograph by W. Richard Wright, used by permission of The University of Akron Archives.

Abe Zaidan at work at the *Akron Beacon Journal* in 1969, with colleague David Hess in the background. Courtesy of the *Akron Beacon Journal*.

Cleveland Mayor Ralph Perk, election night 1971, holding up a broom signifying a "clean sweep" in the election. Future Cleveland Mayor Dennis Kucinich is on the right among campaign volunteers. Copyright Bettmann/Corbis.

Senator Howard Meztenbaum (on right), Abe Zaidan (center), and other *Akron Beacon Journal* reporters in 1974. Courtesy of the *Akron Beacon Journal*.

Ohio Governor John Gilligan (right), Abe Zaidan (center), and Leo Dugan of the United Rubber Workers, 1974. Photograph by Chuck Borsari, used by permission of the Ohio AFL-CIO.

Senator John Glenn (center right), Abe Zaidan (center left), and Senator and Mrs. Frank Church, 1976. From the author's personal collection.

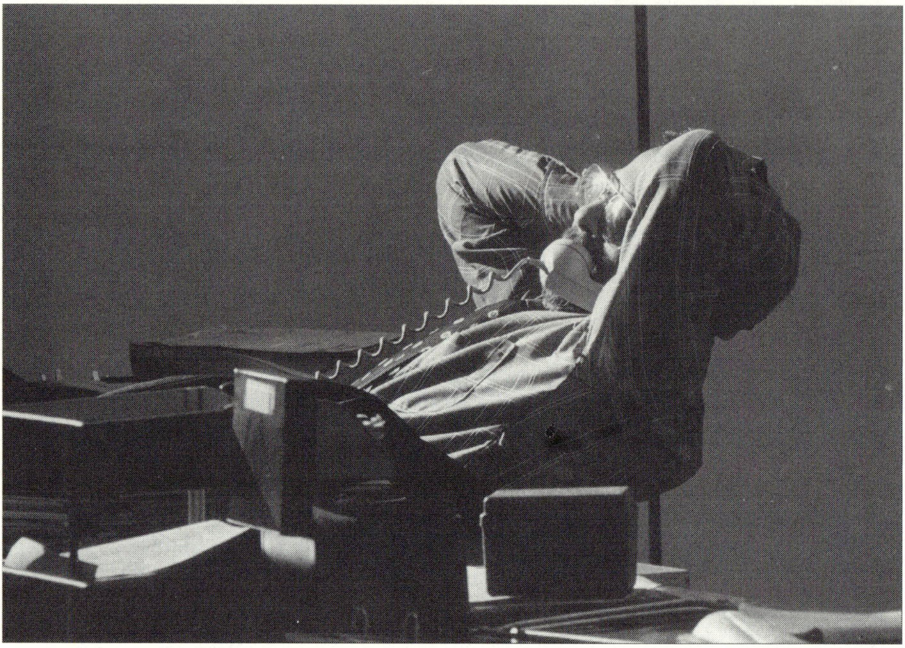

Abe Zaidan finishing up late night work at the *Akron Beacon Journal,* mid-1970s. From the author's personal collection.

Cleveland Mayor Dennis Kucinich, 1977. Courtesy of the *Akron Beacon Journal.*

Governor Rhodes upstaging Abe Zaidan by taking the telephone and calling in a "scoop" to the *Akron Beacon Journal,* 1978. From the author's personal collection.

John S. Knight, editor and publisher of the *Akron Beacon Journal,* 1980. Courtesy of the *Akron Beacon Journal.*

Ray C. Bliss, former chairman of the Summit County, Ohio, and National Republican committees, 1981. Courtesy of the *Akron Beacon Journal*.

Ohio Governor Richard Celeste and Abe Zaidan in 1982. From the author's personal collection.

Cleveland Mayor George Voinovich, circa 1985. Voinovich was later elected Ohio governor and U.S. Senator. Official photo.

Meantime, Rhodes, a lame-duck governor, will be depending on a Democratic legislature to accomplish whatever goals he has in mind the next four years. And if he's only moderately successful, he just might—he wouldn't, would he?—start thinking about a senate career at seventy-three.

When you have the Knack, all things are possible.

Who Killed Cleveland?
Ohio Magazine, March 1979

When you have eliminated the impossible, what remains, however improbable, must be true.—Sherlock Holmes

Cleveland, however improbable, is true. The temptation is always to fight off that notion as if a solicitor from the Flat Earth Society were at your door.

So you keep waiting for the final curtain, for the principals to take their bows amid the din of lusty applause, for the house lights to come on, for the walk back to the parking lot and home to bed.

But that is expecting too much. So you hang around city council chambers day in and day out, waiting for a *denouement* that never comes. Instead, you hear an angry councilman, Bill Lynch, rising during one of the city's frequent political fracases over its financial crisis and declaring for all of the world to record, "We don't believe anybody!"

The precise issue on the floor at the time was less important, it seemed for the moment, than Lynch's emotional definition of the problem. "It's true," I scribble in my notes. "Nobody up here believes anybody." And that's one of the truths that have been nagging Ohio's biggest city for years, right into fiscal default, and now, well beyond it.

The malady has infected many in public life, as well as a great number of average citizens who have not yet found a way to move out to the suburbs. Even the media have been having credibility problems.

As I write this, *Cleveland Plain Dealer* reporters are picketing the paper to protest management's decision to yank reporter Robert

Holden from coverage of the February special election on the proposed sale of the Municipal Power and Light Company and the city's request for an income tax increase. (They didn't think Holden would be *fair* to Cleveland Electric Illuminating Company.) At the same time, the *PD*'s reporting staff was said to be "split" over whether Dennis Kucinich is a good guy or villain, the latter being how the paper's editors regard the embattled thirty-two-year-old mayor.

Not long ago, WJKW-TV embarrassed one of its best reporters, Bob Franken, by publicly "correcting" a Franken news report involving a bank's purported nasty attitude toward the Kucinich administration. Franken stood by the accuracy of his account and resigned.

In apparent desperation, the religion writer at the afternoon *Cleveland Press* argued it would be helpful if the city went after its problems with a series of prayer breakfasts, which *PD* columnist Tom Green promptly twitted as "an abject admission of hopelessness."

For more than a decade, there has been no known middle ground in Cleveland, only an "us and them" mentality that has bred suspicion, distrust, and, of course, disbelief. To suggest, say, to Kucinich's enemies, that he could, maybe, perhaps, possibly, charitably, have some redeeming qualities would be to argue the logic of a partial pregnancy.

But it is an oversimplification to trace the city's death rattle to the arrival of Kucinich at city hall, no matter how his critics would have it. The problems have been around for a long time, exacerbated by a business as usual attitude by previous administrations, a good-ol'-boy relationship between political and business interests, a less-than-attentive press, poor race relations, a declining population that has been conditioned to mediocre city services and the steady, numbing outbreaks of political warfare.

Long before last December's default, there had been warnings of a fiscal disaster. Former Cleveland Mayor Carl Stokes sensed it was coming, but, by an odd *quid pro quo*, an attempt to trade off property taxes for income taxes, lost on both counts.

His successor, Ralph Perk, insisting he could forever balance the books without new taxes, blithely let matters ride for six more years, simply by reassuring the voters that he knew what he was doing.

And Kucinich, who opposed all previous attempts to increase the income tax, came aboard as an antitax operative and friend of the workingman. But until Kucinich's election, the powerful business, labor, and media people found the political climate at least tolerable.

Stokes, the first black mayor of a major U.S. city, made his peace within the black community during the jittery days of civil rights protests in America's ghettos. Perk, a proud ethnic who turned city hall into the League of Nations, was a get-along mayor, full of good news, peace, and ceremony. The *Plain Dealer*'s editor and publisher, Tom Vail, liked Perk's unobtrusive governing, and the mayor, in appreciation, always returned Vail's calls.

The *PD*'s neighborly approach to Perk apparently helped paper over some otherwise difficult times for the mayor. Edward Whelan, a former *PD* city hall reporter, now managing editor of *Cleveland Magazine*, wrote in the magazine in 1975 that his year-end report on Perk for the *PD* was killed for being too critical. Instead, the paper ran an upbeat Q&A with the mayor.

Ironically, Kucinich—whom Perk condemns as a "pathological liar"—landed the *PD*'s endorsement in the 1977 general election after the paper set out to destroy him in the nonpartisan primary. Vail told me later he switched his allegiance to Kucinich (in a matchup with regular Democrat Edward Feighan) because he was convinced the young maverick was a streetwise pol beholden to no one. Another version was available from some PD staffers: after Perk ran a poor third in the nonpartisan primary, Vail figured Kucinich was unbeatable in the general election and, as is his wont, wanted to be first in line to greet Kucinich in the winner's circle.

Such ad hoc alignments of power and influence have long been a tradition in Cleveland, including the courtly days of Louis Seltzer, the *Cleveland Press* editor who regularly fashioned mayors and governors from his stable and, when the mood struck him, disposed of them.

Seltzer had retired by the time Stokes, an impressive young legislator, was igniting black voter awareness in the 1967 mayoral campaign—a personally successful effort that was sharply to establish the city's deep racial division that still exists today. The *Press*, torn by its sedulously nurtured roots in the city's white ethnic neighborhoods and its hankering to fall in step with "an idea whose time had come," agonized over its endorsement, first apparently supporting one candidate, then shifting to another. Finally, it settled on Stokes, as had the *PD*.

In what amounted to a cold turkey showdown between East Side (black) and West Side (white), Stokes won narrowly over Republican Seth Taft. But the election also intensified racial hostility that has, over the years, been expressed in ways (voting patterns on tax issues, for example) that have tightened the noose around the city's treasury. In recent years, blacks have supported school tax levies, but they have been outvoted by whites who view the new money as a boondoggle for school desegregation.

Stokes, meantime, tried twice to increase the unvoted 1 percent income tax by a popular vote. The measures were defeated both times, in 1970 and again in 1971. To sweeten the idea for the voters, Stokes agreed to not seek renewal of a 5.8 mill property tax levy on the 1971 ballot in return for his proposal to increase the income tax to 1.8 percent.

The voters happily rejected the income tax increase and pocketed the savings from the property millage cut, which has cost the city about $140 million in property tax revenue over the past seven years. Offered no alternative, Stokes laid off 1,750 city employees and left office in 1971 with a $13.6 million deficit in the city treasury. Among the contributing factors: a mandatory pay increase for the city payrollers.

Warning enough.

Enter Perk, the former county auditor and a Republican who had long defied the law of gravity by defeating Democrats in Cuyahoga County. He boasted that he could balance the budget without new taxes, create prosperity for his city, and champion the ethnic movement across America.

With Nixon in the White House, and Perk a big-city GOP rarity, Perk also managed to shore up the city finances with hefty infusions of federal funds—millions in urban project dollars that eventually found their way into meeting payrolls.

He also received help from the Ohio General Assembly to enable Cleveland to issue notes and bonds for operating expenses. Many fiscal experts now look back on these schemes as mere expedients to push back the city's day of reckoning.

By 1973, with more and bigger bills coming due, Perk was persuaded to look for help by seeking an income tax increase—a move that was again rejected by the voters, who, by now, apparently believed that each succeeding mayor, by tradition and nothing else, owed himself at least one exercise in futility.

Perk, always flexible in the face of adversity, was busy on other fronts. He gave up the city's sewer and transit systems. Some say he sold them. He says he transferred them. In any event, the sewer system, which went into a regional setup, took in $32 million for the city. The debt-ridden transit system was absorbed by a regional transit operation.

By then, the city's financial maneuvering to avoid deficits here and there had become a classic case of mix-and-match economics, so much so that the accounting firm of Ernst & Ernst reported last year that during a six-and-a-half year period—from January 1, 1972 to June 30, 1978—$52 million in capital improvement money was diverted to operating funds.

There were other warnings that seemed to go nowhere.

•During Perk's first three years in office, the city-voted bond indebtedness dropped from $92.5 million to $61 million. At the same time, unvoted bonds jumped from $0.3 million to $126.2 million. By 1975, the unvoted debt had soared to $144 million.
•By 1975, property taxes comprised only 17 percent of the city's general fund revenue. In 1961, they accounted for 54 percent.
•In 1974, about half of the city's property taxes was used to retire bonds.

These figures were taken mainly from a 1974 two-hundred-thousand-word study of the city's financial structure by two Cleveland State University economists, Edric Weld and John Burke—a study that Weld now remembers as having produced little impact on the city's way of doing business.

But, they noted, "The system appears to be so complex that there may be no one who knows all of its components. . . . There is no present source from which the individual can secure a comprehensive and coherent picture of the city's financial position."

The report lamented "outmoded accounting procedures and a disparity of figures." A few years later, accountants were to shrug in disbelief that the city's books were "not auditable." And soon after his election, Kucinich was saying as much. The two professors also predicted "acute" financial problems in 1978–79 when the 1972–73 notes came due. Said Burke: "I would hate to be the mayor five years from now."

Perk rejects all judgments that he turned over a crippled city to Kucinich, maintaining that he always balanced the budget and left office with a surplus. "If I had still been mayor," he said recently, "the city would never have defaulted."

Perk recalls that he had tried to sell the Municipal Power and Light Company to Cleveland Electric Illuminating Company (CEI) for $158 million—a deal supported by city council but blocked by Kucinich. The revenue from the sale of the plant, which has been losing money for years, would solve the city's financial crisis with a few official signatures on the paperwork, Perk contends.

The plant, which buys its power from CEI and serves about forty-five thousand customers, many in ethnic wards that have supported Kucinich, has a big sign out front that reads: "Power to the People," with Kucinich's name underneath.

In his campaign for mayor, Kucinich chose the sale of Muny Light as one of his visceral issues in painting the city's business giants (Cleveland Trust, CEI, Republic Steel, et al.) as greedy patrons preying upon an economically depressed working class. Clearly, for Kucinich, it was a class struggle. He railed against tax abatement for industry, increased taxes, and the sale of the plant. Muny Light, he contended, was the city's shield against higher utility rates by CEI. Without it, CEI would be a monopoly.

Once in office, Kucinich clung to that position while adding a new wrinkle: the sale of Muny Light, he maintained, would mean the end of the city's $330 million antitrust suit against CEI. But as $15.5 million in short-term notes were coming due last December and default was at hand, the mayor fell back to a compromise position. He proposed a three-member board to monitor Muny Light for eighteen months. If the board determined it wasn't making money, he would agree to sell the plant.

The proposal was sent to city council, which shelved it. The council, out to finesse the mayor at every turn, coupled the plant's sale with the income tax increase on the February ballot. Kucinich shouted another "crooked" deal was in the works, pledged to support the tax increase—and fight the Muny Light sale.

Although Kucinich has a half-dozen or so diehard loyalists on council, his forces are overwhelmingly outnumbered on the thirty-three-member body. In the captain's seat is Council President George Forbes, a forty-seven-year-old black man who has managed to render Kucinich *hors de combat* in each showdown before the council.

Forbes and Kucinich simply can't stand each other, an ugly situation that has produced a stalemate between the city's executive and legislative fiefdoms. In the final hours before the December 15 default, Kucinich batted zero on each attempt to have his proposals heard by council. On the other hand, Forbes complained that the mayor was running his own show without consulting council. At one point, Forbes summed up the problem with one line: "We haven't talked to each other in four months."

Stalemate is a fact of life in the politics of Cleveland. Stokes went to the mat regularly with then-council president James Stanton, a seasoned West Side Irish pol who, like Stokes, assumed territorial rights to sustain his power. Though Perk enjoyed the protective blanket of the press and the corporate community, he had to put up with the assaults of then-councilman Kucinich. (Perk's relationship with Democrat Forbes was a kind of détente in which he chose not to crowd Forbes on East Side policies.) And now it is Kucinich against the whole establishment, and vice versa.

Shut out from city hall, the town's biggies, accustomed to clear access to the mayor's office, are in disarray. Art Modell, who owns the Cleveland Browns and is a front-line civic activist, says a coalition of various interests would not work because there is no way it could get its message across to the mayor. "There's apparently an antibusiness, antibank attitude at city hall," sighs Modell. "Who would listen?"

Cleveland's biggest bank, Cleveland Trust, which has $4 billion in assets and holds $5 million in overdue short-term notes, has taken a wait-and-see attitude—at least until after the February 27 election—before moving to demand payment. And CEI, three of whose directors sit on the Cleveland Trust Board, has withdrawn its offer to buy Muny Light.

Still, Kucinich, who must contend with a stomach ulcer among other things, shows no signs of relenting in his tumultuous brand of urban populism. He and his young staff, having first insisted that the city's treasury was healthier than it was, has managed to improvise various escape hatches when enemies were preparing to lower his coffin. Even as he was forced to ask for the tax increase last December 12, his half-hour television speech deftly splashed the Perk Administration with the sins of bad fiscal management.

"As a councilman," he was happy to report, "I became aware of the incredible inefficiency of Cleveland's city government, of the waste and corruption that exists, of the fat contracts and political plums which city officials habitually handed to their friends and sometimes to themselves."

He scolded his predecessor for "misspending $40 million" in bond funds and of resorting to "flimflam solutions" such as selling Muny Light and other city assets to keep the city afloat. He has a knack for keeping the ball out of his court.

In this respect, particularly when he goes to the streets with cries of "crooks, hacks, and corruption," he obviously believes that events are on his side. His arch enemy, Forbes, has been indicted along with five other councilmen in connection with alleged kickback schemes involving street carnival operators.

There's more: a county grand jury in December indicted William H. Seawright on felony charges growing out of a consulting contract with the Perk administration. And, at this writing, federal, state, and county investigators are sifting through the complex business dealing enmeshed with the Ohio Lottery operation in Cleveland.

In an apparent spinoff of that probe, recent published accounts in the *Cleveland Press* have charged Cuyahoga County Republican Chairman Robert Hughes, one of the most influential politicos in the county, with getting $100,000 in consultant fees for a $2.8 million no-bid rubbish hauling contract during the Perk years.

All this, plus the lesser episodes of reporters being stripped of their assignments for "unfairness," has played directly into Kucinich's mortal combat with the ruling powers.

At the same time, it has intensified the cynicism and suspicions that run rampant in a city on the verge of bankruptcy. Hardball politics, disclosures of great profit from the public treasury, and messy bookkeeping are not unfamiliar to Cleveland's modern history. But they all seem to be converging in a dramatic life-and-death moment that may very well, this time around, be fatal.

In 1979, the city must replace $40 million in bond proceeds siphoned off for operating expenses. It must find a way to pay $40 million in additional short-term notes that come due. Without new sources of revenue, it faces a $45.2 million deficit in current operating expenses this year.

For the year, let's round off the total deficit to about $125 million for a city with a shrinking tax base, a steady exodus of its population (now at 625,000 and plunging), rising fire and police payrolls, a low income tax rate (1 percent—50 percent lower than other major Ohio cities), a voter disposition over the past decade to turn down new taxes, unending feuding and fussing and suspicion of everything and everybody.

Who's to blame?

Everybody is as safe a guess as any.

Kucinich in Underdog Role after Primary
Akron Beacon Journal, October 3, 1979

Mayor Dennis Kucinich, who has always enjoyed playing the role of the underdog, today bore that title again after Republican Lieutenant Governor George Voinovich's victory over Kucinich and three other candidates in Tuesday's nonpartisan mayoral primary election.

The thirty-two-year-old Kucinich trailed Voinovich by more than eleven thousand votes for a second-place finish that qualified him for the November 6 runoff. But the margin of Voinovich's triumph was enough to convince his supporters and some political observers here that Kucinich would not be able to overtake his opponent over the next month in his bid for a second term.

The final unofficial results set Voinovich's margin over Kucinich at 47,743 to 36,515. City Council Majority Leader Basil Russo, a Democrat, finished third with 21,962 votes. State Senator Charles Butts (D-Cleveland) got 19,431 votes, followed by Socialist Workers Party candidate Thabo Ntweng, who had 1,546 votes.

Kucinich, a maverick Democrat whose two stormy years in the mayor's office have seen the city fall into fiscal default, appeared undismayed by the results when he spoke to his supporters at the Cleveland Convention Center.

"We're the underdogs," he said. "We're the underdogs not only to Republicans. We're the underdogs to the money powers of Cleveland which are using their cardboard Republican candidate to try to take over Cleveland and win it for their own profit from those office towers downtown."

He likened the primary to a football game, observing "We're trailing at the end of the half, but as you know, what counts is who's ahead at the end of the fourth quarter."

Voinovich, forty-three, arrived at his election night headquarters in the Cleveland Plaza Hotel at 10:20 P.M. to the cheers of hundreds of loyalists and promptly declared that he was "somebody who's mature, somebody who's proven, and somebody who's experienced in leadership." He added: "Cleveland is the little people's city, and we're going to give it back to the little people."

Voinovich also sought support from the city's spiritual leaders by declaring that, as mayor, he would delegate a "very important part of the decision-making process" at city hall to the "churches of this town."

Although he said he would campaign hard to confront the city's serious problems in the weeks ahead, Voinovich said he would not take a leave of absence from his duties as lieutenant governor. "I'm going back to Columbus tomorrow morning," he said after his victory speech Tuesday night.

Voinovich led the field in Tuesday's balloting, which drew about 40 percent of the city's three hundred thousand registered voters to the polls, in spite of the fact that he lost all thirteen black wards. Kucinich won eleven white ethnic wards.

However, the mayor was only narrowly ahead in those wards, winning his own Ward Seven by only fifty-nine votes over Voinovich. At the same time, Voinovich ran well ahead of Kucinich in the black East Side wards won by Russo.

Voinovich was heavily supported by [the] business and corporate interests that Kucinich has scorned during his first term. Campaign finance reports filed by the candidates through September 12 revealed that Voinovich had raised $144,415 and had spent $106,915.

Kucinich's campaign committee reported raising $75,300 but spending only $16,866.

The mayor charged Tuesday night that "Republican Voinovich's secret fat-cat friends have bought his way into the runoff, but they're not going to buy him city hall."

He urged his supporters to "go back out to the people . . . to every street . . . to every home . . . Let's let all this city know we don't want a money-laundering, fat-cat big-business Republican as mayor of Cleveland."

During the campaign, Kucinich had charged that a $71,000 contribution to Voinovich from the Cuyahoga County Republican Party was actually, in Watergate terms, "laundered" money from big contributors who were granted anonymity.

Voinovich had been a state representative, county auditor, and commissioner before joining Governor James A. Rhodes on the GOP gubernatorial ticket last year. When there was speculation earlier this year that he might enter the mayor's race, Voinovich said he would not be a candidate. However, Republican sources said he was under heavy pressure from the city's business interests to run and was given solid assurances by them that he would be well financed for the campaign.

Kucinich hammered at Voinovich's political alliances throughout the primary and Tuesday night repeated that he intends to make it one of the major issues of the general election. And although the mayor has been at odds with the Democratic Party in Cuyahoga County for years, he appealed for Democratic support in the weeks ahead.

"This election," he said, "is the people against the fat cats; the Democrats against the Republicans; the poor people and the working people and the middle-income people against the rich."

~

Reconstruction: Mayor Strives to Restore Faith in Cleveland
Akron Beacon Journal, December 16, 1979

Greg Krizman politely and patiently tried to reassure the caller at the other end of the line. If the request for a proclamation were resubmitted, said Krizman, Mayor George Voinovich's press secretary, the mayor would honor it.

Bothered by a head cold, Krizman was patting his nose with a Kleenex and trying to tend to the ceremonial requirements of urban government while hounded by reporters preparing first anniversary stories about the city's December 15, 1978, default.

When former Mayor Dennis Kucinich and his staff evacuated city hall last month after losing the election to Voinovich, Krizman said, they cleared out the office files, leaving behind only a batch of stationery bearing the picture of Ralph Perk, Kucinich's predecessor.

Lost in the transition were a lot of requests for the mayor to proclaim special days. Now, a lot of people appeared to be sore because they had not yet got an official word from the mayor—past or present.

"These things are important," shrugged Krizman, "and we're doing our best to handle the requests. Naturally, we want them to have the proclamations."

The same workaday attitude permeated the mayor's second-floor offices at city hall last week in a conscious effort by the new administration to calm the storms of the Kucinich era.

Voinovich casually lunched on cheese and apple slices at his desk, promising to do his best for his city but readily admitting that he had no idea when Cleveland would be liberated from the onus of fiscal default.

The mayor's eleven-year-old son, Peter, spending another schoolless day during the current strike by Cleveland public school teachers, broke open a fast-food container of french fries and a hamburger in the mayor's outer office.

People seemed to be talking in whispers.

Even some of the battle-scarred local reporters were finding the transition too abrupt to take in stride. "This city," complained one city hall reporter, "has gone from being the best news town in America to being the dullest. Everybody is too nice." And that is precisely the image that Voinovich is trying to convey these days as he extends the olive branch to many of the institutions scorned by Kucinich.

"Our major accomplishment," said Will Largent, the new mayor's executive secretary, "is a change in attitude around the city. We've elevated the self-esteem of Clevelanders who feel we're sincere and not a bunch of bastards."

Largent cited as evidence of an improved attitude toward city hall the willingness of some companies to do business with the city again. "Even on little things like shorthand tablets, typewriter ribbons, and carbon paper," Largent said, "we couldn't get anybody to bid on them because the companies felt they wouldn't get paid. We have to regain their confidence in the city, not through words but through deeds."

Voinovich has carried out his first month in office with caution. He has appointed committees to screen candidates for cabinet jobs and has been careful in his public statements about the city's financial future.

A volunteer team of accountants is digging into the financial records of each city department to determine, if possible, the status of the city's funds.

Voinovich resists all questions about the financial picture, but he does suggest that Cleveland is in even worse condition than he at first had feared.

A year ago, the city defaulted on $15.5 million in short-term notes. Five banks held $14 million in notes. Since then, the city has repaid the banks about 25 percent of the principal.

Last summer, the city also defaulted on $3.3 million in notes held by the city's water system. Since the first default last December, the city has not been able to sell bonds and has limped along in a catch-as-catch-can financial operation.

Voinovich says he hopes to regain the confidence of financial institutions so a new agreement can be worked out that will buy more time for the city.

"The banks will do anything that has to be done," says Voinovich, "if they're confident in the city's management and fiscal responsibility."

So far the banks have indicated a willingness to tread water while the new administration seeks a course out of its inherited crisis.

The banks' attitude might have been summed up by Brock Weir, chairman and chief executive officer of AmeriTrust (formerly Cleveland Trust). Although Weir is declining interviews with the press, a company spokesman referred a reporter to an earlier statement by Weir: "I'm pleased by the turn of events in the election, if only for the reason it appears we have established a more civil kind of communication with city government. I think that pleasure is shared by the entire business community. To some extent you might characterize some of us as being in a state of euphoria that dims our perception that the really hard part of remedying the city's problems lies ahead."

Promises of overnight remedies are avoided in Voinovich's low-key effort. The new mayor apparently shares Weir's view that the hard questions about the city's finances are still to be answered.

Voinovich expects the financial review of the city, which will be released soon, will be gloomy. He says he "can't project" when the city will recover from default. And he says he can only hope that Cleveland will be back on the municipal bond market—all but closed to the city by its poor financial rating—"within a year."

Beyond that, he says, "I can only say that I'm not going to panic."

Ohio's Seal of Approval

Ohio Magazine, April 1979

Here they come: Reagan, Ronald; Baker, Howard; Connally, John; Dole, Robert; Bush, George; Kennedy, Edward; etc., etc.

You'll find them all in the *dramatis personae* of the 1979–80 presidential campaign, which has come to be a hyphenated two-year enterprise on the scale of the Great Gold Rush. They want Ohio and will be checking in regularly with the kind of expectations the Wolverines bring to Buckeye Stadium. A win here, and it's on to the Rose Bowl.

In 1976, Gerald Ford needed the presidential seal and the Ohio Republican Executive Committee to escort him safely past Ronald Reagan in the state primary—a victory that handed the hotly contested nomination to Ford. The same day, Jimmy Carter ran up a lopsided triumph over his nearest Democratic challenger, Mo Udall, in Ohio, and Carter's detractors threw in the towel.

Little more needs to be said about how the presidential hopefuls feel about the state. It is important. If New Hampshire gives the political pundits an early opportunity to ferret out a front-runner, Ohio, which winds up the long primary trail in June, is the final test of durability and momentum. The prize is a whole lot of delegates for both primary winners.

So while most Ohioans were preoccupied with the snow drifts in their driveways this year, the candidates were drifting in to the Lincoln Day Dinners and other places to begin their claim on next year's primary. The speeches were predictable and the electorate, it's safe to presume, inattentive.

If there was a wrinkle in the script, it had to be the message that Dole, the Kansas senator who played the heavy on the Ford ticket, brought to nearly a thousand Summit County Lincoln Day Republican diners.

Republicans, he said, can't be against *everything*. Dole went on to advocate his own model of catastrophic health insurance (unlike Kennedy's, to be sure, but nevertheless a studied thrust into an area of deep national concern). He courted black support and talked of compassion for the little guy's problems. On that night, at least, Dole came away as a softy.

Other than reinforcing a few friendships and trying to influence some others, the early arrivals aren't likely to sweep any of the Ohio pols off their feet. The GOP captains in Ohio are wary of premature commitments, and at Democratic Headquarters in Columbus, they're digging in for their man in the White House.

Among those preaching caution to the Republicans is the party's state chairman, Earl Barnes, who has no trouble recalling the wrath of the Reaganites in the wake of the party's endorsement of Ford in 1976. "There are still repercussions being felt in the hinterlands," observes Barnes. "For us to go off now in a lot of different directions is not in the best interest of the party." His advice to anyone who suggests otherwise: "Cool it."

From this distance, it would not be surprising if the party, at some point along the way, starts dabbling with the idea of a favorite-son candidacy in the person of Governor James A. Rhodes, who's been down that road before. On the other hand, the governor, never one to find national politics beguiling, might just say, "Aw, to hell with it."

Although the state's Democrats are facing their first presidential campaign since 1964 with the incumbent on the ticket, there's a sense of uneasiness over their man's public ratings. And that, in turn, is obliquely feeding another issue over whether the party's state chairmanship should be a full-time job.

Steve Kovacik, a Columbus lawyer and Democratic Party contributor, has openly put the question on the table in the context of a possible Kennedy challenge to Carter. Kovacik, Senator John Glenn's campaign manager in 1974, believes the party's current part-time chairman, Paul Tipps (a Cincinnati investor-businessman who draws a fifteen-thousand dollar salary from the party), is inextricably allied with the Carter Administration and has foreclosed on a Kennedy option in Ohio.

"What the hell has Carter given us in Ohio," Kovacik complains in the typically blunt language that has won him dear friends and acid enemies, "that we should be kissing his ring?" He suggests Kennedy would make a good presidential candidate, and, as for himself, he is a candidate for full-time chairman of the party.

"The state Democratic Party," he will tell you, "is a nuthin'. It's broke. It has no voice. No leadership." Insisting that Tipps may be leading the party into a locked-in position with Carter, Kovacik says the question over the state chairmanship shouldn't be delayed until Tipps's term is up in 1980. "That will be too late," he asserts.

There are other rumblings in the party. Attorney General William Brown, who wants to run for governor in 1982, says he'd "like a full-time chairman" and will pursue the idea with other Democratic officeholders.

"I have no animosity toward Paul," says Brown, "but a full-time chairman would give the party a number of strengths in fundraising, continuity in office, and coordination with county chairmen and others. To do all these things, you need a full-time chairman."

Tipps, however, who came in after Jack Gilligan's defeat in 1974, says he has no intention of quitting before his term is up and is keeping his options open after that. He also appears to be unruffled by the doubts about his leadership. "We have done a spectacular job in electing people and raising money," says Tipps. Except for the governor's office, he notes, the party controls virtually everything. "When I took over, the party was $250 thousand in debt," he says. "Since then, we've raised about one million." He's not about to apologize for that record for a part-time chairman.

Nor is he backing off on Carter. "The Kennedy name has been brought up," he says. "But this is political naiveté by the people doing the talking. I'm not a state chairman to gamble with the well-being of the state Democratic Party."

Tipps says he's not influenced by polls showing the president's public approval ratings declining. "I've seen polls go up and down, and the role of a political organization is not to go up and down with the polls."

Still, he leaves open the possibility that the party executive committee may choose another course. That could mean a couple of alternatives to embracing Carter: a favorite-son candidacy or a total hands-off policy on a primary, assuming a Kennedy challenge. If Kennedy stays home, of course, simply put a clip-and-destroy tag on all of the scenarios under current discussion. It would be left to the Republicans to have all the fun this time around.

And back at the war room, the thought of *that* happening will doubtless be of grave concern to combat-ready Democrats for months to come.

Carter in Steubenville: A Presidential Progress
Ohio Magazine, November 1979

When not faced with invading Spanish Armadas or treasonable intrigues, Elizabeth the First of England had a foolproof method of keeping down the costs of maintaining her glittering court while scoring PR points with her subjects. She would make a "royal progress" through her kingdom, putting up at the country estates of wealthy nobles and letting them pick up the tab for the roasted boars' heads and mulled wine. Having the queen and her five hundred closest courtiers drop in for a leisurely week of heavy eating and lavish entertainment was both a great honor and a potentially ruinous expense. A royal progress also gave the monarch a chance to ride through the cities and towns, waving at awestruck peasants and commoners as she passed by.

Today royal progresses are not what they used to be, but the American equivalent—a presidential progress—is a thriving institution. In mid-September, Jimmy Carter and his court of advisors, guards, retainers, supporters, and media jesters descended on Steubenville in southeastern Ohio for a jet-and-TV-age version of a progress. Boar's head was not on the menu, but for the citizens of Steubenville and thousands from the surrounding countryside, it was an impressive occasion.

The president of the United States travels in a style unmatched by mere royalty. Good Queen Bess had no advance men to issue local press credentials or commandeer a wing of the Holiday Inn for a mobile communications center. Elizabeth didn't carry a portable Xerox machine in her luggage.

President Carter has made much of his trips into the hinterlands to answer questions at "town meetings" or to spend the night with "typical" American families. It might be an interesting way to cut the federal budget to have the president always board with strangers, but it would probably become stale after a while.

But a flying visit is another matter, and Steubenville was primed for the presidential appearance hours before the army helicopter appeared across the river signaling Carter's imminent arrival. The Secret Service had been in town even before the visit was officially announced, checking the Steubenville High School auditorium where Carter was to speak, casing the official route, and attending to security details.

A presidential progress is more like a blitzkrieg than a social call. Carter was coming to Ohio via Connecticut, where he was first to address a senior citizens' convention before flying to Pittsburgh for the short drive to Steubenville. According to the White House schedule, which was followed with ruthless precision, the president would arrive at Steubenville at 2:45 P.M., come on stage at the high school fifteen minutes later, stay for exactly one hour of questions, depart for a local restaurant where Democratic worthies were gathered, pump hands and hearts for exactly thirty minutes, then drive back to the airport for the flight to Washington. Not counting the ride to and from Pittsburgh, Carter was to be in Steubenville for exactly two hours and five minutes. It might have taken the Earl of Leicester that long just to get through the formal greeting when Queen Bess rolled up at the head of her throng.

By Wednesday morning, the motorcade route through downtown Steubenville was marked off with steel drums and ropes. The Secret Service men, who all seem to go to the same tailor, paced the street, looking at rooftops for snipers. The weather was unseasonably warm for September and unusually clear for Steubenville. Fifteen hundred lucky citizens had picked up tickets for the town meeting. They were in line by noon and ushered into the un-air-conditioned auditorium by one o'clock. The audience spent two hours in the almost unbearably warm auditorium listening to the Steubenville High School band; the White House staff explained the rules of the town meeting, and the press argued over places on the camera platform. When a White House aide put the presidential seal on the podium a half hour before Carter appeared, the sweaty crowd broke into a cheer.

Outside, the crowds were staking out spots on the curb to catch a glimpse of the president as he swung off Dean Martin Boulevard and then down Fourth Street to the high school. School kids had the day off, and marching bands were posted every block or so to serenade the passing chief executive. Souvenir hawkers were busy peddling peanut key chains, made-in-Taiwan American flags, and commemorative T-shirts. Also on hand was a big contingent from the United Mine Workers of America (UMWA) with signs urging, "Save America—Burn Ohio Coal." For it was coal—or rather Ohio's high-sulfur coal that even in these energy-starved times is lying in vast unsaleable mountains on the ground because of federal Environmental Protection Agency (EPA) restrictions—that brought Carter to Steubenville.

Steubenville is at the heart of a long string of Ohio River heavy industry towns that live and die by coal and steel. Steubenville and its West Virginia twin across the river, Weirton, are dominated by sprawling steel mills that send up giant pillars of smoke and ash. The hillsides are piled with slag, or "gob piles" as they are known locally. Steubenville, which once gloried in the title of America's dirtiest city, has cleaned up considerably, according to locals who remember the days when cars would pull into filling stations first thing in the morning with their windshields glistening from a layer of pure graphite.

On the day of Carter's dash through town, the sky was clear; but that morning there was still a slight whiff of burning sulfur which, to Steubenville natives, is the true smell of home. To them, a little bit of smoke never hurt half as much as a cold blast furnace or a shut-down coal mine. The sulfur smell means the mills are working, and that is always good weather in Steubenville.

The local steel industry is in relatively good shape, thanks to a federal guarantee announced the week before of a $150 million private sector loan to the Wheeling-Pittsburgh Steel Corporation, which employs seven thousand in Steubenville. Carter was to tell the town meeting that it was no coincidence that he had come to Steubenville. The loan guarantee was part of the lack of coincidence.

The coal industry is a different story. The Clean Air Act passed in the environmentally militant early seventies is now drawing a noose around local mines—mines which produce high-sulfur steam coal ideal for power plants but dreadfully dirty to burn without smoke scrubbers that cost hundreds of millions of dollars to install. The immediate issue facing Carter was his position on EPA waivers of sulfur content for the Cleveland Electric Illuminating (CEI) plants that traditionally use southeastern Ohio coal. In June, Carter announced that two Cleveland area plants would be allowed to burn high-sulfur Ohio coal without scrubbers. However, the U.S. EPA set October 19 as a clean-up deadline for power plants. The problem is that many plants that were not exempted are worried that they will have to buy expensive scrubbers to burn Ohio coal, so they prefer to buy cleaner out-of-state coal. The question was: Would Carter intercede under Section 125 of the Clean Air Act to save miners' jobs by requiring reluctant utilities to invest in smoke desulfurization equipment?

The North American Coal Company Number Six Mine in nearby Powhatan had already laid off 750 men the week before, with 270,000 tons of mined coal on the ground and no sure market for it without the CEI exemption. And with four thousand Steubenville miners out of work, the same story was being repeated in other southeastern Ohio mines.

When Carter was asked, "Why can't EPA loosen some of their regulations so that we can move coal through this area?" he replied, "There are laws that bind the entire nation on air pollution standards. . . . One state in the nation has not had an environmental program approved. That state happens to be Ohio."

The UMWA pickets were there to make their point. U.S. Representative Douglas Applegate (D-Steubenville), who had a hand in arranging the visit, was waiting at the Pittsburgh Airport, statistics in his breast pocket. Applegate and U.S. Senator John Glenn had been promised forty minutes in the back of the limousine with the presidential ear all to themselves.

When Carter finally crossed the Ohio River, the congressman, the senator and the president climbed onto the specially adapted roof of the limousine for some old-fashioned political handwaving. The procession moved through Steubenville as fast as the Secret Service could trot. First came the motorcycles, then a truck piled high with cameramen, and then the limousine itself, a shiny black dreadnought of a car with fold-out running boards for the agents. And there was Carter, waving and smiling at the friendly crowds. Right behind came another open limousine with a Secret Service agent crouched on the floor, brandishing an Uzi submachine gun. Behind that came an ambulance from the Pittsburgh Fire Department.

The president hit the high school stage on the stroke of three. The band played *Ruffles and Flourishes*, and the crowd jumped to its feet. For the next hour, Carter demonstrated his tremendous personal powers of persuading a small town crowd that he is a sincere, honest man with a grasp of the situation and the will to help. As Carter deftly fielded questions from several laid-off miners and the wife of a mine owner facing ruin because of the EPA standards, it became clear how "Jimmy Who?" had worked his way across a thousand similar stops in 1976 to become President Jimmy Carter.

The Steubenville area is the rock of the blue-collar Democratic support in Ohio. Carter carried Jefferson County by 7,479 votes in 1976, close to his margin for taking the state's electoral votes. Hanging over the Carter visit like a whiff of sulfur smoke was the Kennedy question. If Carter can't win in Steubenville, he hasn't a prayer in a primary slugfest against Senator Kennedy or in the general election.

In Carter's wake, local Democrats were nearly giddy with excitement. For a few brief minutes, they had a view of the power and grandeur of a sitting president. The steely-eyed Secret Service, the helicopter overhead, and the jostling media horde were proof of that.

The problems remained behind. Carter told them that while he might be able to get a waiver here or a loan guarantee there, Congress was not likely to dismantle a decade of legislation, even in the face of the "moral equivalent of war" on Arab oil imports. Yet Kennedy can't extract sulfur any better than Jimmy Carter.

In downtown Steubenville, the crowds quickly dispersed, leaving the streets littered with Burger King wrappers and empty soft drink cans. The political debates moved into the bars. On Fourth Street, a Steubenville policeman walked slowly home with his wife. Her feet were sore from standing, and she stopped to take off her sandals. Her husband leaned down and rolled up her cuffs. Arm in arm, they strolled home, confident that they had played a minor role in history. The parade had moved on.

All the Candidates' Men

Ohio Magazine, December 1979

In search of a shining knight, Ohio politicians are trying to decide which presidential hopeful holds the most promise—for the country and themselves.

Politicians tend to be optimists. Every four years, their parties suffer through presidential primary elections, the infighting often leaving the parties divided, traumatized, and scarred. And, every four years, the pols believe they will find a painless way to select a party standard-bearer to lead them to the White House. So far, this year has been no different.

For the past several months, traumas have been occurring in both parties in Ohio, the early symptoms of next year's presidential primary. The Democrats, torn between loyalty to the first Democrat to sit in the White House in this decade and fear that he might not figure in the voters' plans for the eighties, have been looking for the most painless way to survive unscathed from what appeared, in early October, to be a certain showdown between President Jimmy Carter and Senator Edward Kennedy.

And the Republicans, much more tentative than they were four years ago, were politely trying to sort out the field of GOP presidential hopefuls, figuring there has to be a winner among them. There was not a consensus as there was last time among the Republican brass for Gerald Ford. John Connally was doing well in the boardrooms with his unflinching confidence that the times begged for his leadership. Ronald Reagan was back, rounding up the conservatives who had gone down fighting for him in 1976 against Ford. Tennessee Senator Howard Baker and former United Nations ambassador and CIA director George Bush cozied up to Ohio GOP moderates, such as former U.S. Senator Robert Taft (for Baker) and ex-attorney general-senator-ambassador Bill Saxbe (for Bush).

Up in Cleveland, Cuyahoga County Republican Chairman Bob Hughes, though conceding that the battle would probably come down to Reagan and Connally, insisted that the party's strongest ticket would be Ford and Bush. And Governor James Rhodes, whose endorsement was coveted by all the Republican candidates, was said to have privately convinced the Connally people that, in his own way and in his own time, he would pull it all together in Ohio for the silver-haired Texan before the first crocus of next spring. Publicly, Rhodes denied an infatuation with any candidate. Among his few quotes on the subject: "It's too early."

That, too, was the escape hatch for many Democratic leaders around the state who were being pressed for a commitment to Carter or Kennedy. Some recalled the "Muskie debacle" of 1972 when a slate headed by then-Governor John Gilligan broke from the starting gate with an impressive endorsement of Maine Senator Edmund Muskie. But by the time of the May 2 primary that year, Muskie had been stripped of his candidacy in the earlier primaries, leaving Gilligan and a busload of top Democratic and labor officials on the sidelines as South Dakota Senator George McGovern swept the national convention.

Politicians remember. "We don't want the Muskie thing to happen to us again," said one uncommitted county chairman. "There's time to work this one out."

But in early September, the White House obviously figured the clock might be running out on Carter in Ohio, the state where Kennedy fever was running high and Carter's own fortunes with the coal miners and steelworkers over the Ohio River were dissipating under the weight of the unemployment statistics. The situation clearly called for action, which translated into a Carter "town meeting" in Steubenville.

On the bright, sweaty day for Carter's scheduled people-to-people visit, the townspeople arrived early with their folding chairs and miniature flags to greet the president's motorcade down Fourth Street past Ed McCauslen Florists and the Colonial Supper Club. A dozen school bands strung out along the route, their majorettes self-consciously striking a pose as the bands played fitfully to welcome the first in-the-flesh president to hit town since 1912.

But although the spectators, some having stood for five hours behind the three miles of rope that lined the motorcade course, waited expectantly for a glimpse of Carter, there also was hint of ambivalence about this president who had carefully staged the event to reassure the folks that he cared about their coal and steel.

A short, red-haired woman who had patiently staked out her curbside view for hours shrugged when she was asked about the president. She said she had voted for him in 1976 but hadn't made up her mind about 1980.

"There are a lot of people concerned about coal around here," she said. "There are a lot of things that could be done, but I don't know whether he can do [the job]." Like others pressed against the rope in Steubenville that day, she wondered whether another president might make a difference, or whether the erosive economic problems of the Steubenville area, where five thousand miners in the outlying coal fields were jobless, were beyond the reach of any mortal.

Such ambivalence, among voters and the worried party pros, had kept White House aides on the telephone this past summer to county chairmen and state Democratic officials across the nation in an ongoing search for clues on how to rejuvenate the president for next year's reelection campaign.

The advice to Carter's political aides has generally been predictable—the president is slipping in such-and-such a county; he needs to be more visible and must come on more dramatically in selling his programs on energy and the economy. "Hell," said one northeastern Ohio Democratic chairman sympathetic to Carter, "he's got to get his butt out here and let people know what he's doing. That makes more sense than anything else."

By early October, however, Carter had yet to start mobilizing his forces in the state that he overwhelmingly captured in the 1976 primary, but narrowly affixed in his victory column in the November election.

At the same time, some county chairmen were fighting a rearguard battle to delay a possible stampede for Kennedy. The party officials argued for a wait-and-see posture until at least the early primaries. Montgomery County Democratic Chairman Joe Shump told his party activists to "be cool. We got a president and he's a Democrat. We've got ample time."

But Shump, whose county went for Carter by 6,245 votes in 1976, also says that an official Kennedy candidacy could alter the picture quickly. "If Kennedy announced," he says, "we'd go back to the drawing boards. There's no question Kennedy would be a formidable candidate in my county. We'd have to reassess the situation." But he adds: "This does not mean an automatic endorsement of Kennedy."

Around the state, such hedging is more the rule than the exception. Says Stark County Democratic Chairman John Meeks, "So long as Carter is the president, I'm supporting him. But there's enthusiasm around here for Kennedy. It's not that Democrats dislike the president; they just don't know whether he can win."

Among the Democratic chairmen feeling the most pressure to break with the White House is John E. Jones, of Franklin County, who says his phone has been "ringing off the hook" with requests for "information about the draft-Kennedy movement." "If I went to my executive committee," Jones noted last month, "and asked for an endorsement of Carter, I couldn't get it." The president's problems in Franklin County have become more acute in the wake of cutbacks in federal installations and the closing of Rickenbacker Air Force Base.

Politicians not only remember, they get nervous when times are bad and it's their man in the White House. They also get impatient and even angry when they perceive a lack of political finesse in the operatives around the president. They groan about amateurish ways that screw up simple political standard operating procedures.

It is the sort of thing they have come to expect from the U.S. Postal Service and of some inept ward heeler, but not from the office of the President of the United States. And when it does happen, there is no consoling a chairman who puts in long hours for little or no pay on the theory that the two-party system works if you can weed out the clods.

So Jones is not reluctant to recall three letters he received from the White House that contained mistakes. The first letter, he says, misspelled his name, which, in his case, flirts with the impossible. The second letter addressed him as the Chairman of Fulton County. And the third referred to him as the Franklin County Clerk. Jones was further bewildered by a White House invitation to attend a conference in New York—on freight trade.

In Youngstown, Don Hanni, the volatile Mahoning County Democratic chairman, also shows signs of restlessness. He is now given to saying things like: "They've got too many Georgia crackers in the White House." And: "Carter's a gentleman, a good Christian man, and his motivations are proper. But he's over his head. I think it will be a long time before the people elect another 'off-the-scene' president."

An "off-the-scene" president, in Hanni's lingo, is an "outsider," a candidate who divorced himself from the party in order to run against it, who raised suspicions about the entrenched, business-as-usual fraternal brotherhood of pols, and who is now counting on them to beef up his campaign.

By the same token, the yearning for a visceral Democrat in Ohio, as elsewhere, has given impetus to the Kennedy bandwagon. So when Cuyahoga County Democratic Chairman Tim Hagan concluded early this year that Carter had, in his view, abandoned old Democratic principles that go back to the days of Franklin Delano Roosevelt, the logical step for Hagan, an unapologetic liberal, was to seek out Kennedy. It was not, however, all that simple.

Those were the days when Kennedy was disavowing all draft movements with words to the effect that he fully expected Carter to run and win, and that he fully expected to support the president. Hagan decided to go ahead with a plan for a "county convention" in which his party would be the first major political organization in the country to support a Kennedy draft.

About three hundred party executive committee members—one-fifth of the membership—showed up for the convention and, in a close show-of-hands vote, endorsed a resolution calling for a Kennedy draft. Although the low turnout stripped the action of much significance, Hagan at least managed to get something pro-Kennedy on the record as a reference point for whatever might happen later. What's more, the event received national media coverage, which never hurts when you are trying to promote a noncandidate.

Now, Hagan sees his draft-Kennedy gambit advancing nicely to the day of the Massachusetts Senator's official announcement. And when that happens, Hagan confidently predicts, "There will be a Kennedy office opened in each of the state's twenty-three congressional districts within ten days. There will be a stampede for delegates. Kennedy is the last hope of the two-party system."

You can also count Steve Kovacik, the peripatetic Columbus political operative and former field commander for U.S. Senator John Glenn, among the "what's-he-ever-done-for-Ohio?" Carter critics. Kovacik, who is raising money for the draft-Kennedy operation in New Hampshire, made up his mind early that Carter had to be dumped. "In thirty-three months," Kovacik grumbled recently, "he's been in the state twice. So when you look at Carter in Ohio, who can he turn to?"

The president can, and has, turned to Paul Tipps, the state Democratic Party chairman, who is less discouraged by Carter's standing in the polls than other Democrats.

Tipps is the president's most viable supporter in Ohio and has maintained an insider's relationship with the Carter White House. That connection paid off early in Carter's presidency when Tipps's close friend, Democratic contributor and Cincinnati businessman Marvin Warner, was appointed ambassador to Switzerland—a post he has since resigned. But beyond such sweeteners, Tipps seems genuinely to like the president. And he contends it is much too early to write his political obituary, particularly in Ohio.

As for Kennedy, Tipps is careful to keep the conversation upbeat. "Ted Kennedy is an extremely popular, charismatic leader who deserves the admiration of all Democrats, including Paul Tipps," says Chairman Tipps. Still, he doesn't see any good reason to get involved in the Kennedy mania with months to go before next year's early primaries. Besides, he adds, Ohio "is not a liberal state."

Curiously, Bill Brown, Ohio attorney general and a Democrat with his heart set on running for governor in 1982, appears to have moved to safer ground after telling *New York* magazine last April that a Kennedy matchup with Carter in Ohio would be "no contest." Clearly, he believed, Kennedy would take Ohio.

But Brown now says "the situation is still fluid," even though Carter's ratings are low. "It's one thing," says Brown, who is given to colorful analogies and picturesque patter in making his case, "to watch one person run down the track and see how slow he is. It's another thing to see him running against somebody and break the tape."

How does this compute for his own loyalty in the contest? "I'm playing this," says Brown, "close to the vest."

Although Ohio is critically important to both parties (the state brings 161 Democratic and 77 Republican delegates to their respective national conventions), it also imposes severe strategic problems on candidates who want to take root early in their campaigns. The state's primary on June 3 is among the last on the schedule—long after New Hampshire, Massachusetts, Florida, and Illinois, and those now famous Iowa caucuses have set the tone and tempo of a presidential race.

Because they have no other choice, the candidates dutifully show up around the state with pleasant handshakes, tough talk, and cast a recruiter's eye on the local political establishment. They announce steering committees, raise money where they can, exude confidence, and make sure that the reporters are at their side. "With your help," the candidates tell the local pols, "we can do it."

But these same local pols have hang-ups about siding too early with a candidate who might not survive through April or May. For people like Ohio Republican Chairman Earl Barnes, it means a delicate balancing act to keep up his official position of neutrality on the wide field of candidates who want to be president. Besides, it does not take much prodding to remember the deep party split that developed four years ago when the state Republican executive committee endorsed Ford and then had to hang on against a last-minute surge by Reagan in the Ohio primary.

As the out-party, the GOP hierarchy has been extending all courtesies to its presidential hopefuls. The only clue to the party's sentiments was a poll completed in August by the Cuyahoga County Republican Party. Questionnaires returned by 312 of 466 Ohio Republican officials queried gave Connally a lead over Reagan, 35.2 percent to 27.4 percent—not enough to scare anybody out of the race or to discourage Bush, Baker, or the other less visible candidates in the preliminaries.

In the same poll, Bush was the leading "second choice" of the party leaders with 22.9 percent. And that, concluded Cuyahoga County's Bob Hughes, was good enough to suggest that Bush would be an excellent running mate for Ford, who hadn't announced anything but was keeping his options open.

Several weeks later, Hughes said he still believed a Ford-Bush ticket would be the strongest the Republicans could put up next year, but he also conceded that the race was narrowing to a Reagan-Connally matchup. "Connally and Reagan are perceived as conservatives, and you can bet that the Republican convention is going to be conservative-oriented," said Hughes.

Ford's chances, according to Hughes, rest on entering the race after New Year's and "finishing strong in Illinois, Ohio, and California—the big ones. Ford doesn't have to go to door-to-door in New Hampshire. He's not running for city council."

In choosing up sides, all the major candidates have picked their share of "names" from the Ohio GOP ranks. Connally brought in

U.S. Representative Clarence "Bud" Brown of Urbana as his state campaign chairman and added Senator Tom Van Meter (R-Ashland) to his national steering committee. Van Meter supported Ford in 1976, but he says Connally is just what the doctor ordered for the Republican Party.

"He looks like a president, acts like a president and talks like a president," Van Meter enthuses. "The sheer force of the personalities involved in this [race] is going to determine the winner. This is not a philosophical battle. Republicans are going to want someone who is not soft-spoken, and Connally fits that description."

Another Connally lieutenant in Ohio is Representative Mike Fox (R-Cincinnati). You can find him at party dinners around the state spreading the Connally gospel in his quiet ambling style. "I think Connally has the ability to excite our party and the nation. He's the only candidate who has the ability to articulate the issues in a way to make the public feel good about the country again. They're looking for leadership, and that's Connally's forte," Fox opines.

Some Republicans aren't so sure about that. They wonder about the electability of a Democrat-turned-Republican from Texas, where they grow all that oil. They also worry about the fallout from the bad publicity Connally received in 1974, when he was accused of accepting bribes from a milk-producing cooperative group while he served as U.S. Treasury secretary. (The bribes were allegedly in exchange for Connally's recommendation to raise the federal milk support level. He was found innocent of the charges in 1975.) Bill Saxbe, who had been the U.S. attorney general during the milk investigation, has a way of getting this across when he is touting his own candidate, George Bush.

"George," says Saxbe, "is as clean as a hound's tooth." At another time he will tell you—referring to Connally—that, "I don't think the voters are going to accept another wheeler-dealer Texan like Lyndon Johnson." By most standards, Bush is the prototype of a Republican presidential candidate. He's paid his dues to the GOP as national chairman; he's served in sensitive government jobs; he's well-spoken; he's somewhere between moderate and conservative; and he's rich. He also has James Baker, Ford's 1976 campaign manager, running his campaign this year.

The entire tone of his campaign is one of Saxbe's "hound's tooth" respectability. But the trouble is, as his own people readily acknowledge, he is not—what's the cliché?—a household name. Baker tried to deal with that obstacle at a Columbus press conference in which he took delight in the Cuyahoga County poll that honored Bush as the leading second-choice candidate. That is not a bad place to be at this stage of a campaign dominated by the hot names of Reagan and Connally, Baker said. The ground could be made up in the primaries, but he conceded, "We've got to win a primary by April 1." That is a good two months before the Ohio primary.

It is still, therefore, Bush's campaign to win. On the other hand, Peter Voss, the Canton businessman who headed Reagan's 1976 Ohio campaign and is on Reagan's national steering committee this time, says, "Everything shows us in awfully good shape. We got a front-runner. And I don't see anybody taking [the nomination] away from him [Reagan]."

Unlike the hurry-up effort to put Reagan on the Ohio ballot in 1976 (when former Voss aide Dave Seffens flew around the state in a small Apache dropping off petitions in the middle of the night at remote airstrips), the Reagan forces have been methodically setting up their operations a year in advance of the Ohio primary.

"We had seventy-two hours to put it together the last time," says Voss. "There's no comparison to what's being done for Reagan in Ohio this time. It's a superb effort."

At sixty-eight, Reagan is taking no chances that there will be another time. By the same token, his age has been one of the negative factors that has led some conservatives into the camps of the other candidates. The choice has been made easier for them this year because they don't have to betray much ideology by turning to younger conservatives in the field. Indeed, if there has been a nearly constant theme to the Republican quest for the Presidency, it is that personalities rather than issues will determine the outcome. Bush is not reluctant to put it in those terms. His (as well as Reagan's, Connally's, and Baker's) position is predictably to the right of the Democrats'. Connally bristles a bit when you mention personality versus issues, arguing that he is the only contender speaking out loud-and-clear on *issues*. But that, too, is predicable, if not wholly accurate.

Robert Teeter, the GOP's public opinion expert, once noted that his postelection surveys of the Ford-Carter contest revealed that issues played a very small role in the voters' choices. Having watched the candidate take their ritualistic bows to the partisan audiences on the stump, I'm persuaded that the greater source of their success or failure is locked in a mysterious chemical interaction that has very little to do with the Panama Canal or SALT II. In the past it has been the candidate who, as Van Meter said, "Looks like a president, acts like a president and talks like a president" who has succeeded in capturing the office of this nation's chief executive. That's chemistry.

Reagan's Fortunes Rising above His Image
Akron Beacon Journal, May 11, 1980

"Among Republicans," the paragraph begins, "there is some uneasiness over Mr. Reagan's qualifications to be president, mixed with respect for his demonstrated vote-getting ability in California. Given the new pragmatism in the GOP, Ronald Reagan may get the nod for president . . . if the convention delegates think he can win, no matter how his experience stacks up against his rivals."

I cheated a little. I left out the dates after "president." They were "1968 or 1972" because the text appeared in the *National Observer's Newsbook* on the 1968 elections. The *National Observer* has long been out of business. But Reagan isn't, although the defunct paper's views are as current in this presidential election year as they were a dozen years ago.

Check this one from the old *Newsbook*: "The gaps in his background are bound to show up, as on a national television program in the fall of 1967, when he was asked his opinion of the SST, the proposed supersonic transport airplane. After a puzzled look at his questioner, Governor Reagan said he had been so busy with state matters that he hadn't had time to look into national issues. He apparently knew nothing of the SST."

All this has a familiar ring this year, recalling Reagan's recent hedging in trying to define parity to some farmers; or his confession that he had been led astray by a couple of four-star generals when he mistakenly insisted that Vietnam veterans had not been entitled to GI Bill education benefits.

You won't find many souls in this complicated world who have perfect recall on all the issues. But in Reagan's case, he's hardly fumbling trivia questions, and the pattern of his awkward responses seems to be a mile wide and at least twelve years deep.

Still, the image of a shallow thinker hasn't bothered him, or the Republican voters, very much in his steady climb to his party's nomination. Some farmers, for example, who find his conservatism quite appealing, were more than willing to give Reagan the benefit of the doubt even if they agreed that he didn't know much about parity. Their attitude: "We are going to teach him, then we're going to elect him."

Maybe it's the *National Observer's* other comment that is propelling Reagan's campaign against an all-but vanquished George Bush. It's the view that perhaps the GOP's "new pragmatism" (circa 1968, remember) would nominate him. (In fact, history will show, the party was even more pragmatic about Richard Nixon that year, nominated him, and got him elected in a photo finish against Hubert Humphrey.)

Republicans say they are trying to be pragmatic again this year, which explains why people like Gerald Ford and Senator Howard Baker, a former president and a would-be president, are beginning to say nice things about the fellow they set out to defeat.

It could be argued, I suppose, that in these two instances both are being "pragmatic" (that is, practical) in the interest of giving the GOP an old college try in November against a president who has his own problems to worry about these days.

But there are many moderate Republicans who have contended during the primary season that pragmatism is one thing and resignation is another.

Can Reagan Control Leaders of GOP's "New Crusade"?
Akron Beacon Journal, July 13, 1980

Sixteen years ago, Phyllis Schlafly helped orchestrate the Goldwater movement with a widely-circulated paperback called *A Choice Not an Echo*—a teeth-baring assault on all that was unconservative in the land. The pages of that book have long turned brown on the library shelf.

But last week, Schlafly was up in Detroit doing her thing again, glowing in triumph as the Republican Party, through its platform writers, was reversing its modern history of support for the Equal Rights Amendment.

In the months ahead to November, I suspect we'll be hearing a lot more from Schlafly and her like-minded ideologues in their fervor to put Ronald Reagan in the White House. And the GOP's moderates, who never have been that good at playing hardball politics over the past generation, will be demoted to their familiar role of helpless bleeders as the Reaganites take control of their party.

In Ronald Reagan, the party's right wing had found a bona fide good ol' boy who has been pacing the sidelines since the '60s with the plea, "Put me in, coach." In a few days, it will be official. He will be in.

But will he be calling the signals? The easy answer is: Of course he will; he's the nominee. But when moral and spiritual fervor set the tone of a campaign, there's also a strong chance that he will become as much the captive of his crusade as he is its leader.

As last week's writing of the platform plodded forward, there was some hope by the moderates that it would loosen up a bit to embrace a wider spectrum of the party. Instead, it grew more conservative with each dotted "i." At this stage of the crusade, there would be no turning back.

And although Reagan doubtless loves what he reads in the platform—after all, he's been saying the same things for years—it's fair to wonder whether he could have changed it if he had wanted to. Remember: the folks who are now in charge in Detroit are the ones that hissed at Gerald Ford four years ago in Kansas City, allowing that he was a "liberal." (With that kind of license, even in politics, it would be easy to presume that William Tell was an advocate of gun control.)

Crusades are hard to control, particularly when the White House is at stake. Barry Goldwater and George McGovern, the most recent pure ideological campaigners, both were swept up in the forces around them and then swept out in November.

Mary Crisp, who tearfully stepped down as the GOP's national co-chairman, said after the ERA's platform defeat that it could happen again this year. But Senator Jesse Helms of North Carolina, a leading hard-liner of the crusade, shrugged that women already have all the rights they "need."

(One curious line in the platform's language was its commitment to "maximum individual liberty and freedom of choice"—which, of course, is precisely what the "pro-choice" people have been demanding in the abortion controversy.)

The national right-to-life organization has come out foursquare for Reagan. And down in Jimmy Carter's home state of Georgia, a group of conservative preachers is preparing for a frontal attack on politics at all levels with something called the Georgia Pastors Forum. They are said to have about sixty thousand members in their churches, and they will, it says here, be rating candidates on such "Christian" issues as ERA, abortion, and homosexuality.

There are similar movements elsewhere, and there will be more on the way. They will be unyielding and will expect the Republican nominee to keep his nose clean.

Get ready for it. This is going to get noisy and even hysterical on both sides. The political process may very well be heading into an emotional breakdown, while a lot of witnesses, at home and abroad, are left to wonder if the country will ever get around simply to electing a leader.

Lightning Strikes Dem Convention: Teddy Electrifies Audience; Tearful Delegates Go Wild

Akron Beacon Journal, August 13, 1980

Just when it seemed that Monday night's violent thunderstorm over Manhattan had moved out to sea, lightning struck Madison Square Garden twenty-four hours later. Senator Edward Kennedy, the defeated candidate, sent a charge throughout the Democratic convention that could leave its mark on the party into the November election and possibly well beyond.

Politics in general, and political conventions in particular, have earned a well-deserved reputation for speeches that are best forgotten. Kennedy broke the rules when he rose to the podium to set his party's agenda for the months and years ahead. There were too many tearful eyes on the convention floor to believe otherwise.

Ironically, his electrifying speech to the Democratic delegates, the Republican Party, and the nation, came too late to save his own candidacy against President Carter—and possibly too late to save Carter, too.

But the Massachusetts senator, who had focused his entire campaign on the meaning of the Democratic Party, was obviously less interested in personalities—his or Carter's—than in calling attention to the keys to his party's survival.

And again ironically, he was heard more clearly in defeat than he was in his unsuccessful nine-month quest for the nomination. As the convention roared its approval in frenzy and tears, the Carter camp caved in on major economic platform issues—the heart of Kennedy's difference with the president during the long primary season.

Afterward, Democrats, with few exceptions, reacted as though something spectacularly new had been added to the grind-it-out business of politics.

"It was a fabulous speech," exclaimed Peter Bommarito, international president of the United Rubber Workers and a Kennedy loyalist. "There were a lot of people with tears in their eyes and a lot of sadness because he didn't win the nomination."

As the URW chief, Bommarito has issued a challenge to Carter to offer the kind of economic program that would generate some enthusiasm among hard-hit union members. "We have forty thousand unemployed rubber workers," Bommarito said, "and I need some assurances that the president is going to do something about it."

Bommarito has flatly ruled out an endorsement of Ronald Reagan or John Anderson. But he doesn't seem eager to jump on Carter's bandwagon just yet.

Ohio's two legislative leaders, Senator Oliver Ocasek and Representative Vern Riffe, both Carter supporters, also were impressed by the Kennedy speech. "It was tremendous," said Ocasek. "With his action Monday night [withdrawing as a contender] and his speech tonight, he did a great deal to bring harmony to the party."

"It was a good speech," said Riffe, "and a speech that was needed. The party is much stronger now than when the convention began. It's time now to start putting it all together to win the war in November."

The strongest dissenting voice within the Ohio delegation came from the state party chairman, Paul Tipps, who has been close to the Carter White House and seemed annoyed by the thrust of Kennedy's remarks.

"It's the kind of speech you make when you're a loser," Tipps declared. "It's easy to make a speech advocating things you're not going to be responsible for."

Whatever effect Kennedy's performance at this convention might have on the party, he at least touched that part of the Democrats' soul that yearns for its traditional values.

The Carter forces, who have been saying that their differences with Kennedy's economic proposals are not that great, so why don't we all get together for the fall campaign, would like to wrap up this convention and get on with the business of beating Reagan.

They won the war Monday night when Kennedy dropped out. But they lost the battle Tuesday night when Kennedy dropped in. Both nights will have their place in history. But folks here are wondering which event will have the more lasting effect on the direction of the Democratic Party.

Carter Finds the Weapons to Begin a Long Struggle

Akron Beacon Journal, August 15, 1980

Jimmy Carter today embarked on an uphill fight to save his presidency with two important weapons that he didn't have a few months ago: a détente with his chief Democratic detractor, Senator Edward Kennedy; and the man the Republicans nominated in Detroit in July, Ronald Reagan.

From an ideological standpoint, Carter is the man in the middle between Kennedy and Reagan. But it was obvious throughout the past week that, for the Democrats, the stronger unifying force behind the Carter campaign was not the patch-up diplomacy with the Kennedy wing. Rather, it was the specter of a Reagan presidency that hung over the delegates, party officials, and Democratic support groups such as organized labor. "If the Republicans had chosen anybody but Reagan," said one labor official, "this ball game might be over before it began. But with Reagan, they've made it an interesting contest."

If anyone needed any reminders of the main issue in the forthcoming campaign, the Democratic rhetoric from the podium in Madison Square Garden reaffirmed concern over the GOP nominee.

On Tuesday night, Kennedy nearly ignored Carter in his broadsides against the president's opponent. Vice President Walter Mondale continued the assault Thursday night. And Carter set the tone of his own campaign by labeling his challenger a captive of a fantasy world.

Beset by inflation, high unemployment, and suspicions that he is well-intentioned but mediocre, Carter countered with a theme that he's likely to pursue through election day: he's made mistakes, but he's also enjoyed some successes and learned a lot. At the same time, he is insisting that today's problems are far too complicated to solve with simple slogans.

"The president," he said in his acceptance speech, "can't bend to the passions of the moment." He accused Republicans of living in a "make-believe world of good guys and bad guys."

Unlike four years ago, when Republican Gerald Ford and Democratic outsider Jimmy Carter broke from the gate with a strong reserve of public willingness to give each contender the benefit of the doubt, Carter and Reagan must reverse serious doubts about their qualifications while trying to keep independent candidate John Anderson in his place.

For Reagan, his problems—voiced repeatedly by some Republicans at the Detroit convention—are his age (sixty-nine), inexperience in foreign policy, and a shoot-from-the-hip image. If he is to capture the broad American center, he also will be pressed to escape the noose of the party's extreme right, rather than welcome it, as did Barry Goldwater in 1964.

For Carter, he must parlay the natural gravitational pull of Democrats from Reaganism with more optimistic economic news and the built-in advantages of being in the Oval Office. A little bit of luck wouldn't hurt, either. That could be a windfall from Iran in releasing the hostages, or some major gaffes by his opponent.

Trailing as he is in the polls (22 percent to Reagan's 47 in the latest AP-NBC survey), Carter obviously will come out fighting. And if the race tightens up this fall, the performances of Carter and Reagan (and possibly Anderson) in their three scheduled debates, including one in Cleveland, could decide the presidency.

As for Kennedy's role in the campaign, it is likely to be more enthusiastic than the cool walk-on part he played Tuesday night. If his supporters are convinced of anything, particularly after his dynamite speech to the convention, it is that Kennedy will be back in '84. That being the case, he will not want to be remembered by the Carter Democrats as the man who turned over the White House to Ronald Reagan.

Many of the Kennedyites left the convention gagging on the thought of a Carter-Reagan alternative. Some even pledged themselves to Anderson. But if Anderson falters along the way, where can they finally turn?

No one understands that, and can profit more from it, than Jimmy Carter.

Part IV

Turn to the Right, 1981–2004

Turn to the Right, 1981–2004

Introduction

Ronald Reagan's election in 1980 began a turn to the right in national and Ohio politics that lasted until the end of the century. It included a twelve-year period of Republican presidential dominance, including Reagan's landslide reelection in 1984 against former Vice President Walter Mondale, the 1988 victory of George H. W. Bush (vice president under Reagan) over Massachusetts Governor Michael Dukakis, and the eventual takeover of the U.S Congress by the GOP in 1994. Ohio and national politics continued to be polarized over this period, ending in the very close elections of 2000 and 2004.

Zaidan commented on this right turn in a number of columns, beginning with a nostalgic eulogy for legendary GOP party leader Ray C. Bliss, the architect of the GOP pragmatic alliances of the 1960s ("Ray Bliss Was in a Special Category: A Man Who Personified Class"). Zaidan found similarities between former Ohio Governor James Rhodes and President Reagan in terms of "politics and posture"; reported on a confrontation between Reagan and U.S. Senator John Glenn, whose own presidential plans for 1984 ended in disappointment; and noted the Democrats' futile efforts against Reagan's reelection bid.

In addition, he offered a poignant picture of Cleveland Mayor George Voinovich, a future Ohio governor and senator, who was then "without a party" in a city where scarce Republicans were becoming rare; and commented on right-wingers old (Robert Welch, the founder of the John Birch Society) and new (Reverend Jerry Falwell, founder of the Moral Majority).

But the Republican presidential dominance did not initially extend to the state level, where Democrats continued to win across the country, including Ohio. Richard Celeste was elected Ohio governor in 1982, after Governor Rhodes left office due to term limits. Assuming that Rhodes's political career was over, Zaidan summed it up in "Rhodes Spoon-fed Believers and Ate Up the Skeptics." But there was one more chapter in the Rhodes saga: attempting to repeat history "all over again," the seventy-seven-year old Rhodes challenged Governor Celeste in 1986. This gambit failed and is reported in "The Fall of an Ohio Legend: Flamboyant Rhodes Fades into History." This essay includes the poignant image of the aged political giant conceding the 1986 election "in the soft isolation of a room at the Cleveland Clinic, where his wife, Helen, was recuperating from surgery." Zaidan bids adieu to Rhodes with a column on his eightieth birthday party in 1989, illustrating the respect Rhodes enjoyed until his death in 2001.

In 1986, Zaidan began writing a regular column for the *Akron Beacon Journal,* the work for which he is probably best known in his home city. A handful of these columns are reproduced here, including the first one ("A New Column—But Will It Get My Goat, Folks?") and the last one ("A Columnist Bids Adieu, Looks Back"). Although not political, these bookend columns reveal much about Zaidan the writer and person. Zaidan left the *Akron Beacon Journal* in 1991, and his farewell column is a rare model of class and grace. The sampling of these columns on political subjects include a brilliant satire of the 1988 U.S. senatorial campaign between then Cleveland Mayor George Voinovich and the incumbent Howard Metzenbaum, with the latter's "dirty little secret revealed at last" (he was from Cleveland!); trenchant columns on the 1988 presidential campaign and President George H.W. Bush; and a reflection on the Kent State shootings twenty years after the fact.

In 1992, the conservative coalition fashioned by Ronald Reagan collapsed for his successor, George H. W. Bush, events that

Zaidan covered for the *Cleveland Plain Dealer.* One reason was a pair of conservative revolts, one led by pundit Pat Buchanan and another by billionaire Ross Perot. The latter ran one of the most successful independent presidential campaigns in history, garnering 19 percent of the popular vote ("Pondering Significance of Ross Perot"). These troubles allowed the Democrats to capture the White House with former Arkansas Governor Bill Clinton, who, like Jimmy Carter in 1976, outlasted liberal opponents for the presidential nomination ("Malaise Chills Usual Heat of Campaigns"). For the third time in five elections, incumbent presidents were defeated by challengers ("Clinton Lead Is Not Yet Unbeatable").

However, Bill Clinton's Democratic coalition did not dominate politics any more fully than the Reagan coalition. By 1994, the conservative coalition had revived: the GOP had taken over control of the U.S. Congress for the first time since the 1950s and made major gains at the state level. Ohio was no exception to this Republican resurgence. Beginning with George Voinovich's election as governor in 1990 ("By George! No Flash, but a Definite Style"), the Republicans steadily took over the state legislature and nearly all the statewide offices, establishing a period of dominance that lasted into the twenty-first century. Eventually, these gains included a majority of the Ohio congressional delegation and the U.S. Senate seats held by the retiring Senators Howard Metzenbaum (occupied by Voinovich's lieutenant governor, Mike DeWine in 1996) and John Glenn (occupied by Voinovich himself in 1998). The net result of these trends was the establishment of parity between the major party coalitions by the 2000 and 2004 elections, among the closest and most controversial in American history.

This section concludes with essays written at the turn of the century, including commentary on the oddities of party politics ("Partied OUT") and political discourse ("Zero Gravitas"). The final piece is an intimate portrait of a giant in his own right, John S. Knight, the Pulitzer prize-winning editor of the *Akron Beacon Journal,* founder of the Knight-Ridder newspaper group, an Akron native, and Zaidan's boss for many years.

In the final section of this book, Zaidan offers an "afterword" on the age of giants.

Ray Bliss Was in a Special Category: A Man Who Personified Class

Akron Beacon Journal, August 7, 1981

It is never easy to relate legendary public figures to the little things that count in most folks' lives. There's a wide lane between the uncommon and the common; and when you find someone who joins those two qualities in a mere lifetime, that's my definition of class.

Ray Bliss—political (though sometimes reluctant) source, needler, lunch-and-dinner partner, memory bank, yarn-spinner, and, most of all, friend—had class.

Others will remember him from all the recorded history of his enormous political talents as a political strategist. Presidents and would-be presidents (Republicans, of course) understood clearly that it would be defying gravity if they failed to consult him during a campaign. National political writers intruded upon his day at his insurance office with phone calls to soak up his wisdom.

Curiously, the pace of these interviews didn't slacken after his "retirement." And just as curiously, his name seldom appeared in a national column. (I always watched for someone identified only as a "prominent Midwest Republican" in those columns and guessed it was Bliss.) Whatever the reasons—shyness, discipline, self-assuredness that one did not need to be quoted to be respected—Bliss often exasperated reporters with his not-for-attribution conversations. But that didn't stop the telephone calls.

Having gone through the same verbal workout with him as a political writer myself, I will concede that side of Ray Bliss is an important part of the record. But it may very well dim in my memory long before the common side of the legend. For example, I will remember him as the thin voice on the other end of the telephone, fretting—to excess, I thought—over whether his boxes of Christmas cookies to certain reporters and editors would be misunderstood.

Considering the arm's length rules that govern most politician-reporter relationships, the smallest gifts can raise the biggest questions. But a long time ago, Bliss earned a special dispensation for these things. He was much too big, much too honorable, to barter with gifts or anything else—large or small.

I will remember him, too, as a fussy man who spent hours of his day worrying about where a reporter would prefer to interview a high-ranking Republican visitor.

And where each speaker would appear on the program. And whether there would be a car at the back entrance or side entrance to the building to return the speaker to the airport. And whether the knives and forks were properly placed at the speaker's table. And whether the speaker would leave town with the best impression of Bliss's beloved Akron.

Now and then I would needle him about the need for such fastidious plans for some of the less formal events. He would feign indignation over my questions, search for some kind of answer (Bliss never considered himself very good as a speaker), and come out with something like, "Well. . . ."

Actually, the reason he did these things as a servant of protocol was simple. It may not appear in Bartlett's quotations, but it has been passed down through the ages: If you can't do something right, don't do it at all. Ray Bliss devoted much of his life to doing things right, no matter how incidental they seemed to others. In his quiet, methodical way, he went about his business with the conviction that even on the fast, bloody track of politics, where reputations come and go in a wash of big bank accounts, scandals, and dirty tricks, there was plenty of room for courtesy, modesty, and clean hands.

He never hesitated to say "please" and "thank you." He had a gentle sense of humor. And he believed that one's honor was more important than any public office. Some parlay, I'd say, for politics or any other profession.

If there were still time to mention that to him today, it would be a safe bet that he would feign indignation, search for some kind of answer, and say something like, "Well. . . ."

And I would understand.

Rhodes Spoon-fed Believers and Ate Up the Skeptics
Akron Beacon Journal, January 2, 1983

It comes as no surprise that among Jim Rhodes's last official acts as governor was a promotion for Liederkranz cheese. Like many of his official acts these long sixteen years that he presided over the state, it was hype for an Ohio-made product that couldn't hurt.

Things-that-couldn't-hurt have generally been the governor's style. Among his first official acts, centuries ago it seems, was a pilgrimage with some shivering reporters to a hole in the Lake Erie ice, the idea being that there might be an economic cycle or two in the ceremonial recognition that Lake Erie fish don't head south for the winter.

Little did those of us who snickered know that the fellow was going to parlay such antics into a record-breaking stay at the statehouse. Ohio's voters were enthralled by a governor who went out of his way to demonstrate the wonderful world of Ohio ice fishing. Whatever good it might have done for the state's well-being remains for historians to mull. For his part, it couldn't hurt.

Like Peter Pan, the governor deftly played to an audience of believers and finessed the skeptics. On the theory that good news is hard for most people to turn down, no matter how far-fetched, he offered them tomato juice in the statehouse rotunda, ribbon-cutting at the Ohio Fairgrounds by dawn's early light, a scheme to build a bridge across Lake Erie, and airports in all eighty-eight counties.

Some of his ideas died in their sleep. Others simply hung around until something better came along. Whatever the case, the governor was able to say, "It couldn't hurt."

Although Jim Rhodes's syntax would come off second best in a showdown with Professor Backwards, he was in fact a skillful orator. Often what he said didn't make much sense, but the believers found it reassuring nonetheless, precisely because of the beguilingly primitive way he said it.

He was, of course, for jobs and progress and against taxes. That much you could sift from his rambling monologues, if not the first time around, at least after years of being hounded by them. His audiences went home humming some of the score, which is one way first-nighters distinguish a good Broadway musical from a turkey.

He was reassuring in a curious sort of way, much as though one would reassure the passengers on a sinking ship that, if it weren't for the water, they wouldn't drown. So it was that he could convince people that, if an old barn hadn't been converted into a national historical site, he might have built a superhighway dead through the hayloft.

He could be flexible, too, in identifying the enemy: In his four terms, Washington was both friend and foe, depending upon the state of the national treasury and the direction that the money was flowing. In the 1976 presidential campaign, he vowed, with a gleam in his eye, to lay off candidate Jimmy Carter. A pragmatic decision. He might, Rhodes explained, have to deal for programs with a President Jimmy Carter.

He also made daring use of the old literary device of suspending disbelief for the sake of a point. Last time he ran for governor, in 1978, he stood against a numbing wind in downtown Cleveland to dedicate a state office building. "Where's the building?" a bystander asked as the ceremony went on before the television cameras. "Over there," somebody nodded, pointing to a half-built structure with its steel ribs still showing. "Ain't even built yet," the bystander said. "I know," replied the other fellow. "But they got to do this now. The election is coming up pretty soon." Next day, the papers reported the building had been dedicated by Rhodes, and that couldn't hurt a candidate at all.

At national political conventions, where people wear outrageous hats to attract a crowd, the governor made news simply by showing up. Not that the reporters expected anything profound from him. The fact that he was there was diagnosed as news. In Detroit in 1980, the word went out from the Ohio GOP grapevine that Rhodes wouldn't bother to come. He always thought conventions were a waste of time anyway.

But he did arrive, as we suspected he would, and teased the national press into believing that he was cooking up a deal between Ronald Reagan and Gerald Ford. The details were, of course, at best hazy. He promised to report back to the press corps in a few hours. He buzzed out of the room and kept the camera crews and political writers pinned down for several hours. He returned well past midnight. The details remained, at best, hazy. The reporters had been reeled in once again.

In a few days, he'll be packing up and leaving the statehouse, for better or worse, and the press corps can go back to writing complete sentences again. He says this time he's leaving for good.

Some folks, however, are a little skeptical. It can't hurt.

~

In Politics and Posture, Reagan Has an Ohio Clone

Akron Beacon Journal, February 26, 1984

Why do I always have a sense of déjà vu when I watch Ronald Reagan at a presidential news conference? Somewhere in my past there was another Ronald Reagan. But who?

No, it couldn't have been my Uncle Jake, a likable conservative cuss whose mind gripped ideas with the force that not even his powerful forearms could muster on a good day. No, Uncle Jake was short and stocky and his teeth had faded and worn after many years of grinding cheap cigars and Mail Pouch. Besides, most of his hair had vanished by midlife, a vanity that passed without comment.

Nor could it have been Uncle Alec, a law-and-order man who somehow got his hands on a police badge and wore it proudly inside his suit coat as he strutted around town itching for a citizen's arrest. More than one tipsy rowdy was impressed by the silvery gleam of that badge when Uncle Alec whipped back his lapel to announce the arrival of the law. But he couldn't have been a stand-in for the Great Communicator. His English was no more legitimate than his badge.

So you strain your cluttered senses as the president rambles through another long answer to a pretty direct question: you try to match up images and . . . and . . .

Voila! Of course. It is Jim Rhodes, the Ohio governor who held the voters in thrall through four terms, deftly handling the electorate and his media critics as though he were cradling a carton of eggs through a wind tunnel.

Like Reagan, there was no easy way to lure Rhodes to a middle ground on a matter that originated on his turf. Nor did he worry much about corresponding truths. "What's that?" "What's that?" he would pepper you if you suggested the possibility of the slightest flaw in his logic. "I don't know anything about that. All I know is that. . . ." What followed was another sermon on jobs and progress.

Like Reagan, Rhodes always managed to come out ahead in his bouts with his critics. If things happened to be going badly on a given day, he had his choice of scapegoats that he used freely: the liberals in Washington; the legislature; and the mysterious "they"—ghosts the governor conveniently invested as the sinister opponents of progress.

Like Reagan, Rhodes was not very tidy about details. He didn't use cue cards to get him through a rare statehouse press conference. But he did round up his cabinet people to answer the questions while he raced around the room passing out press releases. Unlike Reagan, however, the governor excelled in surrounding himself with competent people to run the government while he ran around the world. John McElroy, Rhodes's administrative aide, comes to mind as an intelligent, dedicated Man Friday who quietly worked around the clock to make sure that all of the dikes were secure.

Like Reagan, Rhodes was a gifted performer on the political stage. He had wit, a homey communion with his audiences, and a strong sense of survival. He always knew a dragon when he saw one, and, when he drew his sword, it was pointed away from popular values.

Like Reagan, Rhodes was seldom around when life got sticky. He once avoided a massive civil-rights rally in Columbus by scheduling an out-of-town trip. His office explained that the trip had been scheduled for some time. But in his haste to the county line, he had also scrubbed a speech he was to have given the night before to a friendly audience in Columbus.

Like Reagan, Rhodes enjoys sunshine and palm trees. Reagan has his ranch in California; Rhodes spent countless weekends (and more) at his condominium in Florida. But remarkably, he got away with criticizing former Governor John Gilligan for spending a few weekends at a Michigan retreat.

Like Reagan, Rhodes insisted that politics did not dictate his conduct. Why, he would say, he would even become a Democrat if he thought it would do the state some good. (For the record, he never did, to no one's surprise.)

Like Reagan, Rhodes accentuated the positive. If a tree fell in the woods and there was nobody around, would there be a sound? "All I know," Rhodes might reply, "is that people can do anything." In your astonishment, you wanted to believe.

Finally, like Reagan, Rhodes's command of the martial art of politics was blessed with more than a tad of luck. Just as the slump in oil prices has been a major contributing factor to the control of inflation in Reagan's day, the bright economy of the '60s helped Rhodes with his huge (and federally assisted) capital improvement projects his first two terms. But, alas, as the economy cooled, Rhodes left office in 1982 with little to show for his last term and a $500 million deficit.

Details.

~

Democrats' Plans May Be a Mere Sand Castle Facing GOP Tide

Akron Beacon Journal, May 13, 1984

I am ready for the seashore. The astrological signs are right for it. They are telling me, he who hesitates may never get a better opportunity than now to flee. There is a clear blue sky over the city (at least on the day that this is being written); the Democratic presidential candidates and their entourages have left the state to renew their family feud out West; the president has safely returned to Washington to renew his assault on Congress; and the Cleveland Indians are again making their annual move to the league basement, which, until something better comes along, shall go domeless.

So except for the sunshine, the country is pretty much as I remember it from childhood. Still, there are some loose ends all around, thanks to last Tuesday's election in Ohio, which sent Walter Mondale's quest for the Democratic presidential nomination into overtime. People who want to be president do not normally lose

Ohio, particularly to a fellow (Gary Hart) who the experts insist will not be nominated.

It is easy enough to argue, as many observers are doing these days, that although Mondale has not yet whacked Hart to the canvas, he at least has enough delegate points to be awarded a technical knockout at the party convention in July. There is an unwritten rule in boxing that unless you render the champion unconscious, you won't beat him on points alone. And for the ringsiders who have already declared Mondale the champion-elect, they may accept nothing less than a clear Knock Out to recognize an alternative.

But if Mondale is awarded the nomination without having wrapped it up in the primaries, it will be a sentimental gesture to a loyal and decent warrior whose moment has arrived to wear the crown.

None of this is meant to damn the former vice president. He has worked as hard as anybody for the nomination. He's intelligent, experienced, and has lived the life of a Boy Scout. But on all of the charts, he comes in a distant second to Ronald Reagan, whom history may remember as America's first exclusively made-for-television president.

So what the Mondale story says is that the political parties—what's left of them, at least—are less pragmatic than they used to be in their salad days. They seem more interested in winning battles than wars.

Twenty years ago, the late Ray Bliss, a political genius who didn't care much about ideological warfare, tried to hold the line against Barry Goldwater, not because he disliked him, but simply because Bliss had clearly read the nation's mood and concluded that Goldwater was not electable. Well, he wasn't. And by a landslide, at that. "I don't give a damn whether a candidate is liberal or conservative," Bliss, a conservative himself, often said. "My job is to elect Republicans. That's the only thing I ever have to worry about."

A full-time Republican, Bliss never gave advice to the other party. But if he were on the Democrats' payroll today, the only question he would ask about any of the candidates is, "Is he electable?" With that as his guiding wisdom as the national Republican chairman, Bliss revived a party that had been left for dead in the wake of the Goldwater disaster.

All the signs today indicate that Mondale is not electable in November, but Hart or perhaps another Democrat might be. One of the more prominent signs was hoisted by Ohio's Democratic voters last Tuesday. This should have been Mondale country. With the party's achievers and organized labor behind him in an economically depressed state, Mondale should have had a friendly chorus of supporters singing along with him about cabbages or kings in the White House.

It didn't work out that way. So you have to believe that the Ohio voters, long considered a weathervane for national politics, were trying to tell the Democratic Party something.

But based on the score of columns I have read, and the TV commentaries I have heard since Mondale flubbed Ohio, the Democrats may be the victim of self-imposed inevitability. The delegate numbers favor Mondale; the polls favor Reagan. Hence, the current scenario has Mondale inevitably winning the nomination and Reagan inevitably winning reelection.

Maybe the Democrats could use a day at the seashore, too. They might notice how fast a sand castle collapses when the tide rolls in. Alas, all that work for naught.

Jerry Falwell: the Marcus Welby of Our Moral Ills

Akron Beacon Journal, October 19, 1984

His words are clear and direct, shaped by a voice that does not allow for the slightest hint of human uncertainty. His jaw is firm but unthreatening. His eyes are friendly. He is full of sincerity and good humor. He is the Marcus Welby of the nation's moral ills.

No. He's better that that. Indeed, he may be the very best at what he does. And what he does is shared in this age of the TV pulpit by a lot of others who are very good at what they do.

I came away from Cleveland the other day with that image of the Reverend Jerry Falwell impressed in my mind. He had bounded into Cleveland for a speech to the City Club in behalf of the Reagan-Bush ticket, dashed off a press conference, delivered a textless speech, deftly fielded questions from the audience, and was last seen racing down a corridor en route to his next appearance.

As a celebrity preacher who claims a following of megamillions of conservative Christians, Falwell is the modern incarnation of an old-time circuit rider who preached at four or five crossroads churches on a single morning. He has his own church in Lynchburg, Virginia, but he also has a church-owned private jet that rushes him along an eight-thousand-mile circuit in a single week.

On this day in Cleveland, Falwell was being especially modest about his presence in President Reagan's camp and whatever other controversy that was prompted by the religious right's influence on the Republican platform.

No, he said, he had never boasted that he would get two appointments to the Supreme Court if Reagan is reelected. It was not the first time that he complained about being misquoted.

And no, he said, he was not an issue in this year's presidential election because Jerry Falwell was not in politics. "You can't vote me out," he said. "I've never run for anything."

Besides, he insisted, he hadn't spent much time with the president and probably couldn't influence him if he tried. In that respect, he said, he was only an average American, although I must confess to knowing few average Americans who have spent any time at all at the White House.

Well, Jerry Falwell is, as any American is entitled to be, in politics, but his showmanship and the charm of his own lighthearted denials easily glossed that over in Cleveland. Hey. He was formally introduced as the man who was speaking for the Reagan ticket. Just as the City Club members were reminded that Senator Ted Kennedy would speak later for the Mondale-Ferraro ticket.

Falwell, the spiritual leader of his Moral Majority, has been on national talk shows vowing to work for the defeat of Walter Mondale. He has referred to Reagan as one of the finest presidents since Lincoln. His folks have registered armies to vote on November 6. You need no further evidence to confirm that Falwell is up to his ears in politics the old-fashioned way: Smash the enemy with every weapon in the arsenal.

Hit 'em with morality (that is, abortion, homosexuality, pornography); bomb the critics of the arms race; outflank them with religion, or as Falwell says: "There are forty or fifty million Americans now voting for candidates with moral and spiritual values."

And lest there be any doubt about whom he has chosen as the candidate with moral and spiritual values, the preacher will tell you: "Even if he hadn't showed up [at the first debate], or if he had fallen asleep on the podium, we would still vote for President Reagan."

In recent years, Falwell has had a lot to say about national issues and has frequently found himself in hot water over this quote or that one. Among other things, he has said: "I hope and pray for the day when we won't have any public schools, the churches will have taken them over again, Christians will be running them." He complained that a rabbi who confronted him with the statement on the David Brinkley show had misquoted him. (Actually, the *Washington Post* reported the statement was precisely quoted from one of Falwell's published sermons.)

On other points, he suggests he is less the zealot than the pragmatist. Abortion is murder, he insists; but he also says the right-to-life movement ought to allow for more exceptions in its hard line against abortions.

Although he has described homosexuality in the most graphic terms in a fundraising letter, he also says charitably that he would not ban a homosexual from his Liberty Baptist College campus. But he would discourage both gays and liberals from enrolling there, because he doesn't think they would be comfortable on a conservative campus.

Away from his constituency, as he was at the City Club, Falwell neatly softened the edges of his most provocative positions. So much so that I asked him whether he really had described Senator Jesse Helms of North Carolina, the deep-end rightist, as a "national treasure."

"Yes, sir," Falwell replied emphatically.

For the record, there is that side of Jerry Falwell, too.

Glenn vs. Reagan: "Star Wars," Patriotism, and Peace
Akron Beacon Journal, October 28, 1984

Was that Senator John Glenn at Ellet Hall the other night? The same John Glenn who was forced to the sidelines early in the Democratic presidential primaries because his pale speeches had trouble getting the voters' attention? The same John Glenn whose credentials as a Democrat were questioned by opponents as being too squishy for serious consideration as the party's presidential nominee? And the same John Glenn who aimed for the center of the great shapeless mass that goes by the name of the Democratic Party?

Yep. It was John Glenn who showed up at a rally for U.S. Representative John Seiberling. But even for a partisan occasion, where rhetoric never allows for gray areas between political parties, Glenn exploded with the kind of liberalism that may have astonished some of the others in the hall.

In tone and substance, Glenn spoke without any qualifying asterisks, whether he was railing at the man in the White House or the Reverend Jerry Falwell. He was clearly indignant that Ronald Reagan was quoting him for an advantage over Walter Mondale. (Glenn had challenged Reagan to a debate but says he got no response from the White House.) And that indignation and anger permeated much of his speech.

If we remember Glenn for his rambling oratory on the stump, that image apparently has undergone a major overhaul. Pick an issue and Glenn had a terse assessment for his Akron audience.

Some samples:

On the President's "Star Wars" proposal: "We have a moral obligation to be as hard and as tough as we can to keep weapons out of space." He warned that nuclear weapons could wipe out the world "in a blink."

On Democrats voting for Reagan: "A chicken voting for Colonel Sanders would be goofy."

On the economy: "Wall Street may be booming, but Main Street is suffering."

On women's rights: "Making one woman a justice is not the same as bringing justice to all women."

On religion: He said there was a difference between the "epistles of the New Testament and the apostles of the New Right."

On civil rights: "The president takes his cues on civil rights from people like Jerry Falwell."

After the speech, a Glenn aide said it was the kind of speech that the senator would be giving throughout Ohio for the remainder of this year's election campaign. Contrary to popular opinion, John Glenn can get angry. And I have not seen him in such a snit since 1973, when then-Governor John J. Gilligan and other party leaders asked him to run for lieutenant governor instead of the U.S. Senate.

At that time, Glenn sat in his Columbus office and seethed. He argued that he was being shunted aside to clear the Senate race for Howard Metzenbaum. He accused the party of bossism and vowed to even the score. "I won't let them put me in a box," he declared. He didn't. He ran against the party and Metzenbaum and won the Senate seat in the November election (against Ralph Perk, the Cleveland mayor).

Because of his own laid-back personality, Glenn has long been surrounded by myths about his worth as a politician. He has never been comfortable with the trappings of a political campaign, the awkward quid pro quos that would move him from one point to another to gain some advantage.

But he has long maintained a sense of justice and self-discipline, the latter doubtless the product of his years as a Marine pilot and astronaut. Perhaps too much self-discipline for the loony world of national politics. The style is too bland for an electorate enchanted by slick Hollywood patriotism. The president scores every time he talks about building more military aircraft; it is only fair to recall that Glenn actually risked his neck to fly them. There is a difference.

Maybe that's why Glenn, the ex-Marine colonel, has come out fighting these days. He seems to be defending his honor against an administration that would have you believe that Glenn's party would submit to the Russians abroad and to Satan at home; that the president has a monopoly on patriotism.

The current prevailing view of have-a-good-day patriotism is, of course, nonsense, and beyond slogans. It doesn't require much from the public. But in the wake of Reagan's triumphant visit to the Ohio State campus this week, even a man with Glenn's credentials on matters of "Star Wars" and peace might have a lot of trouble convincing young people that sooner or later they are going to have to deal with reality over style in their lives.

And if Glenn is out of step with the majority on nuclear survival, then we are all in serious trouble.

~

Welch Gone, but Extremism Still with Us in a Free Society
Akron Beacon Journal, January 13, 1985

Robert Welch died last week at the age of eighty-five, leaving the world pretty much as he, in his own mind's eye, found it when he set out in earnest to change it in 1958. That was the year that Welch, a candymaker from New England, organized the John Birch Society, a group that instantly and quite recklessly imposed itself on the nation's conscience as America's last defense against communism, at home and abroad. The society drew its name from a U.S. officer killed by the Chinese communists, claiming him to be the first casualty of World War III.

Like most high-strung crusades, this one often trampled the innocent in the rush to root out the guilty. Not the least of them, in Welch's conspiratorial view of the world, was Ronald Reagan, whom Welch labeled a "lackey" of the communists. And Dwight Eisenhower, he charged, was a "dedicated conscious agent" of the enemy.

When talk of subversion aims that high, it is easy to guess what Welch and his loyal following (perhaps one hundred thousand members at the society's peak in the '60s; half that today) thought about the peons who did share his views. Indeed, he told me what he thought during an informal back-porch debate twenty-five years ago hosted by a Birch chapter organizer in Columbus. (Some debate: he delighted in doing most of the talking, which is something I delight in doing.)

Journalists, he declared, would be the first to be hanged from lampposts when the commies gained total control of the government. I said I'd take my chances on the two-party system, such as it was. But Welch was a man with a cause, and I doubt that he heard a word I said.

The cause was covered in *The Blue Book*, a thick manual in which Welch laid out his strategy against communist subversion. It bristles with the kind of bare-knuckle alarms that mobilized armies of crusaders to head East against the infidels eight centuries ago. History does attempt to repeat itself, and often does.

Welch played for keeps. For example, his training manual referred to an unnamed prominent education leader "whom at least some of us believe to be a communist." Welch doubted that even expensive surveillance would actually prove the educator to be a communist. Instead, Welch proposed a magazine article "consisting entirely of questions to this man, which would be devastating in their implications. The question technique, when skillfully used in this way, is mean and dirty. But the communists we are after are meaner and dirtier, and too slippery for you to put your fingers on them in the ordinary way—no matter how much they look and act like prosperous members of the local Rotary Club."

Welch, operating out of his headquarters in Belmont, Massachusetts, was an overnight sensation with the far right. He opened hundreds of bookstores around the country and a publishing house, produced a couple of monthly newsletters and magazines and a radio program, and insisted on having his literature displayed in public places. The *New York Times* noted last week that the society's paid staff at one point had an annual budget of $8 million.

Curiously, although he professed to be a savior of freedom in America against commie infiltration, Welch had little patience for democratic ideals within his own society. "The John Birch Society," he wrote, "is to be a monolithic society," and it would "operate under complete authoritative control at all levels."

The society reached the mountaintop in 1964 when Barry Goldwater, in a concessionary line added to his acceptance speech for the GOP presidential nomination, told a national audience that "extremism in the defense of liberty is no vice" and "moderation in the pursuit of justice is no virtue." It produced hysterical glee among the right-wingers who earlier had jeered Nelson Rockefeller as he spoke from the same podium.

After the 1964 election, the society's influence gradually waned (although it is by no means dead today). For all of Welch's demands for authoritative control within the society, its leaders began fussing among themselves. Some splintered into other groups, and you began to hear less from Welch himself. Last year, the biggest flap over the Birchers was a report that a couple of their members were San Diego Padre baseball players who spent off-hours passing out society literature.

Extremism, in one form or another, will always be around in a free society; it doesn't have a chance in a closed state. Welch and the others have never understood this. To the extent that our freedoms exist, they will have their say and so will those of us who argue loudly against them.

He tested the system, and I think that, for all the mischief his society has produced, he failed because his premise failed. We are no closer to electing a communist today to the White House than we were when Welch first sounded his alarm. And the reason we aren't resides in the system that makes allowances for the Robert Welches, however troublesome that may be at times.

Voinovich: Popular Mayor without a Party
Akron Beacon Journal, March 3, 1985

Cleveland put on its happy face last week. There, on the front page of the *Plain Dealer*, was a picture of Mayor George Voinovich, Council President George Forbes, and Councilman Earle Turner, each laughing heartily. It was the kind of family scene you associate with the winner of the state lottery. Seldom in my experience with Cleveland politics—politics with a habit of being cruel—have I seen so many public officials enjoying themselves so much.

Well, they had good reason. The mayor had called a press conference to announce that the city's bond rating had been upgraded by Moody's. It meant that a city that had defaulted just six years ago had recovered to the point where it was now considered a better risk for investors. The new rating still isn't in the blue-chip class, but the city is at least one more step removed from the pauper's grave.

On that score, Voinovich can reasonably claim some credit. The six-year recovery from default coincides with his six years in the enormous oak-paneled and tapestried mayor's office at city hall.

Voinovich, who at forty-eight manages to keep his youthful appearance despite the rigors of governing, has a curious hold on the city, not only its money management but the many colliding forces that make up the people who live there. And the latter may have a lot to do with everything else he sets out to accomplish. He is a popular ethnic Republican in an ethnic Democratic city. That gives him a political base much broader than the GOP can claim. The thought surely crossed Jim Rhodes's mind when he enlisted Voinovich as his running mate against Dick Celeste, a Cleveland Democrat, in the 1978 gubernatorial campaign.

But Voinovich also is a man without a party. Oh, he may be cited by national Republican figures as clear evidence that the party has attractive ethnics in high places. But politics regularly deals in cosmetics, and Voinovich happens to be a current convenience.

The reality is something else. For example, as the president of the National League of Cities, Voinovich is trying to make his case for American cities against Reagan administration cutbacks. He testifies before congressional committees; writes letters to the White House calling for urban policies to help "the people and places left behind" in the national economic recovery; insists that the Republican Party has an opportunity to show it cares about declining industrial cities.

"I think I am a Republican mayor with a very good understanding of the uneven side of the recovery," Voinovich said in a recent interview. Citing his own city as an example, he said: "We're out of intensive care. But we still need good medical attention."

So far, there isn't much evidence from the White House that what this urban Republican mayor is saying has changed many attitudes. Certainly not when he insists: "Cities have taken more than their share of cuts. In fact, we've been on the front line of taking government cuts."

Nor is Voinovich thrilled by suggestions from on high that perhaps there is more that cities can do to help themselves. He argued that he has not avoided the hard choices in running his city: he has gone to the voters six times in five years with revenue issues. In 1981, he managed to win approval of a city income tax increase to

2 percent, from 1 ½ percent. In the past five years, Voinovich says, the city paid off $41 million in debts.

You sense that Voinovich wonders whether the White House is willing to make the same hard choices through defense spending cuts and increased taxes to get its house in order on the federal budget deficit. In any event, he's not in the mood for sermons on better management of the city treasury.

"I haven't given up on the White House," he says. "I still hope I can educate them."

The mayor hasn't had much more luck with the Republican Party in Ohio. For awhile, he considered running for governor next year. There were even some people alive in the party who thought he would be the party's best choice against Celeste.

But there is somebody else who has convinced the Republicans, including Voinovich, that he intends to run. Yep, Jim Rhodes, who, even in retirement, continues to dominate all things Republican in the state. No, not all things. Only the things that matter to Rhodes.

Voinovich withdrew from consideration, saying that he would seek a third term as mayor. He was polite about it. "Why shouldn't he [Rhodes] run if somebody is not willing to take it away from him?" Voinovich asks.

No, he says, Rhodes's presence did not influence his own decision to stay out of the race. His explanation: "I just feel down deep in my heart that my work in setting a new foundation and tradition in Cleveland isn't finished."

Perhaps. So why do I keep wondering why his fadeout as a possible candidate for governor wasn't met with an outcry from the Ohio GOP of "Say it isn't so, George"? The silence wasn't deafening. But it was moderately loud and, to me, certainly clear.

~

For Rhodes, This Doesn't Look Like a Miracle Year
Akron Beacon Journal, September 23, 1986

It is supposed to be the political season hereabouts, but so far it is not. Voters seem to be in a postelection mood—relieved that a long period of noisy partisan combat has ended and eager to get on with their lives. But that is normally a November mood, not September's, when the emotions of politics start rising as quickly as the autumn leaves fall.

From that, it would be fair to assume that voters are really saying this is not their year for dramatic reprisals at the polls. Johnny Apple, the *New York Times* correspondent who has been tracking campaigns in other states, senses a similar pattern across the land. Last week at the Akron Roundtable, he observed that, politically, we are in a "year of non-change."

Perhaps Ronald Reagan has something to do with that. The voters, at least a majority of them, have settled in comfortably with his presidency for nearly six years and for the most part have preoccupied themselves with matters (or so they presume) beyond politics. Whatever the case, the political landscape in Ohio—short of an earthquake—may not change very much after the November elections.

For Jim Rhodes, the Republican candidate for governor, there's an irony here. As one whose long political career has thrived on a quite successful formula of doing his thing, his way, without the slightest variation or concession to the politics of change, Rhodes now finds himself faced with the same rules working against him.

On the day of Apple's Roundtable appearance, a *Beacon Journal*-University of Akron statewide poll showed him to be trailing Governor Richard Celeste by twenty points. Rhodes has been behind in the polls in other races that he ultimately won, but this time around he must overcome not only his opponent but a strong feeling within his own Republican Party that it will take more than a miracle to save him. That is translating into an absence of enthusiasm among the party pros that is every bit—maybe moreso at this stage of the campaign—as deadly to him as the indifference of the voters. That should not come as any surprise. Back in the primary there were obvious clues. He drew only 48 percent of the GOP vote against two opponents, which should have been a clear warning that the former four-term governor's popularity was on the wane.

To the Republican majority that voted against him, his nomination was all the more unpalatable because there was good reason to believe that Celeste was vulnerable this year.

But they have lost their appetite for battle, and for the first time in all of Rhodes's campaigns since 1962, I am hearing—in September!—concession statements from otherwise loyal Republicans. Rhodes, of course, hasn't quit. He won't. He will drive himself to the end, because it worked so well in the past.

This time, however, it is going to be a lot harder to perform a miracle because he still hasn't convinced many of his own people that it's possible, particularly in a year when a lot of folks seem to be in a mood to leave well enough alone.

The Fall of an Ohio Legend: Flamboyant Rhodes Fades into History

Akron Beacon Journal, November 6, 1986

James Allen Rhodes, the most dominant politician in Ohio in the past quarter-century and perhaps since they started electing governors in the state, is history.

The man who roared into the governor's office in 1963 and went on to win three more terms along the way was discharged from the ranks in Tuesday's election in a landslide that destroyed his bid for still another political comeback at seventy-seven.

Moreover, it decisively transformed political legend into reality: Not even Jim Rhodes, who made a career of sustaining his loyalists while disarming his critics, could go on forever. If he erred in returning to the ring this year, it was doubtless because he believed the legend more than anyone else.

In the end, Rhodes, who so frequently stood in the winner's circle, was left to concede defeat to Governor Richard F. Celeste in the soft isolation of a room at the Cleveland Clinic, where his wife, Helen, was recuperating from surgery.

For those who had witnessed his buoyant arrival as the victor over Governor Michael V. DiSalle in 1962, the contrast suggested cruel finality. But as one who had administered defeat to others with astonishing regularity, Rhodes at least may have had a notion in recent weeks that his fate was sealed. Republican insiders say he started preparing himself last month for what, even to him, seemed inevitable.

Unlike his earlier triumphs, Rhodes never managed to get the crowd into the game—even against an opponent who was projected to be vulnerable this year. Gone was the beguiling Rhodes magic that had held him in good stead over the years: the inexhaustible energy, the flamboyant themes, the cracker-barrel wit of the coal miner's son that he was, the optimism, the unorthodox pre-yuppie political style that endeared his verbal gaffes to his audiences.

In his last round of combat, a televised debate with Celeste Sunday night, the debate judges instead saw him as a desperate man, stunned by his inescapable predicament and swinging wildly.

Never had the contrast been more pronounced. Here, after all, was the man who had commandeered the state Republican Party in 1962, reshaped it into his own image, preempted Republicans and Democrats from taking his crown, controlled party delegations, dealt Democratic legislators right out of their shoes, survived all questions about his policies and personal integrity, established his own state of mind as Ohio's credo for more than two decades, won obedience from the would-be renegades in his party, and still managed to find time to become a multimillionaire.

(On his fortune, Rhodes insisted that it came about through solid investments during the four years from 1970 to 1974, when he was forced to the sidelines by an Ohio constitutional limit to two consecutive terms as governor.)

Much of Rhodes's success derived from his sharp political intuition, his genius for keeping his opponents off balance—and not a small share of luck that brought him into office against a weak opponent during a strong national economy.

He preferred pragmatism to ideology, technically operated as a Republican, but often said he'd become a Democrat if he could get one of his pet programs adopted. That may have infuriated some GOP purists, but where could they go? On the other hand, he enjoyed the admiration of some of the veteran sharks in the Democratic Party. As Charles Carney, a former congressman and state legislator from Youngstown, once put it ever so respectfully: "With Jim Rhodes, you could always cut a cake."

Rhodes was an expert on how to cut a cake in the bartering—the shrewd flexibility—that is the essence of political survival.

Watch him in action in the 1964 presidential campaign: first assuming that the Republican nominee, Barry Goldwater, was a loser (an excellent assumption), Rhodes, as governor, made a brief, perfunctory appearance at a Goldwater rally in Columbus and quickly departed.

Later in the campaign, he began to believe that Goldwater might win. Contrary to the wishes of the late Ray Bliss, the state GOP chairman, Rhodes released the Ohio delegation to vote its wishes on the first ballot—a tactic that sealed Bliss's enmity forevermore.

At presidential conventions, Rhodes's offbeat antics, to which the Ohio press corps had long been resigned, were a novelty to national reporters whose attempts to interview him invariably fell short of producing a semblance of coherence.

Some of Rhodes's confidants, including Cuyahoga County Republican chairman Robert Hughes, insisted that Rhodes was a shy man who felt uncomfortable around the press. But it also may be true that Rhodes understood his limits perfectly and cleverly converted them to political assets to entrap and at least humor his skeptics.

He loved the game and all of its show biz trappings, whether he was pitching Ohio tomato juice, stuffing down hot dogs at the Ohio State Fair, or telling a salty joke in selected company.

When reporters tired of his rambling discourses on "jobs and progress," he would go right on repeating it a week later, a month later, a decade later.

When Republicans argued that he was not partisan enough, he ignored them, as he spent much of his political career ignoring most criticism. Instead, he made it clear to a reporter at the 1976 GOP convention that nominated Gerald Ford that he wasn't about to criticize Jimmy Carter. "Carter might get elected," Rhodes said in his clippity-clip style. "I might have to talk to him about some programs."

From the beginning, Rhodes promised programs. Mostly, bond-financed construction projects that would require no new taxes, he said. Against DiSalle, an unpopular governor who had been cast by his opponents—which included most of the Ohio press—as tax-mad, Rhodes swept into office on a landslide, which he deftly converted into the state of mind that was to accompany him into his later successful campaigns.

The formula was simple: No new taxes, accentuate the positive, dispatch the negatives with self-effacing humor, and keep the faith that something good will come of it. (Remember this vintage Rhodes line in 1982? "The Democrats used to say I wasn't fit to sleep with the hogs. The Republicans defended me and said I was.")

Ohio loved to laugh at such carefully contrived innocence, which made Rhodes all the more conscious of its political benefits. While some labor leaders berated him as the stalking horse of big-business interest, they also had to swallow the fact that many of the rank-and-file voted for Rhodes, who led them to believe he would never raise their taxes (he did anyway) and somehow put every Ohioan to work.

He was equally influential with newspaper editors, promising to deliver whatever they wanted for their hometowns. "I'm for everything," Rhodes could say with a straight face.

And to enhance his standing with blacks, one of his first Cabinet appointments went to the late W. O. Walker, publisher of a chain of black-oriented newspapers in Ohio.

The style had its price: state services—welfare, mental retardation, education—which had been in terrible shape anyway, grew worse under Rhodes's austerity program. But as political liabilities, they were no match for the assets of the more visible and highly touted—some real, some imagined—construction projects that bore Rhodes's imprimatur. Rhodes, of course, knew that.

Unsurprisingly, there always has been a tendency among some of Rhodes's critics to count him out. When he lost to Robert Taft in the 1970 Republican senatorial primary after the tragic bungling of the Kent State University antiwar demonstration, Rhodes was thought by some observers to be washed up.

Exactly one year earlier, when he was finishing his second term as governor, *Life* magazine charged him with a scandalous involvement with the mob. His guardian angel appeared to have deserted him. But he bounced back to defeat Governor John J. Gilligan in 1974 and Celeste in 1978.

Small wonder that he has for so long held the state's collective political mind in awe. And small wonder that his keen sense of timing didn't alert him that it was time to quit when he was ahead.

Too late now. Jim Rhodes, for better or worse, is history.

~

A New Column—But Will It Get My Goat, Folks?

Akron Beacon Journal, July 13, 1986

I read the other day that the army has given up on a two-year experiment to enlist a special platoon of goats to clear out a twenty-acre tract at Fort Dix, New Jersey. Anybody who has lived around these friendly scavengers for no more than a minute or two can swear to the fact that goats are not that fussy about what you set out for lunch. So the army's plan for a cheap cloven-hoofed landscaping service held more than a little promise.

But as it has been said often, every solution causes a problem. And the brass eventually discovered that the anticipated savings were all but offset by the care and treatment of an elite corps of twenty-nine goats. So the creatures now have been dispatched to a South Jersey farmer who, I presume, has a better idea about catering to big eaters.

I need to talk to that fellow. Beginning today in this space, and continuing for what we casually project for eons, I have been enlisted to write four columns a week, which translates—in my less lucid moments—into a nightmarish vision of a column an hour, with time out on Sunday to change the ribbon on the computer.

There isn't a hair's difference between the appetites of goats and columns. I knew that going in. But when Dale Allen, the editor, proposed the idea to me, bravado overtook my better judgment. After more than three decades in this business, you get that way. Don't tell me I can't do it, you argue with yourself. Make them think that you can do anything—despite the daily personal screw-ups that remind you that haven't come *that* far, baby.

So four columns it will be, a fact of life that will force me to pay more attention to the daily horoscope for those neat little urgings to go, "Complete all unfinished work. You will be pleasantly surprised by an upturn in your financial picture." Or: "You are passing into a phase of more productivity. Seize the opportunity. And for heaven's sake, stop pitying yourself."

The topics? Good question, and I can't answer it precisely. Having held forth on the Sunday Commentary page for the past three years, I will make a confession: There were too many Wednesday afternoons when I didn't have the feeblest notion what I would be writing the next day for the Sunday column. Now I may be able to say that in quadruplicate.

Opinions? Sure, but I must add this footnote: I constantly surprise myself with the number of things on which I have no opinion at all. (Should pachysandra be planted six inches or a foot apart?)

Human interest? Hopefully, lots of it. Most readers are human, perhaps even a majority of those who write unsigned diatribes to columnists, and if you can find a way to make a column interesting (the national average is one of three), you will have more readers. I don't need to tell you that this is a tenet of Journalism I.

People and places? Yep, especially about the regional scene.

Topics? Whatever. Some light. Some heavy. Some desperate.

Get the idea? Yeah, you and me both.

And now I'm off to see that farmer on how he figures to feed all of those goats.

~

Metzenbaum's Dirty Little Secret Is Revealed at Last
Akron Beacon Journal, July 19, 1988

One of the more substantive issues emerging in the U.S. Senate race in Ohio is a charge by Senator Howard Metzenbaum's opponents that he is from Cleveland. Although the issue has brought howls of "dirty politics" from the senator's camp, I can tell you right off that the accusation is essentially correct. I know it sounds like a boast, but I must confess that I've known about this political time bomb for some time.

At least, oh, twenty years. It was back in 1968, I think, that I first met Metzenbaum, and, being the aggressive young reporter, I promptly went for the heart of the political discourse: "Nice to meet you, Mr. Metzenbaum. Where are you from?"

"Cleveland," he said, without demanding that we go off the record.

I've always appreciated his candor on that occasion. Twenty years ago, not everybody that you stopped in Public Square was quick to admit that he or she was from Cleveland. Some began by fudging: "Actually my parents were from Bowling Green." Or: "My company transferred me here for three months, two weeks, and five days." Others simply waved off the question and rushed to the first car with out-of-state license plates.

Now, after all these years and two U.S. Senate terms in his diary, Metzenbaum's native ties to Cleveland are being used against him by his opponents. Curiously, they are not from Indianapolis or Wheeling, but from *Cleveland*. In fact, Metzenbaum's opponent is George Voinovich, who happens to be the mayor of Cleveland.

Be that as it may, I have read that Voinovich's media crew is running TV political commercials in Columbus and Cincinnati to inform the voters in those towns that Metzenbaum is not from Indianapolis or Wheeling, but Cleveland!

In some respects, it is understandable why the Voinovich people have set out to prove a *double* negative in Ohio's southland. People who live in Columbus and Cincinnati traditionally have had no confidence in people from Cleveland—a distrust that appears to have begun back when the mapmakers misspelled the city founder's name. (The opposite is not true. People who live in Cleveland are not generally aware that Columbus and Cincinnati have been ceded to the Union.)

On the occasions that I have toured southern Ohio with politicians, Cincinnatians have approached me about my own residence.

"Akron area," I would say.

"That's Cleveland, isn't it?" they would cryptically reply—the way John Wayne would say Dodge City.

"Well, no. We have our own city government and streets."

"Still sounds like Cleveland to me," they would say huffily. "What brings you to town?"

Rather than answer the question, I would praise the Cincinnati Reds or put in a good word for Woody Hayes over in Columbus. Somehow, it always eased tensions a bit.

There are some risks involved, of course, in labeling Metzenbaum a Clevelander down south. The senator might retaliate with

TV commercials in Cleveland accusing Voinovich of being the mayor of that city. No one is quite sure how that revelation will play up north. But, again without boasting, I can report that the charge is substantially correct.

This Campaign Is Suffering from an Identity Crisis
Akron Beacon Journal, November 6, 1988

Well, here we are in the closing hours of another presidential campaign, still debating who we are not, or otherwise trying to prove a negative.

It all started when Senator Lloyd Bentsen, the Democratic vice presidential candidate, coolly told Senator Dan Quayle, his Republican counterpart, that Quayle was not John F. Kennedy. It was an instant hit, playing in headlines across America and Europe.

Since then, Quayle has gone three better in the name-dropping competition, insisting to everybody that Michael Dukakis is not Harry Truman, John F. Kennedy, or Franklin D. Roosevelt. Rather, Quayle swears that Dukakis may be Walter Mondale, Jimmy Carter, or George McGovern. But like so many things in a political campaign, that is only Quayle's opinion.

There was a time when Quayle probably would have accused Mondale of being Hubert Humphrey or McGovern of being Eugene V. Debs. But why live in the past? Mondale and McGovern aren't running this year.

If there had been time, the Democrats might have put together a consensus that George Bush was not Woodrow Wilson, King James, Winston Churchill, Queen Victoria, Alexander Hamilton, or—heavens!—Nancy Reagan.

To which Bush quite likely would have replied that the governor of Massachusetts was not Socrates, Zorba the Greek, Homer, Helen of Troy, Aristophanes, Alexander the Great, or Melina Mercouri.

Of course, we've all known these things for some time, so we have to wonder why so much precious time has been taken up in what should have been a serious campaign fitfully arguing over who all of the candidates are not.

Great leaders of the past have always said, "I am me," and have gone on to get elected without a single sensible challenge to their identity.

Proving negatives began taking on new meaning, however, when Richard Nixon looked us all in the eye and said he wasn't a crook. At the time, his political enemies would have loved to have pointed an accusatory finger at him and declared: "Even if you are not a crook, sir, you are certainly not Abraham Lincoln, either." Fortunately for the health of the nation, Nixon's enemies decided to forgo a counterattack dragging Lincoln into the argument. Instead, they thought it better to let the public decide whether Nixon wasn't what he said he wasn't. The outcome wasn't pretty.

So much depends on one's assumed image these days that we may never again know who anybody is when he or she comes asking for our support. Hairstyles, for example, can change in one sitting at the barbershop. Transformations are much simpler today than when Mom used to scold us with: "I'm not going to let you go out looking like that."

"But Mom!" we'd plea.

"You heard me!"

Careful, there, politicians. By raising questions about your opponents' true identities, you are approaching a dangerous level of public discourse. In the confusion of mistaken identities, it won't be too long before all candidates will begin to look like their opponents. And where will that leave the poor voter?

You know the answer as well as I.

James Rhodes's Birthday Bash Was Bipartisan Affair

Akron Beacon Journal, September 17, 1989

They hauled out Jim Rhodes—his favorite one-liners and all—for a big birthday party in Columbus last week. "Number eighty," said the red-white-and-blue banner above the Aladdin Shrine Temple stage. But it could have been eighty-four, or fifty-one or sixty-three. Except for the extra flesh sagging the jowls of the ex-governor's courtiers, and the landslide of gray-white around their beaming faces, nothing much ever changes in the presence of James Allen Rhodes.

But eighty being a nice round number, it was time, some of the guys in the front office decided, for them to pay their fondest respects to one of the last—perhaps *the* last—of America's anecdotal pols, a pre-TV creature who still brags openly about being a product of the southern hills instead of some eastern finishing school—and has mostly success to show for it.

The evening could not have gone better for the honored guest if he had planned it himself, and those who know Rhodes intimately would have hardly bet the farm against that possibility.

Officially, according to a souvenir booklet handed out to a thousand or so $100-a-ticket donors, the event was "produced" by Ohio Senate President Stan Aronoff, a Republican from Cincinnati ("ARN-off," Rhodes repeatedly barked), and Ohio House Speaker Vern Riffe, a Democrat and quadrennial suspect as candidate for governor. The booklet itself was assembled by another Rhodes pal, Tom Dudgeon, a newsletter author.

As is his custom, Republican Rhodes favored Riffe, with whom he has cut more than one poker deck, with his most complimentary remarks. Ignoring the likely presence of a couple of GOP gubernatorial candidates for the ceremonies (Cleveland's Mayor George Voinovich and Hamilton County Commissioner Robert Taft), Rhodes bubbled that Riffe would "make a great governor for this state."

Riffe, meantime, reminded everybody that he was born in a little town (New Boston) just thirty-five miles south of Rhodes's birthplace of Coalton and the two loved to talk about old times, and they never forgot where they came from. Riffe, perhaps the most influential politician in Ohio, was humble on this evening. He said he learned so much from Jim Rhodes. "We don't believe in deals," he said. "We believe in helping people."

Nobody seemed to mind.

After all, the theme of the evening was bipartisanship, which, if you can imagine this, brought Rhodes and his twice-Democratic rival, Governor Richard Celeste, together on the podium awkwardly leading the Ohio State Fair Youth Choir in several choruses of *The Battle Hymn of the Republic.* Some of the astonished witnesses declared the duet to be a unique moment in the history of the world. More likely, others supposed, it was a triumph of a Hollywood special-effects crew.

The audience, made up of the usual political militia so easily mustered in the state capital—officeholders, aides, payrollers, lobbyists, aspiring achievers—politely stood or sat through the program with a minimum of cross talk.

During Rhodes's thirty-minute speech, which was universally upbeat and rambled from anecdotes about an "elderly lady" to pleas for semiconductors, one could follow the talk by reading the lips of all those who had heard the lines before. No matter. "I am what I am," Rhodes declared. "And what you see is what you get. And what you don't see, you may not want."

And as he has been known to do, he praised former Ohio Senator Frank Lausche as his idol (although it didn't seem quite that cozy when the two battered each other in a governor's race in 1954). He said he liked the way Lausche answered questions. He said Frank would give you three answers to every question. Jim allowed that that was a good way to get ahead and, as many of us know, spent much of his long political career perfecting it.

Bob Hughes, the Cuyahoga County Republican chairman who spent two decades as Rhodes's top banana in this part of the state, made it down to the party from Cleveland. A chain smoker who figures that the fun of politics will be diminished in the absence of "Ol' Jimmy," Hughes scanned the hall as brigades of politicians ambled by, and smiled: "Look at them. Twenty years from now, 90 percent of the people won't even remember who any of these people are."

We'll probably find out at Jim Rhodes's hundredth.

If Taxes Go Up, President Needs Heavy-duty Alibi
Akron Beacon Journal, May 29, 1990

The only real debate centering on the White House today is not over whether Vice President Quayle's on-the-job training qualifies him for an honorary degree at Wellesley, but whether President Bush intends to go along with a liberal, socialistic, commie-inspired, money-grubbing, economy-busting tax increase.

The whole debate is interesting because it rests solely on Bush's insistence during his last campaign that the state of the national economy is best understood by lip reading. If you are weary of references to that term, now you know how his opponents felt as he methodically moved his lips on the hour and quarter-hour to trounce Mike Dukakis.

But the Bush folks now fear that any concession to taxes by the president would force all of his political friends to concede that he lied to the voters. I personally think those fears are overdrawn. But it does make you wonder about the empty state of Bush's loyalists today in that they have been unable to engage in some clever damage control to get him off the hook.

There is no denying, of course, that candidate Bush went around telling everybody to read his lips when people innocently asked how much extra his presidency would cost them.

But I ask all of you who claim to have paid the closest attention to the campaign: did any of you actually read his lips? I mean, did you look to your neighbor and say, "I read George Bush's lips when he was standing in the muck at Boston Harbor, and he said, 'Dukakis polluted this harbor thing, and I'll never raise taxes' "?

Of course not. What's more, I don't think there are two people alive today who can honestly say that upon reading Bush's lips, they were satisfied that he formed those immortal words.

Voters almost never do what they are told to do by politicians, so it was quite natural that while some people had already made up their minds to vote for or against him, nobody ever read his lips. If they had, then a strong case could be made by Bush's image-makers today that he actually said, "Don't kid yourself: Of course, I'll raise taxes."

That strategy would be a major breakthrough for the Bush forces. It could be said that closer inspection of Bush's lips (via the most up-to-date computer images) clearly shows he did not promise what everybody thought he promised. Hence, he would not be betraying the public trust (that is, lying) by coming out for a tax increase to save the republic.

The rest would be easy. The public would have to accept the fact that Bush was honest, and that if voters were confused by the lip-reading slogan, they had nobody to blame but themselves for not paying attention. And since voters will never admit that they were fooled by politicians, they would suffer in silence.

And after a while, they would forget it altogether, or call it a Democratic plot to salve their conscience. But that would last only until 1992 when the Democrats forget to put up a candidate.

Running without opposition, George Bush would agree to set aside lip-reading once and for all, which would show you what a decent winner he can be when the pressure's off.

All of this is such a simple scenario, I wonder why all of the president's men are spending so much time trying to find synonyms for taxes.

May 4 Tragedy Needs Forgiving, not Forgetting
Akron Beacon Journal, January 28, 1990

When trouble erupted at Kent State University on May 4, 1970—a dark date in American social history—a young sociology professor named Mike Schwartz was walking across the Indiana University campus in the glow of a warm spring sun. He and some other faculty members had been actively working to depressurize student unrest over U.S. military policy in Southeast Asia.

"And then," he recalled one day last week, "I got the news about what happened at Kent State. I sat down by a fountain on the campus and burst into tears. I just couldn't believe that the government could turn on itself that way."

Nearly twenty years later, Schwartz has an additional reason for remembering the tragedy. He has been KSU's president since 1982 and, in one way or another, has had to deal with the enduring costs of that day's madness—the lingering anger, the widest spectrum of public attitudes, the damage to the university's image, the need to make certain that the moment will forever be too significant to be purged from public memory for the sake of convenience.

What's more, Schwartz says he is fully aware that come May 4, 1990, all of the threads from the bloody event—four students killed, nine wounded—will doubtless be woven into a day of commemorative ceremonies on the campus. Society, after all, has a tendency to seek greater meaning from history on anniversaries that end in zero or five.

In this instance, "May 4," as the coded version has come to be known, will be twenty years old.

So on that day, George McGovern, a vigorously antiwar former senator and presidential candidate who, ironically, may be no more than a vague political figure to a new generation of college students, will be the principal speaker on the program that will dedicate architect Bruno Ast's granite memorial on a knoll near where the shots were fired.

Schwartz says he's prepared for the day that will likely bring the national media to the campus and thus broadly reassociate KSU with state-sponsored bloodshed. "I don't really know what to expect," he told me. "But I have no misgivings. I think we've really come to terms with our own history, and I want the rest of the people of the state to do the same. I don't want anybody ever to forget what happened. What I'm interested in now is *forgiving*—not *forgetting*."

Along with that, he hopes to be able to project a thriving university to all comers—a school that took one of history's strongest punches and dramatically recuperated to astonishing good health. "After May 4," he says, "it seemed to me that the university was treated as the rape victim who was blamed for the rape, and a heavy price was paid. Enrollment declined. The professors didn't want to stay here. Morale was terrible. In almost every conceivable way, the university was given up for dead. But slowly it made an unbelievable comeback."

To support his argument, he will be able to say that KSU has a record enrollment—thirty-two thousand students at eight campuses, nearly twenty-four thousand on the main one—despite the fact that it has stiffened its academic requirements for student applicants.

He will tell any skeptical visitor in the crowd that KSU today ranks behind only Ohio State University and the University of Cincinnati in obtaining National Science Foundation money in Ohio for research. He will point out that KSU now offers doctorates in fifty fields and has a widely recognized library with more than 1.7 million volumes.

When Schwartz completed this random list to me, I told him KSU's detractors would write it off as self-serving. "I know," he said. "But I say it has been a helluva comeback for the university. And all I'm asking is that the detractors recognize it and rejoice in it. I want them to know that what was here twenty years ago is not here now."

I asked him: "Between now and May 4, what will you be thinking about?"

He didn't hesitate: "What's going through my mind? Four dead kids. All unnecessary deaths and maiming. None of it had to happen, nor happen here. That is the biggest part of the tragedy."

Schwartz has earned the right to talk about comebacks. Twenty years ago, he wept. Some people didn't.

~

By George! No Flash, But a Definite Style

Akron Beacon Journal, January 13, 1991

At 11:12 P.M. Tuesday, November 6, a middle-aged man with boyish looks and well-known in the fitting rooms of politics as a person of few extremes walked onto the stage of the Hyatt Regency-Ohio Center ballroom in Columbus and, after shaking hands with a couple of his congratulatory friends, exclaimed to an exuberant crowd:

"Wow! What a victory! I gotta tell you that it's really hard for me to believe that the grandson of immigrants who couldn't read, write, or speak English was elected governor of the State of Ohio!"

For anyone who had followed George Voinovich's relentless political career, which unofficially began as president of the Ohio University student body back in the middle '50s, there was ample reason to share the governor-elect's astonishment.

Here, after all, was a fellow who could quip that the first thing people around the state wanted to know about him was whether he spoke English. And that former governor Jim Rhodes, with whom he ran tandem on a statewide ticket, could do no better than to pronounce his name correctly about once in every five tries. (Gerald Ford once scored a near-hit with "Vukovich.")

Moreover, only two years earlier, Voinovich, a personable but scarred old pro at fifty-four who has always seemed to be ready to run for one office or another when the clock strikes midnight, had been relegated to political oblivion after a ruinous lopsided defeat at the deft hands of Senator Howard Metzenbaum.

For a person with a less-developed sense of personal destiny, a 608,000-vote shellacking in the U.S. Senate race would have been quite enough encouragement to set out on a different course to earn a living.

But Voinovich could easily argue that he had seen misery before and lived to tell about it. For example, Voinovich was swamped in the 1971 Cleveland mayoral primary by Ralph Perk, another Republican ethnic in a city where ethnicity is as flagrantly visible on the political stump as a forehead tattoo. He then scored an impressive victory in the race for Cuyahoga County auditor in 1972, defeating Democrat Julius Krupansky by more than two hundred thousand votes.

And within a few years, while still in the county auditor's office, he was thinking seriously about a statewide race for auditor but then was persuaded to run for lieutenant governor as Rhodes emerged from retirement to defeat Dick Celeste for governor.

That was in 1978, and all of the names remain familiar today.

Having recovered from his loss that year to win two terms as governor, Celeste, who was constitutionally barred from seeking a third term, will relinquish control of the office on Monday. And Voinovich will try to fill the role—as governor and Republican Party leader—that Rhodes once seemed to have reserved for himself in perpetuity.

~

A few weeks after the election night huzzahs have become a pleasant memory, George Voinovich is sitting in the living room of his small, unpretentious home on the far east side of Cleveland and comparing his two most recent election night experiences.

"When I took on the Senate race," he says, "I knew it would be difficult all the way and that if I won it, I would have to do everything right. But I ran out of money and had no money for TV."

(Actually, Metzenbaum spent about $300,000 more than Voinovich, a relatively narrow advantage in a $17 million race. A large element contributing to Voinovich's defeat may have been an incredible political commercial accusing Metzenbaum of favoring child pornography.)

When Voinovich contrasts that disastrous night in 1988 to his big victory over Democratic Attorney General Anthony J. Celebrezze Jr., he breaks into a faint smile. "I can tell you this," he says. "It's a helluva lot easier being an early winner than being an early loser."

Janet, Voinovich's ebullient wife, sits at his side on the sofa and also recalls that dark night. "The best thing about it," she says, "is that it came to an end. I never knew the final vote. I only knew it was a loss."

Voinovich nods. To this day, he says, he still hasn't looked at the final figures of that defeat.

It is an absolute of politics that there is very little relationship between a political campaign and governing. Campaigns are built on outrageously broad premises that are intended to be reassuring without offering much substance.

During his campaign against Celebrezze, Voinovich often mentioned that he wanted to be the "education governor"—a pop term these days for governors and presidents. Such oratorical shorthand has come to have go-for-the-gut immediacy about it and, depending upon the situation, can be replaced with such other nonthreatening words as "environment" ("environment governor") or "peace" or "tax-free."

In the evolution of sloganeering, these self-labeling terms are even leaner than Jim Rhodes's campaign aphorisms, most memorably "Profit is not a dirty word in Ohio."

Voinovich also was given to summarizing his goals as Ohio's next chief executive by declaring that he wanted to "improve the quality of life" of every Ohioan. That kind of talk may be easily excused in the dreamy reaches of campaign rhetoric. But it hardly offers a clue to the sort of man who will guide the state through what will likely be some lean economic years.

If you are looking for a clue to George Voinovich, you may have to leave the public spotlight and return to the Voinovich home, a place that spoke both of the past and the future on that late-autumn afternoon. It sits just down the street from a gazebo overlooking Lake Erie. Many of the homes in the snug neighborhood are nondescript but neatly kept—a glimpse, at least, of simple Old World sturdiness and pride.

He bought the home in 1972, says Voinovich, who is of Serbian-Slovenian descent, "from a Lithuanian. Before that, we lived just five blocks from here."

The home has the lived-in air of casual permanence about it: older furniture, some antique crockery, scarcely a hint of modern excesses—all very much in the Voinovich mode and a breed apart from what one might expect of a fast-track politician these days. The hint of the future is strewn about the living room floor and on the dining room table: stacks of paperwork, some of which say, "Seminar for new governors."

That scene, which seems locked in some previous era, brings to mind the words of Alex Arshinkoff, the Summit County GOP chairman who was the first to endorse Voinovich for governor. "You'd never see him drive a Cadillac," Arshinkoff said. "That's just not in his makeup. Slovenian people, by nature, are very conservative fiscally. George will run state government that way—tight."

And apparently intent on sustaining his style, no matter his rank.

"Even when George was lieutenant governor [part of 1979 before Voinovich left the job to run for mayor of Cleveland], we continued to live here," Janet says. "We never did move down to Columbus."

Voinovich doesn't plan to be spending a lot of time running around the state giving speeches and "doing a lot of PR." Rather, he expects to be busy as a hands-on governor looking after every detail. And he will continue to devote time to his family, with quiet Sundays and dinners at home.

"I'm already blocking out my time that I will be taking off," he says. "I've got to get away [from the job] with Janet, or I can get pretty mean."

Bob Hughes, the Cuyahoga County Republican chairman, describes Voinovich as a "dedicated family man" and says he saw a change in Voinovich's perspective on politics after George's and Janet's nine-year-old daughter, Mollie, the youngest of their four children, was killed by a van as she walked to school in 1979.

"Her death," Hughes says, "deeply affected George and Janet—George in a sense that it changed his perspective and made him a much cooler and much more sensitive and perceptive person. He realized that politics was not everything in his world. He likes to reserve whatever time necessary for his family."

~

Look then for none of the good-ol'-boy showmanship of Rhodes, who thrived on county fairs, after-dinner stand-up routines, and a lot of ubiquitous horsing around in the provinces while his cabinet handled the affairs of state. Look for none of the soaring—if unattained—visions of Celeste, who had a thing about participatory democracy and New Liberalism political affirmations in behalf of the Commoners.

Most likely, George Voinovich will be content to grind it out as a man in a discount-house business suit, working carefully between the foul lines while seeking a political consensus in the legislature to achieve his goals.

Having developed his political instincts as a Republican in the Democratic and often tumultuous arena of Cleveland, Voinovich managed to survive quite well with an acute understanding of political turf. As mayor of Cleveland for three terms during the '80s, he remained largely unscathed by partisan crossfire by avoiding major confrontations with the former all-powerful Democratic president of city council, George Forbes.

"As mayor," Cuyahoga County Commissioner Tim Hagan, a Democrat, says of Voinovich, "the city council was thirty-one-to-one Democrat. So George cut his deal with George Forbes and let Forbes run the city."

Voinovich, of course, would dispute the notion that he was no more than the ceremonial mayor of his city, a title often associated, with stronger evidence, with Perk. But it also is true that Voinovich maintained a relatively laid-back profile in contrast to his predecessor, Dennis Kucinich. In fact, it could be argued in the post-Kucinich era that nothing short of daily mayhem at city hall would have cast Voinovich as a hyperactive chief executive.

Oh, there were minor disagreements with Forbes and occasional media criticism that he spent more time out of state either on official business or on vacation than he did managing the city's affairs.

But after the Kucinich years, Voinovich was given generous credit, particularly by the business community, for restoring peace and quiet—often described as "normalcy," a relative term to be sure—to the city's day-to-day operations. And it didn't hurt his image as the miracle healer of Cleveland's economic wounds—the consequence of default—that in contrast to Kucinich's headlong assaults on the private sector's achievers, Voinovich quite willingly supported millions of dollars in tax abatements as a handsome incentive for downtown developers and lived by a theme of "accentuating the positive."

(Voinovich's disposition to working with business leaders has been quite evident in the people he named to head screening committees to recommend twenty-two cabinet-level appointments. Many of the volunteers are business executives.)

As a state legislator, county auditor, commissioner, and mayor, Voinovich has accumulated the kind of political experience that will prepare him for the uncertainties of his new job in Columbus. In that respect, it's hard to overestimate the benefits of a rigorous Cleveland-style political education, where partisanship, ethnicity, and race have long been elements of one's apprenticeship. To have suffered such conditions as long as Voinovich has, and to have emerged with fresh energies, is certainly a positive sign of his durability against whatever odds.

But Columbus is not Cleveland, and Voinovich's success as governor will depend on a quid pro quo with a Democratic House of Representatives under the unyielding command of Speaker Vern Riffe, an operative with boundless powers to shape legislation in his own image.

Voinovich may also face another kind of problem in the Republican-controlled Senate, where there could be awkward demands from his own party that he raise the Republican banner on pet GOP issues.

Between these two houses, Voinovich will have to find a route in advancing his campaign promises of sweeping reforms in ethics, campaign financing, and education. At the same time, he will have to hold bruised egos to a minimum in carrying out his pledge to houseclean the government from basement to attic.

"We'll crack the bureaucracy," Voinovich says in a matter-of-fact way that hardly sounds like a wild-eyed boast to rope in the more than sixty-five thousand employees on the state payroll.

When told that a lot of other governors have come into office with the same lofty ambitions and have failed, Voinovich delivers up that faint smile again and says, well, it can and will be done, so just watch him.

That leaves people like Hagan, a veteran himself of the trenches along Lake Erie, wondering how well Voinovich can possibly fare in Columbus, which is comparatively far from the madding crowd up on the lake. Says Democrat Hagan: "George Voinovich is a decent and fairly civil human being. And he damn well may have leadership ability. But he's totally untested as a politician because he's never had to expend any political capital on an issue. And despite his nonsense that there is no Republican or Democratic way to run the government, he'll find out from the Republican Senate that there is a Republican way to run the government. He's going to be tested like he's never been tested before in public life because he's always held himself above partisanship."

Now, Hagan says, the real question is whether Voinovich will be able to say no to Republicans. "I don't know," Hagan says. "He didn't say no to Forbes [a Democrat]."

Voinovich could not have carried the state so heavily in November without the added support of Democratic voters in Summit, Cuyahoga, and Lorain counties—long considered Democratic preserves but backing the Republican candidate this year. But it is also true that the big money that poured into Voinovich's campaign lifeline came from Republican wallets—$1.2 million from Summit County fund-raisers alone, according to Arshinkoff. President George Bush made it to Ohio four times on behalf of Voinovich and other Republican candidates. So Voinovich's political lineage was quite evident throughout the campaign.

Still, some Ohio Republicans now insist that partisanship will not be a decisive factor in defining the Voinovich administration. "He won't be a strong ideologue," says Cuyahoga County's Hughes. "George recognizes he's governor of all the people. He'll listen to Republicans, but he's more of a chief executive officer than he is a politician. He will be a no-nonsense administrator and woe to any of his associates who get into trouble. They'll be gone."

Hughes was referring, of course, to the oft-documented ethical problems that plagued the Celeste administration through two terms and served as perhaps the leading issue in Voinovich's defeat of Celebrezze. If you asked the GOP operatives in the Hyatt-Regency the evening of Voinovich's victory speech to identify the smoking gun that brought down the attorney general, they unhesitantly replied with a single word: "Celeste."

Ethical purity in government, however, is as elusive as finding a diamond without imperfections. And already, before Voinovich has even entered the governor's office, the *Cleveland Plain Dealer* has raised questions about Paul Mifsud, Voinovich's confidante and campaign manager who will become his chief of staff. The newspaper wondered about the propriety of a travel agency with which Mifsud is associated making some of the travel arrangements for the inaugural ball. If nothing else, the issue, a speck in the scheme of ponderous government today, suggests how easy it is these days just to give the *appearance* of impropriety.

Like Hughes, Summit County's Arshinkoff regards Voinovich as a tight-fisted manager of public money. "He's a professional when it comes to running the government," Arshinkoff says. "He will cut the waste in government, cut the number of employees, cut the costs, get into the bowels of government and get rid of the waste. He'll run the state tight."

As for partisan demands, Arshinkoff says: "When all things are equal, George is a Republican. But he's not going to put the Republican Party ahead of good government."

Roy Ray of Akron, the Republican whip in the Ohio Senate, which has a twenty-one-to-twelve GOP majority, doesn't think the party will present any serious problems for Voinovich when everyone gathers in the coming weeks to focus on new legislation. "George is a hard worker and a realist," Ray says, "and we all want to cooperate with him to do the best job for this state that we possibly can. I seldom get excited, but I do get excited over the prospects of working with George."

~

Voinovich will enter office under a cloud of budgetary problems—a projected $1.5 billion deficit in the 1992–1993 biennium. And the situation could worsen in a deep and prolonged recession. Even if he succeeds in trimming the "fat"—which is always there to be trimmed—there invariably is something to take its place. Besides, the trimming must come for the leanest side of the state budget because so many of the programs, like education and human resources, are fixed in stone.

This year there's likely to be an avalanche of news reports about projected budget cuts and projected untouchables, each followed by a lot of wailing and hand-wringing that will demonstrate the imperviousness of the government pie. (Among the biggest cut-preachers of all-time was former President Ronald Reagan, whose administration ran up the biggest deficits in the country's history.)

Still, to give Voinovich his due, if there is ever the slightest zeal detected in his view of government management, it is his unyielding belief that government is not shrink-proof. His efforts to prove it as governor will doubtless be one of the top spectator sports in the early months of his regime.

But there is something else to watch, too—Voinovich's demonstrated political independence and his willingness to reverse his own positions when the situation calls for it.

As president of the National League of Cities, he was a visible critic of the Reagan administration's urban policies, arguing that they were hitting the urban poor the hardest. He ridiculed Reagan's plea to "stay the course" by likening it to "what Hirohito told his kamikaze pilots." At a National League of Cities meeting in Atlanta in 1980, he declared his anger over the imbalance of Ohio money going to Washington and the federal money that was coming back. "We've been systematically screwed!" he asserted.

When the Republican Party was casting about for a gubernatorial candidate for the 1978 election, Voinovich was among those younger Republicans who argued that the party needed a new face and that it would be wrong to tie its fortunes again to Rhodes. Was it then a feat of pragmatism that Voinovich eventually agreed to join Rhodes to shore up the ticket in Cuyahoga County?

And upon being elected lieutenant governor in 1978, Voinovich often denied that he would leave Columbus to run for mayor in 1979; then, as expected, he announced his candidacy. One of the deciding factors was that despite Rhodes's grandiose plans for his lieutenant governor, the governor could only function as a single act and Voinovich became extra baggage to him the day after the election.

Voinovich has all but resorted to saying "read my lips" in rejecting any suggestions of a possible tax hike to erase projected state deficits. He prefers to talk about "responsible solutions" instead. But if he eventually determines that there are not enough of those kind of solutions to go around, it would be well to remember that Mayor George Voinovich, the realist, called for—and eventually won—two increases in his city's income tax, calling these hikes "life or death" matters.

That is strong language for Voinovich, who normally seems quite content to defy the gravitational pull of blatant political rhetoric. On the other hand, it would be wrong ever to say never in charting his new course in Columbus. He might just prove you dead wrong.

A Columnist Bids Adieu, Looks Back
Akron Beacon Journal, February 19, 1991

Today's column will be my last appearance in this space.

The column, which began in July 1986 on the Lifestyle page and crossed the room to the Metro page in June 1990, has been eliminated by the *Beacon Journal.* According to the paper's editors, it lacked sufficient readership to justify its existence. In their words, the column "didn't work." In response, I am leaving the *Beacon Journal* to take a fresh look at some long-delayed personal writing ventures.

But it isn't my intention today to dwell on a management decision with which I quite naturally disagree. Instead, I prefer to look back over nearly a thousand columns and say that if anyone is innocent enough to take on such a task, there is no better place to do it than in the Akron area.

Over the years, I learned that my column's back yard was not so small as to be provincial. Nor was it so large that both columnist and reader dealt with each other in absolute anonymity. I also learned that if you give the readers half an ear, they'll provide more column material than you can possibly assimilate in twice the column's frequency.

If you guessed somewhere along the line that I'm a fan of this area, it proves that we have had something in common—even if you wore an Indians T-shirt and I continued to honor my childhood crush on the Pittsburgh Pirates.

Over the past month, I've had occasion to wonder whatever gave me the brash idea that I ought to be a columnist in the first place. After all, where does it say that a mere mortal can claim some special gift to belabor the masses with uninterrupted treatises on such diverse subjects as Casey Stengel, Ronald Reagan, Copernicus, Giuseppe Verdi, and the conscientious chef at the Greek restaurant?

Did anybody really need to know about that trip to Ireland in which my wife finally caught up with gravestones of her ancestors? Or about my fortieth high school reunion—my first concession to such rites—that left me awkwardly poking among the faces to see how many I could remember? And did you really have to follow me around the muddy fairgrounds track at Burton before sunup in order to understand that antique collectors have their bizarre moments?

Of course not, but. . . .

There were times, of course, to be serious. A column that attempts to mirror events three or four days a week cannot honestly escape those times, and the last couple of pieces that have appeared here reflected my deep concern and dread of the Persian Gulf War. Though some of us might think otherwise, not every word can be turned into some disc jockey's tasteless gag line.

The Start of It All

Still, it was humor that got me into this column business in the first place. That was more than twenty years ago when Jack Knight insisted that our trade was slipping into a dull void and wondered aloud whether there wasn't something we could do about it at the *Beacon Journal.*

By chance, I happened to write a now-forgotten piece that caught Knight's eye. He relayed his feelings to Ben Maidenburg, who, in his memorable take-no-prisoners style, ordained that I come up with two or three light columns a week.

It scared me to no end. But I also knew that if I had any future in this business, there was no way—in Ben's words—that I could disappoint Jack Knight.

A Political Detour

That series of columns ended when I became political editor, but it taught me that there are a lot of days when a columnist ought to commune with readers by sharing our mutual grievances about a society that keeps bumping into itself—which means all of us—in ways that leave us no choice but to force a half-smiling sigh.

Nearly a thousand columns later, I have decided, too, that all writers survive not through the tolerance of their editors but through the tolerance of their readers. So, having survived this long, I think it would be only fitting to close by telling any of you who has read this far that I have been grateful for your interest, advice, ideas, and even the occasional scolding.

It's been fun, folks.

~

Malaise Chills Usual Heat of Campaigns

Cleveland Plain Dealer, February 17, 1992

As the eight hundred people at the recent Summit County Republican Lincoln Day dinner were leaving the Tangier restaurant, a woman observed that the crowd was somewhat subdued for an event that is essentially a political pep rally.

True. There had been few crowd responses during the evening that threatened to lay waste to the main ballroom. One could argue that Republicans are usually a pretty straight bunch, anyway, and once they have downed their chicken Parisian, there's little else of consequence left to the evening.

But in touting the army of local candidates on hand that night, GOP Chairman Alex Arshinkoff was at his ebullient best. And the main speaker, Lt. Governor Michael DeWine, the party's challenger to Senator John Glenn this year, promised to be a feisty candidate with a bulldog's approach to changing the old order on Capitol Hill. Still, his zingers drew more of a courteous handshake from the crowd than a hearty "give 'em hell" send-off into the trenches.

Does this spell hard times ahead for the Republicans?

Not so fast. Last week, I heard from an old friend in California who has long served Democratic causes as an officeholder and party worker. So far, she wrote, the Democrats' presidential campaign has been uninspiring. She would doubtless vote to leave the Oval Office empty rather than reelect George Bush, but. . . .

Well, like many other Democrats these days, she's suffering in silence, hankering for another Democrat to enter the race. "Gore, Gephardt, Cuomo," she wrote. In the constricted time frame of presidential politics, February can be election day eve for potential candidates in the wings. The question for those Democrats who belong to the anybody-but-the-New-Hampshire-five crowd is whether wishing will make it so in 1992.

The frustration is understandable. Even as the New Hampshire primary worked its way through its final lackluster week, the Dems' campaign seemed to be competing with the Earthwinds balloon to see which would be launched first.

Neither party can take much joy in the public image problems of the other side. Thanks to the deadening effects of a woeful economy, the public seems to be wondering whether there is any politician alive today who can reverse the current slide. And if there is, where is he or she? Not in New Hampshire.

On the other hand, the easiest way to pass the buck these days is to lay all the sins of the universe on the politicians. Historically, they have been the most convenient, and often most deserving, targets.

Yet every other institution today is struggling with its own internal management problems that are not a part of the electoral process. Rather, they reflect breakdowns in some of the basics of making good things happen in the workplace.

According to what I've been reading, more and more companies face devastating morale problems created by indifferent (maybe that's too kind a word) communications between the bosses and their staffs. One survey said that 85 percent of American workers believe their bosses are not in touch with the problem. That leads to depressed morale, frustration, and resentment. It's not how companies can hope to compete in a world market.

Some are reacting by hiring consultants to find out what's the matter with the companies they're supposed to be managing.

Jimmy Carter once used the word "malaise" to describe what ailed the country, and it didn't take some voters long to turn to Ronald Reagan to escape into a new decade of simply feeling good. Now, a dozen years later, with a serious malaise upon us, *Newsweek* took up the subject in a cover story examining what's wrong with the "feel-good" movement.

The article deals with the hyping of self-esteem among young people as a means of preparing them for a healthy life on the planet. But it says things have gotten so out of hand that the movement has produced "an explosion of awards, gold stars and happy-face stickers for the most routine accomplishments of childhood. Most children's sports teams now automatically give trophies for just showing up."

The article concludes that a feel-good world is fine, but wonders what will happen to kids when they find out that life isn't like that at all.

Maybe a lot of despairing adults are finding that out, too, no matter what they're being told on the political stump today.

Clinton Lead Is Not Yet Unbeatable
Cleveland Plain Dealer, August 7, 1992

When Mae West breezily observed that "too much of a good thing can be wonderful," she could have easily been describing the current mood in the Democratic camp over Bill Clinton's lofty standing in the national polls.

The repetitious ratings, one reinforcing another, are suggesting that President Bush has been all but mathematically eliminated from the race. At the same time, Dan Quayle's eyes already seem to be fixed on 1996.

Well, it's August, and although enjoying a big lead in the polls may be more pleasurable for the Democratic team than a couple of weeks at the seashore, you won't find much talk on either side (with possible exception of George Will, who is in a big-time sulk) that we are standing in the path of a landslide.

Clinton's twenty-five to thirty-point lead in some of the major polls, says John Green of the Bliss Institute of Applied Politics at the University of Akron, is "by no means insurmountable." Put an asterisk besides that. It could be insurmountable unless certain things occur. "Bush is in a whole lot of trouble," said Green. "But if the Republicans have a good convention—a big if—he could take off ten points from Clinton's lead right there. The Bush people would be delighted if, by Labor Day, he was only ten points behind. But all of this assumes that Bush starts doing some things right. He has to begin by articulating some direction for the country."

Green added: "The state and local Republicans are ready to go, but the president keeps tripping on his own feet." True enough. While Bush was trying to make some points on the stump, his campaign staff tripped him up with a press release that aimed below Clinton's mid-section. It effectively put the president on the defensive in the evening newscasts, which in politics, is akin to blowing a tire while demonstrating a new car.

There has been a great rush to suggest a formula for success for Bush, but some things are beyond his control this late in his administration. This week, for example, as he tried to rev up some conservatives out West with fightin' oratory, the latest figures showed unemployment claims rising again. Such negatives, the experts said, are likely to nag him into November.

The Republican locals, as expected, will remain upbeat for public consumption in the hopes that a windfall may somehow rescue the president from his plunge in public affection: a major goof by Clinton, an international situation that will allow Bush to dominate the show as commander-in-chief, a glimmer in the lifeless economy.

The rationale for cutting losses never changes. If one is destined to lose at the top of the ticket, the margin should be close enough to protect other candidates down the line.

In Summit County, for example, Republican Chairman Alex Arshinkoff counts among his can-win races this year the Democrat-held offices of county executive (Tim Davis), clerk of courts (Diana Zaleski), and recorder (Ralph James). The latter jumped up from nowhere on Arshinkoff's charts after James's arrest on a drunken-driving charge.

So in these pre-GOP convention days, Arshinkoff is echoing the party liturgy that Clinton can only spell serious trouble for the taxpayers. Referring to Clinton's proposals for social programs, Arshinkoff says: "You're going to have to raise taxes to pay for them. I'm not sure that Americans want the billions and billions in added taxes to pay for these programs."

Arshinkoff also joined those GOP partisans who question whether Clinton would be ready to handle the complexities of foreign policy as an "on-the-job trainee," and promised more to be said about that as the campaign progresses.

That will be a hard sell to the public worried about what job will be eliminated next back home. Besides, as long as a smiling Saddam Hussein can go swimming in the afternoon while lackeys talk of taking over Kuwait, he will be a prickly reminder that we once had him on the ropes—and let him go.

The foreign policy argument is easily diluted by the fact that few presidents have ever had any foreign policy experience—Ronald Reagan among them, unless you count California as an alien land.

I agree with the University of Akron's Green: Clinton's huge lead is not insurmountable. But Clinton will have to lose in order for Bush to win.

Pondering Significance of Ross Perot

Cleveland Plain Dealer, September 18, 1992

Two questions that are shaping the script of this season's presidential campaign are: (1) Is God a Democrat or a Republican? (My hunch: Independent); (2) Will that really matter if Ross Perot decides to play God in the final month of the campaign?

To some political movers and shakers like Alex Arshinkoff, the Summit County Republican chairman, the first question is inconsequential in spite of the well-documented evidence that a couple of "Pat" moralists—Robertson and Buchanan—are preparing to swallow the GOP apparatus whole by 1996. That's paraphrasing the Reverend Pat.

What he really told his Christian Coalition conference delegates last year was: "We want . . . as soon as possible to see a working majority of the Republican Party in the hands of pro-family Christians by 1996."

Having produced more than half of the delegates to this year's nominating convention in Houston, Robertson and his allies aren't doing too badly in their bid to theocratize a secular political party that once could boast of eagerly embracing Fords as well as Lincolns.

Arshinkoff insists, however, that there remains a clear separation of church and party hereabouts. "There's been a long tradition of strong political parties here—Democrats and Republicans—and a tradition of strong churches that stay busy doing good things in the community and worrying about everybody's souls. Religion is not an issue in this county. In fact, if anybody wants to work, I can use all of the volunteers I can get. There aren't enough."

That leads to the aforementioned second question about the heavenliness, or lack thereof, of Ross Perot. It is on this point that Arshinkoff hears thundering trouble from the skies.

First, however, you should know that political analysts operate much like the laser beams that "read" the numerical values of each musical impulse on a compact disc. In the process, the numbers are assembled and amplified into the Cleveland Orchestra's account of a Beethoven symphony—which is the good news. Or a heavy-metal blast, which, for much of the older population, is the bad news.

President Bush's people, including Arshinkoff, have been assembling numbers from every direction to orchestrate the outcome in November. You shouldn't be surprised to know that, so far, the numbers have produced, as a poet once said, the sound of one hand clapping for the president.

The state polls have shown Bush running at least ten points behind Bill Clinton, and some knowledgeable insiders are concluding that the president is even in deeper arrears among the Buckeye voters. According to one poll, Perot, who is on the ballot, is getting about 7 percent of the vote in Ohio, most of it coming from Bush.

Arshinkoff is even less cheerful about Perot's impact on the Ohio ballot. "If he becomes a candidate," Arshinkoff says, "he'll get 20 percent to 22 percent of the vote in Ohio."

If?

Arshinkoff amends that conjunction to read "When," and adds, in an unhappy voice: "You don't spend $18 million not to run."

His reasoning runs this way: Perot is getting a free ride from answering the hard questions while Bush and Clinton bound around the country fielding unpleasant references to their careers. "If I were a businessman worth $4 billion," Arshinkoff asks, "would I have kept my name on all of the ballots if I weren't running? It's like saying that you're half pregnant."

Indeed, Perot has been tantalizingly vague about his plans for Halloween month. A few days ago, he said he might reenter the race to goad Clinton and Bush into a serious discussion of the deficit. On the other hand, he left open the possibility that he might ask his loyalists to support Clinton if the latter came up with a satisfactory plan to reduce the deficit.

In preparation for a possible do-it day, Arshinkoff says the media and the voters ought to be asking some tough questions about the Texas billionaire, to wit: "What's he doing for a living these days? What foreign companies is he doing business with? Is he prepared to disclose his business transactions?

"Pat Robertson is not our problem," Arshinkoff says. "Ross Perot is our problem. The stability of the two-party system is at stake."

Not to mention the stability of the twelve-year GOP occupancy of the White House.[1]

Partied OUT

Northern Ohio Live, February 1999

When is a political party not a political party? Let's not get all that technical and think about it in the textbook sense that to be competitive, a political party must necessarily operate with (1) lots of money, (2) reasonable agreement among its people about its message to the common folks, (3) a coherent organization that, among other things, guarantees its candidates' names are all spelled right on the mailers, (4) professional staff to run its headquarters, and (5) a forceful and articulate (choose one) chairman, boss, military strategist, or anyone else who can sustain pain and disdain while plotting the demise of the party's enemies.

If you can accept the notion that a political party could be something much less than the living organism defined above—and still win some elections—you are looking at the Summit County Democratic Party, which has become something of a microcosm of the state Democratic organization.

In contrast to the county's Republican team, which functions as a well-disciplined brotherhood of Avis-style, we-try-harder, upwardly mobile underdogs, the Dems in recent decades more nearly fit the definition of the late Governor Michael DiSalle, who once described his fellow Ohio Democrats as a collection of fiefdoms free of any pecking order from the top. (After the November massacre of the Ds on the state ticket, one wonders whether even DiSalle's words were too kind.)

Fiefdoms? Well, Democrats do control Akron city hall, where Mayor Don Plusquellic's huge popularity has yet to wane in a dozen years in the office; Democrats have resided in the congressional seat since 1970, and the current occupant, Tom Sawyer, is safely settled in the job; the county executive, Tim Davis, is a Democrat, although scandals have besieged important people in his office, leaving for the time questions about his own culpability. Look around and you will find Democrats all over the county government, including sheriff, auditor, and treasurer, as well as a clean sweep of the thirteen Akron City Council seats.

So who needs a political party?

Not so fast.

Methodically and undramatically, the Republicans are catching up in a county where Democrats have long held a registration superiority. (After all, Akron voted for McGovern over Nixon.) The decline of the blue-collar tire industry, dissipating the once powerful United Rubber Workers unionists, and the rise of white-collar jobs associated with polymer research at the University of Akron, have changed the landscape considerably. Add to that the twenty-year reign of the politically adept Alex Arshinkoff, the late Ray Bliss's handpicked county GOP chairman who stepped into the job at the age of twenty-four, and the GOP have closed the political gap.

Republicans have moved into the state senate seat that once belonged to Oliver Ocasek and now have a three-one majority in the Ohio House seats that are solely within the county's boundaries. Arshinkoff also has erected a ladder from the Republican-held county prosecutor's office (which the Dems lost in the wake of a scandal nearly twenty years ago) to the judicial system, moving up—by appointment—assistant prosecutors to various vacated court seats. Eight of twelve common pleas judges and five of the eleven municipal judges are now Republicans. Democrats have long looked at the GOP's fundraising ability, particularly with corporate leaders hereabouts, as a source of the Ds eroding strength. Dems gasped when Arshinkoff announced a $1.2 million take at the party's annual finance dinner last summer. But the Republican chairman, who drolly casts himself as "just a poor Macedonian boy who wants to get ahead," will have none of the poor-mouthing talk by Democrats. "If you add up everything that the mayor, the congressman, the county executive, and all the other Democrats raise for their own campaigns, it comes out pretty equally with us. The only difference is that we raise it as a party, they do it individually," says Arshinkoff.

Nor will he concede that the Democrats—unified party or not—are in trouble in the county. "In their worst years since the Great Depression, their election results have always been better than ours. All we have managed to do is strengthen the two-party system in the county, which is what everybody should want. We can be competitive now. Fifteen years ago when we filed candidates, the Democrats laughed. Today, they don't know where we might be competitive." It's also true that of the twenty-seven races on the Summit County ballot in November, the Republicans won thirteen.

Russell Pry, who is in his first year as the Democrats' chairman, insists there is evidence that Democrats, who have regularly bemoaned their separateness, have a new sense of collegiality. "We're starting to see officeholders take more of an interest in the party," Pry says, noting that Akron's mayor contributed $17,000 from his campaign treasury to Democrats running in November. He added that the party raised $150,000 on its own. Still, he adds a note of caution about the rise of a tightly centralized party: "We operate differently from the Republicans, and we always will."

Jim McCarthy, the veteran Democratic county auditor who took no chances in November by spending about $95,000—three times his normal outlay—to hold off his Republican challenger, sees better days ahead. He praises Pry for "bringing strength and ability" to the party.

The mere fact that a county officeholder is applauding the party chairman is newsworthy of itself. Pry's predecessor, labor leader Jim Frost, was regarded among the officeholders as being too attached to union work to be of much value to their political missions. A mission not helped when Frost's predecessor, Nancy Treichler, came to office after the party officeholders' endorsed candidate (Robert Gippin) for a Board of Elections seat—the crucial first step leading to the chairmanship—was rejected by one vote by the precinct committeemen! The image of sour-faced officeholders will be a lasting one with Democratic activists.

By that measure alone, the Dems can honestly lay claim to progress. But they've got a long way to go before they can hold a candle to Arshinkoff's tightly organized GOP.

~

Zero Gravitas

Northern Ohio Live, October 2000

Here I am, no farther than the second paragraph of a book review in the *New York Times*, and the writer is already talking about "voters who are troubled by [George W.] Bush's lack of gravitas." His *what*?

At the risk of not minding my *e pluribus unum*, I would bet you a vintage *Oxford English Dictionary* against a dozen of your finest Latin crossword puzzle reference books that whatever else might trouble the voters in Peoria and Bucyrus today, gravitas is not on the list. Scan all of the New Deals, Square Deals, Fair Deals, New Frontiers, and maybe Manifest Destinies, and, alas, gravitas very likely is not even an asterisked footnote. (Be honest about it: Would you want a gravitas in every pot?)

Yet the pundits on the TV talk shows, when dismally failing in their efforts to find something clever to say about the current presidential campaign, are drenching us with gravitas gush while loftily pondering whether Bush has more or less than Gore.

I'll be honest about it: If you had mentioned it to me six months ago, I would have guessed that gravitas was a shortstop for the Texas Rangers. That purely wild guess was promptly corrected by Dave Hess, an astute former Capitol Hill national correspondent, who was sure it was the New York Yankees. "Or was it the Red Sox?" he offered meekly.

As a former political editor, I confess to regressing to the old boisterous union halls of the United Rubber Workers around Akron for my understanding of what troubles voters. You didn't have a hard time figuring out where the conversation was going if you were in command of a few key words: a "dog" was a hotdog, "suds" was beer, and that "dirty SOB" (with or without gravitas) was the opponent.

It was left to perceptive sidewalk political gurus like the late Francis "Pooch" Maile ("That's Francis spelt wid an i," he firmly cautioned me upon our first meeting) to trash the starch in modern political discourse. As one of the URW's top political operatives, Pooch would have been immediately suspicious of anyone who sprang gravitas on him. "Huh?" I imagine him muttering in his husky voice.

Pooch was quick to size up a situation in simple terms. And nothing was said on a first-name basis. If he did lapse into referring to third parties by name, it often missed the mark, as with somebody he named Butch McGillicuddy—which, I later discovered, wasn't even close. "Hey," he would begin any telephone call, whether at midnight or just before dawn. "It don' look too good for our man. He's sayin' too many dumb things. They're two-blockin' him."

Although I've cleaned up some of this, you should at least know that "two-blocking" to Pooch meant that the opponents were mauling his man by tackling him high and low. No, gravitas won't do.

The bad news for the national pundits is that gravitas—whatever it means—is not doing much to define the presidential race where I come from. When I mentioned it to Russ Pry, the Summit County Democratic chairman, he was unmoved. "I haven't heard that word," he says. "I wouldn't know what it means."

Over at Kent State University, Jack Gargan, a highly respected political science professor, was slightly less dismissive. "My impression is that it is used increasingly in a political context. I'm not aware of seeing it in other contexts. It connotes the notion of seriousness and maturity. It may be a word whose life span passes quickly."

That led me to John Green, the director of the Bliss Institute of Applied Politics at the University of Akron. The trail became warmer.

"I actually got a call from the floor of the Republican National Convention by a national political correspondent, who asked me whether I thought Dick Cheney had gravitas," says Green, who is often called upon to reflect on the political landscape in the national media. "It's really a governing word, not a political word," Green says. "It says, 'Is this guy serious enough, and has he prepared himself enough for the job?' "

But, Green adds, it is more commonly used in measuring a presidential appointment to, say, a cabinet position where the appointee is expected to look and act in the manner that will impress those with whom he must deal in the job. Say, more like Henry Kissinger than Robin Williams, I assume.

I know, I know. That's a lot of fuss over a word that is causing too much fuss among the major media thinkers on Sunday morning talk shows and national columnists. (My guess is that gravitas drew its first breath when George Will mentioned it at a Georgetown soiree. People picked up on it, batted it around their offices the next morning and, when they couldn't find it in their dictionaries, concluded that it was important enough to use to keep impressing their neighbors.)

But we live in that kind of an age when we are able to communicate in meaningless ways to millions of people that sit on this end of the television set. So Al Gore is now "Alpha Al" (Hey, Pooch. Get it?), and an op-ed page headline blares: "Al's got his mojo, but he's not sure how it's working," courtesy of a Maureen Dowd column. I would say that, if Al Gore is hip enough to know what "mojo" means, he's far from being the stiff that some people say he is.

I tried out "mojo" on a Saturday brunch group of a well-read retired businessman, a former theater-TV critic, a lawyer, a college dean, and a political science professor. There was some fumbling around—nobody likes being unhip—but frankly, I was dealing with soggy guesswork, and the conversation drifted off to the Cleveland Indians and why nobody knows how to pitch anymore.

Still, I can't help wondering whether gravitas has anything to do with charisma, which was once the litmus test used by political pundits, even though voters seemed more concerned with health care, Social Security, education, crime, war, and peace. Come to think of it, I never hear anybody talking about charisma anymore.

Think it's gone off to play shortstop for the Seattle Mariners?

Remembering John S. Knight[2]
December 2004

On the evening of October 26, 1977, John Shively Knight entered the ballroom of the Tangier restaurant with an uneasy glance at one of the many tables that had been prepared for the dinner event. "Where are the cards?" he asked in a low hurried voice. "Did you remember the cards for the questions?"

I'm sure he fully expected me to tell him that we had overlooked the cards. "Here," I said, snatching some three-by-five cards that had been partially covered by a napkin. "We didn't forget them."

"Oh," he said with unconvincing approval, as I led him to the dais for an evening that I feared could go either way on the occasion of his eighty-third birthday.

More than two months earlier, as president of the Akron Press Club, I had invited him to be the speaker at the club's first journalism awards dinner. He was not enthusiastic about the idea, suggesting that he had reached an age where he had lost some of the forceful clarity that had characterized his rise to preeminence as an editor and publisher. I had offered him several dates to accommodate his schedule. He would fuss with his calendar and then reject a date for whatever reason. Finally, I mentioned that we simply had to schedule the Press Club dinner no later than October 26.

"But that's my birthday!" he said. Of course, who could forget it? For the next twenty minutes, it was parry and thrust across his desk in his office at the *Akron Beacon Journal.* But he began to warm to the idea as I told him that the event would serve both to launch the awards program and at the same time acknowledge his birthday.

Still, something else was troubling him. "I try not to get involved in programs involving newspaper people," he said. "They don't know how in the hell to do these things and always manage to screw it up." I repeatedly tried to reassure him that this time it would be different. Finally, he looked away, said nothing for a minute or two as he reflected on his decision. He then turned to me and said, "Oh, I'll probably be sorry as hell for this. But okay, I'll do it if you work with me on the speech."

At the time, I was the paper's political writer and had developed a professional relationship with him that frequently produced casual, friendly chats and some disagreements with him on anything that he thought was worth talking about. But none of this prepared me for the following weeks of editing his speech. The first three pages of his draft contained his impatience with fuzzy-headed editorial writers who were incapable of taking firm positions on issues. I told him that while there was no mistaking his own position in the opening section of his speech, it was also true that a relatively new editorial page editor (David Cooper) was at the *Beacon Journal* and perhaps this was not the time nor the occasion to be taking shots across the editorial writers' bows. Somehow I persuaded him to save his disdain for the sorry state of editorial writing for another day. The first three pages of the draft were cut. At last the final draft, a metamorphosis of words, commas, and transposed paragraphs was ready except for one minor point. My wife Nancy read it and noted that Knight had attributed a quotation to the wrong poet. When I warily reported that to him, he whirled around to the library shelf behind his desk, drew out *Bartlett's Familiar Quotations*, and . . .

"Oh, yes . . . she's right," he said, a little embarrassed. "Well, let's change it," he ordered. He sent a note to Nancy thanking her for her vigilance.

So there we were, Nancy and me, sitting next to him on the dais as the program began. He complained that the light was not strong enough, that he wouldn't be able to read his text. I coaxed him to put on his glasses, which he had refused to do, vainly refusing to make a concession to age. He had also warned me that the program could not go beyond 10 P.M.

Okay. And there would have to be more light. Okay. And . . . and . . . and.

They wheeled in a big birthday cake, and he pretended to be surprised by all of the attention ("What's that?" he asked. "Happy birthday, Mr. Knight. You know," I said) in front of an audience of about three hundred. Following the speech that spanned the current state of newspapering, politics, and his other favorite topics, the questions were sent up on the cards. At 10 P.M., I whispered to him that it was time to go, as he had requested. But by now he was happily into the flow. He shrugged me off. "You still have more cards," he said. We went on for another half hour or so.

The evening, I believe, was important in understanding the life of Jack Knight. Revered and respected in his city of Akron as an international media figure, a tower of civic responsibility, and a professional Pulitzer Prize-winning journalist of the first order, he was beginning to reveal the growing insecurity and uncertainty in his own voice that only the aging process could produce.

As one who met with him regularly when he was in town—all at his request; I didn't presume that I could volunteer as a confidant—it became more obvious that he was fearful of the consequences of his passing as they influenced the future of his newspapers. He once read to me a letter from his grandson, John S. Knight III, who feared that, in the hands of his grandfather's successors, the newspaper group would lose its journalistic soul and become solely a bottom-line operation. Jack feared the same. He had hoped that perhaps his grandson would carry on the Knight tradition of exemplary journalism. But that wasn't to be. Young John was murdered during a robbery in Philadelphia, where he was working for the *Philadelphia Daily News*. Insofar as a deeply saddened Jack Knight was concerned, the line of succession, as fragile and perhaps as remotely possible as it was, had come to a tragic end.

Around the office, Knight was a familiar figure to his staff, a subdued contrast to his favorite executive editor, Ben Maidenburg, whose angry voice could be heard across the newsroom when he questioned a breakdown in somebody's judgment. Knight preferred to chat one on one, stopping by a reporter's desk at the end of the day with his paper under his arm. A deeply-rooted Republican, he nevertheless encouraged disagreement within the paper, and it was not unusual to find a signed column by an editorial writer opposing the *Beacon Journal*'s presidential candidate endorsement.

Despite his economic conservatism, he was strongly opposed to the Vietnam war. When George McGovern ran for president in 1972, he visited the *Beacon Journal* and met with several editors. Before the session began, he looked across the table to Knight and thanked him for his financial contribution to his campaign. (It was, of course, based on the senator's opposition to the war, as well as Knight's disdain for Richard Nixon.)

"I should tell you, senator, that my contribution does not commit this paper to endorsing you for president," Knight said.

"Mr. Knight," McGovern replied with a grin. "The way my campaign has been going, I can tell you that I need the money more than the endorsement."

Although Knight was keenly interested in national politics, he was attentive to the city's political scene and had been active in the county Republican Party in his youthful days. He and Ray Bliss, the Akron insurance man who earned the title "Mr. Republican" for his political wizardry as state and national chairman, formed a natural bond in Akron. They were friends, but carefully remained within the bounds of their individual careers in matters involving the welfare of the city. I don't recall ever seeing Bliss in Knight's office, although the parade of politicians, from presidents to councilmen, never ceased on the third floor of the *Beacon Journal.*

Bliss respected a political writer's prerogatives, maintained a courteous low profile, and, much like Knight, gave the highest priority to a disciplined mind. And much like Bliss, Knight repeatedly fretted over the imbalance between elected Democrats and Republicans in Akron. "When," Jack would write to me from Miami, "are we going to do a long piece on the problems in the Republican Party in Akron?" (He even scolded the Republicans in his Press Club speech.) It was not enough for me to point out that the city was a Democratic mother lode that had been created by the predominance of unionized rubber workers over the decades.

Bliss had repeated some of his own concerns about the party to me in a lengthy rambling lunch on August 4, 1981, in which he seemed to want to go over a number of things that troubled him. Among other things, he said he hoped that, as chairman of the University of Akron Board of Trustees, he could work out some internal problems there. He died two days later. On that morning, there was a letter from him in my mailbox that eerily transcended my efforts as metropolitan editor to muster a special group of reporters to cover the life and times of Ray C. Bliss in the few hours to the noon deadline for the big home edition. Courteous as ever, Bliss wrote that he enjoyed the lunch and talked about having another meeting.

In his later years, Knight dutifully voted on election day and then called me with the early turnout in his Eighth Ward Precinct. The *Beacon Journal* was an afternoon paper with several editions. Knight would return to the office to await the first edition and then arrived at my desk with a hurt expression to note that his report on the turnout was not in his paper. I apologized that we were unable to report it for the early edition but would certainly have it in the next one. A small matter, but Jack Knight at that moment was more interested in being a reporter than the fellow who owned a giant group of newspapers.

For all of the minor adjustments along the way for a professional relationship with Jack Knight, I never wavered in my respect for him nor my interest in being fully prepared to hold my footing on any differences of opinion that arose. To his credit, he never said my views were not welcome. Indeed, he encouraged them. But if we were to disagree politically, I had damn well be ready to defend mine. And he did the same. If that is a definition of a great journalist, then Jack Knight, regardless or whether he owned one or a hundred and one newspapers, was a great journalist.

Part V

Afterword

An Age of Giants and the Present Age[1]

The columns and articles reprinted on these pages represent an age that seems lost in ancient history, though no more than a generation past. In politics, particularly, the velocity of change has swept us into a day that has been reshaped by forces that will doubtless make even today's landscape unrecognizable in relatively little time. If anything, these forces are accelerating at such a pace that one can predict their consequences only at the risk of being quite loony. Political crystal balls are now the faux jewels of the purely self-deluding.

Changing times? Begin with television, with its repetitive twenty-four-hour news cycle's ability to elevate and implant even the smallest nonevent in the viewer's consciousness well beyond its significance simply by reproducing it, drip by drip, every thirty minutes. Then, of course, there are the dizzying hordes of real and imagined experts, with carefully crafted misshapen proofs, who have custom-tailored their way into the studio (often for a good price) to duke it out with a subliminal nod and wink to their partisans, fully aware that, with a little luck, their "best" lines may even be salvaged in the next morning's papers. The historical media highlights, in the manner of recording a costly dropped pass in the end zone, will surely memorialize how right-wing columnist Robert Novak, in a fit of scowling anger during a real-time TV verbal scuffle, uttered a naughty word and stalked out of the studio. For that, CNN promptly suspended him.

The point of demarcation between news and entertainment is now indistinguishable as the electronic media (and, unfortunately a greater number of the print media) have all but vanished. Too often, what passes for "news" today is no more than contrived partisan studio debates by the program's regular hired hands that appear to be staged as an absurd hockey match with each side wildly slapping shots at the opponent's net. It is a slightly more laundered version of the show that Jerry Springer has already perfected. The partisan guests loudly suggest that there is nothing of substance that cannot be brawled to the highest level of mindless entertainment, with ample time out for the commercials that pay their salaries. (Whatever else you may say about them, they are carefully fashioned to *entertain*.) In turn, political candidates and their loyalists enlist expensive cosmeticians to remake them into the requisite camera images that will endear them (alas, not always!) to an unsuspecting public. The lesson of a sweaty, heavy-browed Richard Nixon in the day of starkly sinister black-and-white TV in combat against a more telegenic John Kennedy has not been forgotten by the modern political stagecrafters as they prepare their national tickets to convert the whole land into their very own theme parks. At the same time preening photo-ops, those carefully designed nonevents of expense-free exposure to the masses, could be more accurately described as "photo-optical illusions." (Was President Bush really sharing Thanksgiving turkey with the GIs in Iraq? Or, as we later learned, wasn't it an ad hoc prop in a game of "Let's Pretend"?)

The TV trail has placed increasingly enormous burdens on campaign pocketbooks that have made relative wealth a key factor in determining the "more qualified" candidate for the seat. Unfortunately, neither TV's inclination to entertain the viewer (read: Cable News 101), nor the heaps of cash to deliver it to potential voters, has yet demonstrated that either has informed the public very much nor inspired greater numbers to rush to the polls on election day. Indeed, studies have regularly reported that Americans appear to be more misinformed and less interested than ever in national and international issues. As Stephen Hess, a senior fellow at the Brookings Institution and former White House speechwriter, lamented in the *American Journalism Review*: "I don't want it to sound like I think Americans are dumbbells. [But the U.S.] is simply the most apolitical country in the world."

Can we assume that greater dependence on TV—along with the explosive rise of jabbering radio talk shows with their own narrow ideological political agendas—is actually responsible for contributing to the delinquency of the electorate? Or does it reflect a culture in which millions of viewers prefer to sit in thrall in the presence of adolescent "reality" shows—shows that are supposed to startle but instead sickly entertain an increasingly jaded citizenry?

There are, of course, other factors at work: The networks are now the subsidiaries of huge non-news corporations with shrinking priorities for their news operations, which are denigrated as their least profitable programming. At this writing, NBC, CBS, ABC, Fox News, and CNN have eliminated twenty-three foreign bureaus since 1988. In the same *American Journalism Review* report on the decline, John Schidlovsky, director of the Pew International Journalism Program, described the retreat from foreign bureaus as "perhaps the most negative development in journalism in my lifetime."

At the same time, many newspapers, including the *Akron Beacon Journal,* have eliminated their own staff reporters in Washington and shaved statehouse coverage as cost-cutting measures. In the 1970s, the Ohio Statehouse Press Room teemed with highly competitive reporters from the state's daily newspapers. (The least secure among them would quietly pass among the veteran reporters at their typewriters, peering over their shoulders to get some hints on how to approach his own story. We learned to elbow one in his paunch as he passed by.) Journalism was, for us, a privileged experience of long hours and low pay for the daily challenge of seeing one's byline over a story that would annoy a serious competitor who had taken the day off to attend a funeral.

Although *Columbia Journalism Review* reported in the spring of 2004 that there are "2,200 fewer full-time editorial employees at newspapers since 1990," the cutbacks aren't the result of dwindling profits. As the journal further notes, "most newspapers and TV news operations are incredibly profitable." Average profit margins for newspapers rose from 13 percent in 1991 to nearly 20 percent in 2005, a healthy increase which, *CJR* noted in an editorial, was "more than double the average profit margin of the Fortune 500."

Hmmm. . . .

Another troubling aspect of the retreat from serious political reporting turned up in a study by the University of Southern California Annenberg School of Journalism and the University of Wisconsin. It reported that political ads on local TV newscasts outnumbered local election-related stories three to one. In the nation's fifty largest media markets, only 37 percent carried any election stories at all! This isn't entirely an overnight phenomenon. As early as the 1970s, the local nightly TV news literally began to turn over the staff-covered political story to the profitable political ads. I recall one happy-voiced Cleveland anchor opening his show with a headline-grabbing few-seconds-long film of opposing gubernatorial candidates entering unnamed buildings with the voice-over: "The gubernatorial campaign came to Cleveland today."

Oh? If so, no matter. He never returned to the story in the newscast. Locally, as the studies have shown, it has only gotten worse. No headlines, either.

Added to the modern media-politics mix is the growth of extremely well-funded and well-connected single issue groups that demand absolute obedience to their social and religious credos. That became clearer than ever as President George W. Bush rode into a second term with considerable help from evangelicals energizing the anti-same-sex-marriage voters, the latest peak in the so-called cultural wars that towered over other concerns among religious conservatives. Such "values" have had a profound influence on public policies all the way up to (and back from) the Oval Office, where Bush glowingly ascended among the nightly televangelists as—can we say it?—*America's first honest-to-God Christian president.*

In the 1960s, such "wedge" issues as school prayer, abortion, and gender seldom if ever snuck into the political debates. The script of the 1964 Goldwater-Johnson presidential campaign was played out largely on the Cold War (that is, commies everywhere), the hot war in Vietnam, and civil rights at home.

The "Red Scare" hysteria was thrust into the mix during the postwar McCarthy Era, in which some people were led to believe that even President Eisenhower was a communist or at the very least a "comsymp." Such nonsense led to the breeding of numerous "patriotic" groups, the most prominent of which was the John Birch Society (with the help of a lot of retired military wackos). I sustained the full force of the society's apocalyptic motives in an interview with its founder, Robert Welch, on the back porch of a Columbus physician. (Physicians seemed particularly attracted to the radical right's message, probably because of their growing fear that the nation was on the brink of socialized medicine.) Actually, Welch, a New England candymaker, was not that hard to figure out. He was simply trying to build a platform for a presidential candidacy with a constituency of frantic Red-baiters, but fell far short of his impossible dream.

As editor of a small liberal magazine in Columbus from 1963 to 1967, I found myself on many mailing lists of nutty right-wing publications that didn't hesitate to merge communism and civil rights under one subversive heading, with regular smears of Martin Luther King and other black leaders. (Boy, how some of the southern conservative pols came around to be counted in honoring Dr. King upon his death!)

But my biggest nuisance was an Ohio State journalism professor whom one would think would know better. This fellow thought it was clever to highlight his correspondence with my address in red ink spelling out "comrade". I finally put an abrupt stop to it in a letter to him from my lawyer with a formal typed address in very legible ***black***. Finally coming to his senses, the prof rightly decided that his political passions, however sincere, would not protect him in an American court of law.

Never far from the center ring was the nation's economy—or, as the late Ohio governor James Rhodes made a career out of reminding us: *"It's jobs and progress, folks!"*

Ahhhhhh . . . Jim Rhodes. A college dropout from southern Ohio, he was a hybrid of Huey Long, George Babbitt, and the Music Man with a summa cum laude in raw political instincts that one seldom encounters among today's cast of bland characters.

No Ohio politician of the last century was more skillful at evasive humor and an elusive (exasperating!) political style that successfully delivered his audience to the polls for four terms in the governor's office. Despite the high-strung times, Rhodes, a sort-of Republican who was dismissive of political labels as trivial pursuits, was hardly an ideologue. At other times, he roared that if he had to switch to the Democratic Party to guarantee the success of one of his pet projects, that would be fine with him.

In contrast to today's lockstep and largely colorless (not a pun, but it could be) GOP, Rhodes confounded everyone in 1964 by hurriedly removing himself from a Goldwater introduction in Columbus, leaving others to shepherd the senator through his campaign visit. He then crossed up the savvy State Republican chairman Ray Bliss by releasing the Ohio delegation immediately upon his arrival at the national convention in San Francisco to vote its preference (obviously Goldwater), rather than holding out on a subsequent ballot for a more moderate candidate—say, Nelson Rockefeller—and certainly one with a better chance to unseat LBJ. I once asked Rhodes whether he had any regrets about what some member of his own party considered a political double-cross. "What's that? What's that?" Rhodes, the exquisite rope-a-doper, shot back, as he usually did, playing for a few seconds time, when a reporter seemed impertinent to him.

"NAWW!" he barked in a voice that signaled it was time to change the subject.

Over the years, Rhodes acted purely on visceral inclination as a one-man road company, with the Ohio State Fair as the centerpiece of his annual itinerary. His sit-whittle-and-spit brand of self-deprecating humor fully amused the friendly Ohio electorate that shared his "vee-zhun" of how the state should be managed. But more importantly for Rhodes's political survival, the state's developers, bankers, and other high rollers loaded up his campaign treasury with more than thoughts of sugarplums in their head—with the quid pro quo, of course, that in Rhodes's "Wonderful World of Ohio" his financial backers would have a free hand in doing their things. Rhodes was nothing if not a conduit to massive construction contracts across the state that included new universities, highways, and whatever else could lay one brick on top of another without a moment's planning for the operating costs to maintain them.

To the skeptics in his own party, he freely offered advice on how to win over the voters. He once scolded Richard Nixon for raising foreign policy issues in the 1968 presidential campaign. Rhodes insisted that "lunch bucket" issues were all that mattered on election day. As national reporters wandered in from outside of the state and the Ohio delegation hotels at conventions, they finally conceded, albeit with glazed eyes, that with Rhodes, what they saw was all they were ever going to get—*ever!*

Or as the late Bob Hughes, the chain-smoking Cuyahoga County Republican chairman and Rhodes ally, impishly asked me: "Did you see the look on that reporter's face with the way that Rhodesie [sic] answered his question?"

Rhodes (sigh) was not merely an Ohioan. He *was* Ohio—in suit, tie, and culture.

Even in his later years as campaigner, Rhodes moved about the state like a talent scout to add another act for his delighted audiences. After being joined on the stage at Scioto Downs in Columbus by Miss Ohio to announce his candidacy for governor, Rhodes snagged Hughes and airily noted that the beauty queen had gone over well with the crowd. "Give her fifty bucks and have her come to our next stop," he commanded, assuming time, place, and acceptable talent fee for an attractive young woman whose name he couldn't quite remember. Lighting another cigarette, Hughes laughed, "Rhodesie is something else." I didn't hang around to find out whether the $50 changed hands.

Although I had been one of his biggest critics, he always met me with a friendly "Dr. Zaidan" greeting, which I understood to be his attempt at mock-heroic humor. At his eightieth birthday party, a mass gathering of Republicans and Democrats in Columbus in September, 1989, Rhodes shouted to me that he had included me "in the book." He was referring to the commemorative booklet produced by Stan Aronoff, the Republican president of the Ohio Senate, and Vern Riffe, the Democratic speaker of the Ohio House. (Notice the "bipartisanship" of yesteryear.) Rhodes had inscribed my copy of it with a flourish of adjectives:

To Abe,

One of the great newspapermen of this nation . . . True—accurate and reliable. With my Respect.

–Jim

Of course, I didn't believe a word of it. Once again, Rhodes, with more than a hint of sarcasm, was being playful with his words.

Rhodes's enormous one-on-one success through his self-promoted folksiness and back-channel command of heavy campaign contributions—much of it encouraged by his midnight telephone calls to business leaders with guarantees of "no new taxes"—seems a Stone Age away from today's meticulously fashioned candidate *images* striving for picture perfection on the TV news. Rhodes would have puzzled for awhile over the newest entry in the modern political playbook: the Internet. My hunch, however, is that he would have felt a lot more comfortable simply being Jim Rhodes than infusing himself with blogaphilia, an alien technological world that he would not make much effort to understand. For him, naw . . . no need to.

~

That was then. Today, the electronic-at-your-fingertips phenomenon is bringing a cacophony of new voices into our homes and offices from the so-called bloggers operating beyond the traditional parameters of the mainstream media. Some of the information is useful, some is questionable, and even the careful reader can be duped by clever polemicists who create their own sphere of online "journalism." It can be safely assumed that the Internet will increase its influence on the shifting political landscape. Still in its infancy as a political tool, the Internet demonstrated a singular ability to speak to an increasing army of potential voters in the 2003–2004 political campaign, raising millions of dollars to boost the early fortunes of Howard Dean and elevating the clout of such liberal organizations as MoveOn and America Coming Together—all at minimal cost to the candidate and the organization.

So swift has been the success of computerized fundraising that *New York Times* columnist Frank Rich concluded that the "political establishment has been blindsided by the Internet's growing sophistication as a political tool. . . ." Joe Trippi, manager of the Dean campaign, entered his fascination with the net in his book, *The Revolution Will Not Be Televised*, insisting that there will never again be "politics as usual" with the presence of online fundraising, political commentary, and instant communication right in your homes. For Trippi, we should no longer refer to the "Information Age," but rather the "Empowerment Age" that distributes information to anyone who can turn on a computer.

Although John Kerry lost in a contest whose outcome was still being debated long into the new year, no one benefited more from the Internet. His windfall success in fundraising through unaffiliated liberal organizations (MoveOn, ACT, and others), as well as his own, was astonishingly enriched by Internet appeals that nearly matched Bush's bulging treasury.

Suddenly, and unpredictably, the 2000 presidential campaign became ancient history, buried in the more than half-billion dollar signs of 2004. The new operative number was "527," which referred to the McCain-Feingold campaign finance legislation that created the "independent" fundraisers in 2002. It permits "independent" advocacy groups to raise money for whatever their causes so long as they do not advocate a candidate. Publicly, anyway, inasmuch as there are no secrets about the direction their heavily enriched tides are flowing.

What new and greater impact they will have on our political culture in subsequent campaigns, working to our benefit or betraying us, I can't say, although there seems to be no dispute that the continued decline of powerhouse political parties is moving at a quickened pace as the Internet-induced fundraising puts the political contributor on a one-on-one basis with the candidate or a 527. Simply put, says Tim Hagan, former chairman of the Cuyahoga County Democratic Party and gubernatorial candidate, "527s have now replaced political parties."

A postelection study by the Center for Public Integrity dramatically supported the conclusion that a huge gorilla had joined the political circus. The Democratic-oriented 527s raised $229.9 million; the Republican-oriented, $90.1 million. The study also tracked the money spent on broadcast advertising in the so-called "battleground states." Unsurprisingly, the leader was Ohio ($9.7 million). Battleground? Bush's 119,000-vote edge over Kerry in Ohio was formally court-challenged for months before it finally faded into little more than the losers' permanent suspicions.

As a former political writer, I can only add that such work, cradled in the technologies of the day that generate robotic, impersonal responses from the ether, wouldn't be nearly as much fun for me today as it was when the stories were on the streets, in the noisy union halls, and in the smoke-filled rooms, rather than the high-rent district of TV studios, the televangelists' pulpits, the clubby-class's $10,000-a-plate fundraisers, and the frantic digital voices of the Internet today.

At the Democratic national miniconvention in Kansas City in 1974, I happened to look down to the floor from the balcony at the Illinois section one afternoon before the delegates had gathered. Seated alone—*alone!*—was Richard Daley, the powerful Chicago mayor. It seemed to be the opportunity for me to dare to meet the legendary political boss.

As I approached him, he turned to me with a cold stare, obviously noticing my press badge. Da Mare was not particularly fond of the press. Still, I had to meet him.

"Hello, Mayor," I said, as he studied me with the practiced eye of a politician who carefully measured his potentially troublesome visitors. "You don't know me, but. . . ."

"No, I don't," he snapped, fixing his eyes on the badge.

"Well, I merely wanted to tell you that my wife is from Chicago, and, when you were the Cook County Clerk of Courts, you signed our marriage license.

His expression changed quickly to a grin. Springing from his chair, he shook my hand. "I did, did I?" he said, still grinning.

"Yes, sir. You did sign the license."

"That's good to know. Yessiree . . . Thanks for stopping by," he said, adding: "And please tell the missus that the mayor said hello, will ya?"

At that point, the disparity between a seasoned street-hardened Old Pol and a curious journalist vanished. I can't remember a moment that repeated the mayor's instant visceral response—Good Lord. The *missus?*—to someone who might have voted for him. Who could match it today?

As for today, for further evidence of what I can still make out in the blurry marathon of modern politics, read on.

~

One afternoon in 2003 as I was watching a cable network newscast, the program was interrupted by modern TV's version of an apocalyptic early warning system.

So that one would be struck by the gravity of this intrusion, the words "BREAKING NEWS" slashed the screen. A live overhead view recorded the traffic on the freeway below. But let the voice-over explain the drama taking place—live, mind you—to be archived, for heaven's sake, in the viewer's mind forevermore:

"Kobe Bryant is on his way to the courthouse!"

Huh? Here was the very same fellow who was also on his way to becoming an even greater TV celebrity than when he vaulted to professional basketball superstardom as a slick dribbling and slam-dunking Los Angeles Laker. Add the seductive all-season element of an incomparable professional athlete having to respond to a charge of *sexual* misbehavior—and what do you have? Exactly what the cable folks eagerly diagram for their audiences when more substantive news has them nodding off. (A network legal analyst described it as the "public's enduring fascination with trials." To which could be added: "TV's enduring fascination with the things that fascinate the viewers.")

If more than half of America had no idea of whom the animated on-site telecast was *breaking its news,* it was their loss for not getting with The Program these days. The cable was there to force-fill-in your blanks—war or no war in Iraq and other such things. With Kobe Bryant, the news perps were working with considerable experience from the day when O. J. Simpson was tracked from above as his white Ford Bronco cruised down the freeway ahead of a convoy of police cars in a modern reprise of the Keystone Kops.

It was another case of cheap news coverage with high entertainment value: *celebrity athlete*, plus *alleged scandal*, plus *motion* and—sit back and take your mind off the weightier matters in all of our lives. And, many show-biz months later, the criminal case against Bryant was pitched out by District Judge Terry Ruckriegle for the simplest of reasons: the female victim decided she didn't want to testify! For TV-land, it will be remembered as nothing more than another episode of instant gratification against a world of real tragedies.

We are living in an age of pop politics, pop crime, pop Ben-and-Jen celebrity journalism, and even embedded-Geraldo Rivera–pop war as the networks, old-line and now cable, try to hang on to what's left of their fractionalized audiences. Just as great operatic stars "cross over" to record pop music, politicians are increasingly engaged in the kind of antics from *Saturday Night Live* to Leno, Letterman, King, and Imus that they hope will play to their electoral advantage. (I have long regretted that, as a former newspaperman, I must concede that, for pure entertainment value, there's no way that the printed word can compete with the in-your-face possibilities of the tube.)

How else to explain the moral convulsing over Janet Jackson's now-you-see-it, now-you-don't exposed breast at the Super Bowl's halftime extravaganza? The most troubled voyeur of this ancient burlesque-house striptease was the Federal Communications Commission, then headed by Michael Powell, son of then-Secretary of State Colin. With expressively displayed indignation on behalf of Moral America, it showed that it could convulse with the best of them, and concluded that it would serve the twenty CBS-owned affiliated stations right if it fined them $550,000 for unintentionally giving America a nanosecond peek at you-know-what. The media immediately dived in with what some described as a "wardrobe malfunction." Others referred to it as "Nipplegate"—adding the curse of Gatehood to the bulging darkly-honored list since Nixon's plumbers were overly active.

Really, folks. If the nation should fall, will an exposed nipple be the, eh, indiscretion that opened the gates of hell? But in the current era of TV's ludicrous entertainment values, a nipple is obviously a nipple is obviously a nipple for the older networks, even though those who are so inclined won't have any trouble finding them exposed quite regularly in far greater detail on the cable pay channels. (CBS obviously hadn't taken former Attorney General John Ashcroft seriously when he added still one more vignette to the ongoing cultural wars by draping the breasts of a statue at the Justice Department. I can only imagine what he would have done, had he hung around long enough, with the taboo parts pruriently (!) exposed by Michelangelo's mammoth *David* or Manet's fetching *Olympia.*)

Such moments, however, do reflect television's rush to fill in those precious moments with its own version of Sin-fotainment. Celebrity misdeeds, murder trials, sexual naughtiness—all exported to your living room, interspersed with erectile dysfunction ads (some of which are now prominently displayed behind the batter's box at Major League stadiums for the TV viewers who could not be blamed for the metaphorical confusion of hitters swinging Louisville Sluggers).

The *Salt Lake Tribune* was forced to react with an enough-is-enough editorial as the national media invaded the city to report on a local murder case (Lori Hacking, the victim). Referring also to the endless Hearstian national coverage of the murder of Laci Peterson and trial of her husband, Scott, the *Tribune* brilliantly captured TV's debilitating forces at work on the nation's uninformed citizenry as countless media posses galloped into Salt Lake City seeking the surrender of one more tiny gem for their readers and viewers.

The *Salt Lake Tribune* wrote: "A nation full of people who know more about Scott Peterson's defense strategy than they do about Donald Rumsfeld's is not a nation that shows much ability to govern itself." Elizabeth Auster, a senior writer in the *Plain Dealer's* Washington, D.C., bureau, added her own incisive comment to the *Tribune's* editorial. She observed in her Sunday Op-Ed page column: "Cases like Peterson's and Hacking's fit perfectly into a news diet increasingly built on tasty little tapas—gossipy snippets that are easy to digest and cost little in thought. . . . So what if we lose the ability to distinguish what matters from what doesn't. We may not be informed. But at least we'll be titillated."

In the Blue state-Red state days, weeks, and eternity following the November election, as pundits endlessly fussed over the impact of "moral issues" on the outcome, there could be no doubt that TV was taking its cues from the pulpits of the religious right. CBS and NBC crossed the line of timid self-censorship by refusing to accept commercials by the United Church of Christ, which lamented the "exclusion of gay couples and other minority groups by other individuals and organizations." The networks meekly explained that such references were too controversial. CBS preposterously added that it was guided by the fact that Bush was supporting a Constitutional amendment to ban same-sex marriage.

With Bush's support from evangelicals commanding the national dialogue, justified or not in measuring their actual strength, the O'Reillys and Limbaughs didn't hesitate to join the chorus as indignant lay preachers to defend the nation against the terror of prurient interests.

There was, for example, the *pas de deux* of Nicollette Sheridan, of the newly minted (and quite successful) *Desperate Housewives* cast, offering Philadelphia Eagles sensation Terrell Owens an apparent full frontal bare bosom peek in a commercial on *Monday Night Football*. Limbaugh, long under investigation for his own alleged drug-gulping excesses, gasped to his audience that he was "stunned" by the sight, although he sort of contradicted himself by saying he couldn't believe what he saw—or didn't see.

One could easily be critical of the tastelessness of these TV moments, but I would argue that they are no more harmful to the public domain than the skewed priorities of the noisy cable talk shows, the unapologetic cowardice of the major networks—cowed somewhat not only by conservative Christian groups but also by the fear of reprisals from the FCC—and the tiresome repetition of marginal entertainment in the name of news by the celebrity newsmen who spend a lot of their time hoping to part the seas.

The stuff of theatrical excess—rather, extravaganza—was clearly on view in the lingering Terri Schiavo case and the death of Pope John Paul II. In both instances, TV simply couldn't let go of what the *Times'* Frank Rich lamented as the tasteless "culture of death" to construct audiences not only for the networks but also for the politicians who saw opportunities to secure their bases. Rich wrote: "Once the culture of death at its most virulent intersects with politicians in power, it starts to inflict damage on the living."

Broadcasting and Television Magazine expressed its own disdain for the round-the-clock fixation on the tragically stricken woman, noting: "Terri Schiavo's predicament has existed for years but, for the media, the literal life-and-death struggle is impossible to resist. To jaded media-watchers, however, she is just more fodder—easiest to cover by not straying too far from the emotional argument."

At the same time, another pseudojournalistic culture was rising to the surface with revelations that the White House was exploiting other channels of "news" engagement with the public to support its pet policies. Conservative radio talk-show host Armstrong Williams was paid $240,000 (no heavy lifting required!) by the Bush administration to hype the "No Child Left Behind" program to an unsuspecting audience; Jeff Gannon, a phony news reporter operating under an alias, managed to get credentials representing an equally phony news organization to position himself among the White House press corps with friendly administration questions at "news" briefings; the administration spent nearly $100 million on self-serving TV news clips with "reporter" Karen Ryan—broadcast by local television stations as authentic reports that the Government Accounting Office preferred to criticize as "covert propaganda." And never have so many marquee journalists "made" as much news as they reported. Incredibly for a reporter of his rank, Bob Woodward (Watergate chronicler) managed to embed himself in the Bush administration's inner-sanctum for a couple of books that flattered the president. Although he is an editor on the *Washington Post*'s payroll, his bosses said he seldom came into the office while working on the books that included information he had withheld from his own paper. Judith Miller of the *New York Times* was treated by some of her colleagues as a heroine for going to jail to defend the First Amendment, even though much of her information on the buildup to the Iraq war came from a discredited Iraqi exile and proved wrong. None of this improved the image of journalists, although, as the year ended, reporters were far more aggressive toward the administration than during the early days of the war. Even Ari Fleischer, the former Bush press secretary, noted reporters' increasing frustration with the White House. The *New York Times* quoted Fleischer: "It's constantly getting worse. It's accented and compounded now because this administration is more secretive." And that was before Vice President Dick Cheney failed to tell Bush that he accidentally shot a friend at a Texas ranch!

But clearly, the government, historically never satisfied in the way the press reported its warts, is becoming ever more sophisticated in the electronic age in providing its own version of manufactured news.

It might be fair to ask, I suppose, whether public officials are any more culpable in this shell game to influence the public than are the TV news packagers who opt for the entertainment values of another day in the life of Michael Jackson.

~

In the 1970s, Senator John Glenn, a liberal fellow from a small town in Ohio, turned down an opportunity to appear on the popular *Mary Tyler Moore Show* on grounds that it was a Mickey Mouse way to win votes. No matter, the program replaced him with Betty Ford. The space hero had always insisted to me that he had more than enough publicity from his historic orbit and could live happily without further huzzahs. That explained why he refused to approve a floor demonstration in his behalf by the Ohio delegation at the 1976 presidential convention in New York City—cooling the fervor of his supporters to market him as a potential vice presidential running mate with Jimmy Carter. An unassuming gentleman who never bothered to learn the requisite dance steps on any political stage, he succeeded in Ohio but never got very far as a potential presidential candidate. Among other things, the word within the media-political coatrooms was that, even though he had been a daredevil Marine combat pilot who as a test pilot had broken the speed record across America, he was, you know, sort of sincere nice-guy squeaky-clean dull, someone who honestly enjoyed the gift of his favorite cranberry bread (baked by my wife Nancy) I delivered to his Ohio home near Columbus. He also predictably sang "Beautiful Ohio"—off in a corner, largely for his own amusement—as others whooped it up at a wild staff-organized party.

He was an exception. Instead, we have Arnold Schwarzenegger (a guaranteed "10" for celebrity appeal, although the novelty is wearing thin) announcing his candidacy for governor—where?—on the Jay Leno show. Ross Perot declared his presidential intentions on Larry King's program; Senator John Kerry, in the midst of an early in-house political meltdown, rode onto the Leno stage on a borrowed Harley Davidson motorcycle, fully designed (in leather jacket and jeans) to convince the audience that while his craggy appearance has often been compared to Abe Lincoln's, this was one senator who was hip to the most simpleminded tastes of modernity. (He later added to the legend during the campaign by appearing in TV photo-ops as a hunter and a windsurfer, which apparently didn't impress the machos enough to swing them away from a Texas by-God rancher.)

For state-of-the-art chutzpah, who will ever forget President Bush's dashing arrival on the aircraft carrier, a la James Bond, delivering the kind of spirited *Mission Accomplished* film clips that might be converted into campaign gold. As the war raged on through the summer of the presidential campaign, the film remained in discreet storage somewhere. For pure visual spectacle, however, it outclassed any of those hokey old Hollywood versions of Caesar's triumphantly returning Roman legions.

Talk about the rush-to-celebrity tastelessness—it is never far from the script! How about enthralling the viewer, nanosecond by nanosecond, with the Michael Jackson saga? At the moment of his reluctant entrance from the TV wings, the world appeared to stop on its axis. Enough of Iraq and corporate layoffs and Wall Street mischief. The story topped the network TV and hourly radio newscasts, hurtling into the ensuing trial coverage in April 2005 with exclamatory cable reports to America and all-the-ships-at-sea that began—God forgive me for repeating the exact words—"BOMBSHELL RELEVATIONS"—which simply meant that more trial stories were arriving.

Here was the very latest on a terribly troubled pop superstar who was on the minds of countless equally troubled fans. (Names, I learned in some journalism class, make news.)

From the start, CNN again declared our vision of the events on the screen as "BREAKING NEWS" as Jackson was led into official custody for fingerprinting and whatever else with his back to the cameras. MSNBC chose "FLASH NEWS" for the alert to its highway-to-highway coverage of the Jackson motorcade, reporting at intervals the number of minutes separating Jackson from his arrival at the sheriff's office where it would take, we were told, about one hour to process him. And so it went, with more celebrity history in the making. The Jackson extravaganza finally ended on June 13, 2005, much as it began, with extreme coverage. The only exception was the news that he was acquitted on all charges.

All of this nonsense was promoted by well-paid adult professionals in the TV business, mind you. Forgive me for my impatience with the current state of news packaging that must sustain twenty-four hours of empty air space each day with a lot of "Gee-Whiz Split-Screen Limited-Time-Offer" animations. As one who developed an early habit of reporting the news through a clackety Smith-Corona rather than a state-of-the-changing-art computer and digital camera, however, I simply want to alert you to the cranky old-fashioned side of me.

But consider the consequences of the media's herd journalism as we were led into the oil fields and cities of Iraq. Few of those in media power dared to dispute the official White House weapons-of-mass-destruction line. In retrospect, there has been an increasing number of *mea culpas* from such venerable institutions as the *New York Times* and *Washington Post*—fewer from the TV crowd—that they, well, might have done a better job reporting the corresponding truths of our actions so carefully spun by the White House and apparently heavily dependent on outsourced disinformation from exiled Iraqi con man Ahmad Chalabi. Until his eventual outing as the wallet-stuffed (with U.S. dollars) Wizard of Oz with a power-grabbing agenda, Chalabi was a regular visitor on network TV, accorded the courtesies of a VIP insider at the White House, who sat just behind First Lady Laura Bush in the balcony during President Bush's State of the Union speech.

How did he get this far without exposure to his darker side? How, indeed, did we miss the undertow of the biggest story of our generation? Either the national media weren't paying attention or were swept up in the war fever reminiscent of the days of Randolph

Hearst. (Can you imagine what havoc Hearst could have caused in the world with TV monitors and Internet at his fingertips for the sinking of the *Maine*?)

Since 9/11, when patriotism and fear dominated the agenda, the obsequious national media have finally started to examine their own questionable deference to the official administration line.

"Our news culture, and not just TV news, muffed the run-up to a war," complained Frank Rich in his *New York Times* column. Unfortunately, he and others have concluded, the media would not take on a popular president. Some of the lemmings in the media have grudgingly admitted their failures. At the *Washington Post,* where reporters complained that the prewar coverage left much to be desired, Executive Editor Leonard Downie Jr. was quoted by his paper in August as saying that he regretted the imbalance of the coverage. "We were so focused on trying to figure out what the administration was doing that we were not giving the same play to people who said it wouldn't be a good idea to go to war and were questioning the administration's rationale," Downie conceded. "Not enough of those stories were put on the front page. That was a mistake on my part."

Up the road at the *New York Times*—along with the *Post*, one of the two dominant eastern newspapers that often shape the agenda of the politicos and the other media—there were also serious second thoughts about its failure to balance the prewar discussion. In a July 16, 2004 editorial, the *Times* sighed that it had become a part of "groupthink" in devaluing the war's doubters about weapons of mass destruction, adding that the paper "should have been more aggressive in helping our readers understand that there was always a possibility that no large stockpiles existed." The sage *Times* editors might have begun their aggressive reporting by checking the discredited in-house reporting of Judith Miller, who relied on Chalabi for her scoopish death-and-destruction scenario of WMDs in the hands of Saddam Hussein.

Meanwhile, *The New Republic*, an early supporter of the war, conceded in June 2004 that "the central assumption underlying this magazine's strategic rationale for the war now appears to have been wrong." Considering the gravity of the scenario, these were historic concessions by the marquee players in the media.

But the 2004 presidential campaign also reflected a dramatic shift in the voices shaping the public mind. Michael Moore's anti-Bush documentary *Fahrenheit 9/11* set motion picture box-office records for its genre, grossing more than $119 million while drawing the wrath of the administration's supporters. Hollywood added a new version of *The Manchurian Candidate* and left it up to the moviegoer to figure out the contemporary political clone. Several other politically inspired films were making the rounds with less fanfare. It would be a fair guess, however, that the rise of such politically embedded films was having its share of influence in the assault on the electoral process.

Joining the battle for the electorate, the powerful Sinclair Broadcast Group was poised for an unprecedented thrust into broadcasting partisanship. Run by officers friendly to Bush, Sinclair ordered more than forty of its stations to air an anti-Kerry "documentary" ten days before the election. But faced with the loss of advertisers who wanted no part of the public controversy, Sinclair offered a diluted version of the original. Unfortunately, you may expect to see more of this as television falls into the hands of fewer and fewer owners who, like Fox's Rupert Murdoch, have certain political agendas.

At the same time during the 2004 campaign, the publishing houses were releasing a flood of books bearing directly on—for or against—the man in the White House, an impressive number rising to the elite bestsellers list. In 1964, the heated Goldwater challenge to Lyndon Johnson produced no more than a few diatribes. On one Sunday in August alone, the *New York Times* featured reviews of three books about John Kerry. Nor was the political biography—a generously inaccurate genre—absent from publishing. In August, following the release of still another book allegedly about Hillary Clinton by one of her severest critics, the *Washington Spectator* noted that more than seventy books about the senator now reside in the Library of Congress—still somewhat behind the 250 about her famous husband.

Curiously, despite the spread of cable talk-shows as part of the new political culture mix, polls indicated that a surprising number of folks got their updates on the news from Jon Stewart on cable's *The Daily Show*, a comedic recasting of the day's events. Oh? Unimpressed by the "straight" news shows, the Television Critics Association lauded it as the best news and information program of the year. Does anybody doubt that no one among the noncomic news peddlers at the major networks thought *that* was very funny.

Obviously, all of the media are sharing in smaller fractions of their audiences—a far cry from the monopoly of the major networks of yesterday. I should add here my own bias against the glamorous seven-figure TV news princes and princesses who arrive at their offices each day in limos and pretend to know what will play, or not play, in Peoria. This disconnect should be obvious to anyone privy to the insider mentality of the cupbearers on the Georgetown circuit.

But let's be fair about this: TV's fascination with bizarre news priorities—entertainment over substance, the entertainingly trivial over the critically important—has had some admiring copycats in America's newspaper offices. Decades ago, when wrestlers and Ed Sullivan were the celebrities, curiously awed newspaper editors began taking their cues from the TV "news" budget, figuring that if a story was reported on the 11 P.M. local news, it must indeed be worthy of reporting it to the readers in next morning's new columns. (On the other hand, the theory grew that if something *wasn't* on television, it never happened.)

As an irregular night city editor at a the *Columbus Citizen-Journal* in the early 1960s, my night's work was never complete until the managing editor emerged from the publisher's darkened office with a scribbled list of items he had copied from a local TV newscast.

"Do we have this?" he asked urgently, reading from the list. There had been a minor traffic accident with no injuries. But television had done what it does best: film of a creased fender with the drivers outside their cars babbling to police.

No, sir. We didn't (and shouldn't) have had it. But the managing editor, all eyes on the black-and-white screen, prevailed. A paragraph would appear the next morning noting the mishap. It never occurred to the boss that there were probably a dozen or so similar accidents that day that were not recorded in our morning paper simply because the TV cameras had chosen to report only one for its audience.

Such addiction to the TV screen didn't stop there. Years later, at the *Akron Beacon Journal,* the late Paul Poorman, editor of the area's dominant news medium, nevertheless worked to cross-pollinate it with whatever TV station would take his cue. He had visions of daily TV news programs originating "live" from a designated area in the newsroom. There were several trial runs, but, to his dismay, the idea never saw daylight. Later, he and others, including this writer, appeared on a news program originating at Channel 45/49. It, too, met an untimely but well-deserved end. Newspaper people usually make lousy TV personalities.

Poorman had insisted that the TV medium offered a gaping path to vast unseen audiences and presented newspapers (that is, the *Beacon Journal*) with a huge opportunity to reinforce their subscriptions by riding piggyback on the tube. I believe the media consultants call it "synergy," the kind of word that never fails to increase their fees.

Nice try, but it was little more than a hanging chad on how readers judge the hometown paper.

Although I had majored in broadcast journalism in college with youthful dreams of becoming another Edward R. Murrow—my roommate, an obliging art major, had painted the Murrow standard program opener, "This is the news," on the clerestory of our dormitory room—I eventually returned to earth with the reality that I had a horrible broadcast voice and doubtless would have a slightly better shot at becoming Ernest Hemingway. (Young people often dream!) Besides, with TV looming as *the* medium, I knew that I could never bring myself to smile at a camera when there was nothing that really amused me. No matter. In my family, it didn't make a whole lot of difference, because they gave up in despair when I refused to be a doctor or a car salesman.

After college and a couple of inertial years in the Air Force, I worked for newspapers and as a magazine editor in Columbus (where I began the long trail of reporting on the life and times of Jim Rhodes). The lure of Jack Knight drew me to the *Akron Beacon Journal.* I had known of Knight's towering presence in the newspaper field, which had inspired excellence in many of his papers.

On my first day at work, I had arrived with my left hand heavily bandaged from a serious cut suffered during our move into a house in Cuyahoga Falls. Knight's office was in the northwest corner of the city room on the third floor. Each day, he came out to chat with whomever was available about whatever was on his mind. Somehow he managed to see my bandaged hand and casually walked to my desk. "Hi," he said, "I'm Jack Knight. What happened to your hand?" It was my first encounter with the man whose Sunday columns—"Editor's Notebook"—were widely read in his vast newspaper group as well as by presidents and their wannabes at campaign time.

I told him about my accident. He listened intently. "Take care of yourself," he said tersely, and turned away. As I grew to know this self-assured but forever-inquiring figure, it became obvious to me that it was impossible to overestimate his value not only to his own newspapers but also to the equilibrium of the entire industry. It's doubtful that another will come along someday who will equal his serious insights as a working journalist, his compatibility with his staff, his enduring faith in young people, and, of course, the purposeful business acumen that created the Knight newspapers empire.

"As long as I am alive," he once told me, "and as long as my name is on this newspaper, I will never tolerate anything that would in any way embarrass it." He applied the same standards to everyone in the business. Although he had made a fortune with his investments in newspapers, he prided himself more on being a Pulitzer Prize-winning journalist than a businessman.

A moderate Republican who vigorously opposed U.S. involvement in the Vietnam war and who refused to endorse Richard Nixon's reelection because of the Watergate scandal (he annoyed Democrats, too, by declaring his neutrality in the race), Knight would never retreat from bullies on any side, but he always encouraged others to have their say. He also professed a strong sense of humor and decided that I should add some levity to the paper as an offbeat columnist.

However, the greater test for me under Knight and Ben Maidenburg, the paper's combative conservative executive editor, arose when I was named the political writer—a sensitive job handed to a guy who was far more liberal than those in the front office. But, to their credit, neither Knight nor Maidenburg interfered with the content of my Sunday column. Ben would give me the silent scowlish treatment on any morning after my weekend column disrupted his breakfast. But a few hours later we would go to lunch together without a single reference to what I had written.

As for Knight, whether he agreed with me or not, he preferred Socratically to probe my logic—and grammar.

A sample of vintage Knight, the editor: I had written about some meetings at a national political convention and noted that a congressman had spoken to his caucus and that when he was "done" he invited a few delegates to dinner. Impishly, Knight, with his keen eye for subtle meanings, sent the column to me from Miami, where he had settled in for the winter, with the word "done" circled in red.

In the margin, he wrote: "Medium well or rare? "

Knight and Maidenburg, a Knight loyalist to the core, loved to thrash out issues with others on any matter, the outcome of Sunday's pro football games not excluded. A deliberative man, Knight would not agree to a five dollar bet with me on a pro football game until Friday, insisting he wanted to allow as much time as possible to consider the possible outcome of the Sunday matchup. Once he came to my desk to collect on a bet in which his team, which lost, beat the point spread on a Hail Mary touchdown pass as the game ended. I told him a gracious person would pardon the bet under these circumstances. "Young man," he replied in an imperious tone, "why do you think I spend so much time studying these things before I bet with you? Five dollars, please."

Knight and Maidenburg often disagreed with each other on politics. Maidenburg solidly backed Jim Rhodes as governor; Knight had other ideas about the quality of the chief executive in the statehouse. As the political writer, I had a golden opportunity to side with Knight in this instance.

~

In the late 1960s and in the '70s, politics had one foot in the past and one in the future. Local and state politicians still counted on newspapers to carry their messages in news stories and paid ads, but

TV was beckoning with its highly successful pretenses of political realities—from bumper-sticker soundbites to the excesses of attack ads.

There were hints of deeper systemic changes in 1968 when a no-apologies liberal Democrat, John Gilligan, upset Senator Frank Lausche, an old-line conservative who had been around as Cleveland mayor, governor, and senator for an eternity, in the party's primary with a major assist from the Ohio AFL-CIO. But Gilligan, a former congressman from Cincinnati, failed to sustain his momentum in the general election. Having angered George Meany, the hawkish head of the AFL-CIO, with his dovish views on the Vietnam war, Gilligan found himself with tepid labor support in the fall campaign and was defeated by Ohio Republican attorney general William Saxbe. Earlier, Lausche, sulking from his loss, stood in the cold outside a half-constructed building in Cleveland to endorse Rhodes and credit him with another example of bricks-and-mortar leadership.

At the same time, labor lost one of its most powerful advocates, Vice President Hubert H. Humphrey, who was defeated by Richard Nixon in the 1968 presidential race—a campaign in which Humphrey could not fully extricate himself from President Johnson's increasingly unpopular policies in the quagmire of Vietnam. There was upheaval, too, on the Republican side. Nixon saw fit to force out the party's national chairman, Ray Bliss, the brilliant architect of GOP success after the 1964 Goldwater debacle. Nixon, an inscrutably private person in many respects, obviously rationalized that he would be more comfortable with his own man in place, one who could be counted on to march to his orders.

For the hometown political writer, however, it still meant embracing the late Tip O'Neill's judgment that "all politics are local"—from the quiet Saturday night partisan dinners to honor the party worker of the year at a forgettable restaurant, to the raucous gatherings of Democrats (Republicans, it should be noted, were always genteel) to elect a new chairman, choose a delegate to something, or simply to have some well-disguised fun.

Cleveland, for example, was essentially a one-party system made up of various Democratic factions whose loyalties shifted with the days of the calendar. There were the Kucinich Democrats and the George Forbes Democrats and the Irish Democrats and the Slovak Democrats and the West Side-East Side—I could go on. Choosing sides became so confusing that the *Plain Dealer* endorsed two of the three mayoral candidates in the nonpartisan 1977 race and then endorsed Dennis Kucinich, whom the paper disdained in the primary, in the general. Knight was astonished by the flip-flop. But the *Plain Dealer*'s publisher, Tom Vail, a princely socialite who would interrupt an interview to accept a phone call about his tennis plans on Long Island for the getaway weekend, was clearly puffed up by the attention drawn to the paper's endorsement of a thirty-one-year-old populist. He cheerily told me there was really a change of heart at his paper because Kucinich had a firm streetwise understanding of the city's problems which somehow went undetected by the *PD*'s editors in the primary!

Unconvinced, some of the paper's critics downed their evening swigs of beer with the thought that Vail had decided that Kucinich was going to win anyway and wanted to join him in the winner's circle. I happened to be working as an out-of-town reporter in the *Plain Dealer*'s newsroom when Kucinich arrived to claim his victory. Standing next to him was Vail. "Well done," Vail purred. "Well done."

Slight in stature, with a heavy pillow of dark hair crowning his boyish appearance, Kucinich could easily deceive those who underestimated his self-assured determination to run the city according to his combative plans. A bright, tireless pol who worked late into the night to prepare himself for whatever enemy attacks would come in the morning, Kucinich took his message to the steps of major banks, which he saw as an evil presence in the city, successfully fought to retain the city's municipal power system, and, in brief, repeatedly drove his opponents to maddening frustration. His updated version of populism was clearly on display in his recent bid for the Democratic presidential nomination.

You needn't have spent much time on Kucinich's trail those days without recognizing his genius for sizing up his next political opportunity after whatever political setback. It didn't surprise me that he held on to his impossible presidential bid as long as he did because it gave him a platform for his opposition to the war and support of other liberal causes right up to the convention. Don't ever underestimate his energy and intelligence that is inured to political warfare. He will be heard from again.

The succession of changes at city hall that produced such extraordinarily diverse politicians as Carl Stokes, Ralph Perk, Dennis Kucinich, George Voinovich, Michael White, and Jane Campbell have often revived the city's deeply-rooted ethnic, racial, class-conscious divisions that attracted national attention. Reporters from major eastern newspapers popped in and out of town trying to define in modern terms what was not really new in old urban cultures. For me, it meant commuting from Akron to Cleveland each day (and night!) to record the latest combat casualty, whether it arose from the city's financial default, the failed recall of Kucinich, or the latest round of name-calling, which seemed to be the least of the city's problems.

Until Carl Stokes's election as mayor in 1967, Cleveland's political culture was dominated by white ethnic sensibilities. More than one observer noted the "Balkanization" of the city's neighborhoods into Eastern European communities, each with beckoning church bell tower and a foreign language newspaper. The East Side blacks accepted the arrangement and voted for white Democrats. By 1967, the mood offered Stokes, an attractive state legislator, his best opportunity to advance to Cleveland's city hall. Handsome, airily articulate, and apparently capable of wedding East Side and West Side in relative peace, Stokes gained the support of the corporate establishment. In troubled times, Stokes would be their best investment.

It didn't quite work out that way. Subsequent rioting, hostility in the police force, rising tensions on both sides of the Cuyahoga River that physically divided the city merely exacerbated the older social and economic order that had long beset the city. Many of the problems, including a desperate school system and a beleaguered treasury, remain. None of this would surprise Stokes's successors up to the present day.

~

The Democrats' strong bonds with labor formed a powerful political base. The Ohio AFL-CIO, which once reached a membership of one million, deservedly took credit for the election of Jimmy Carter in 1976. With money and manpower and a disciplined get-out-the-vote game plan, the union put Ohio into Carter's column by a hair over President Ford. Still, you began to sense that the Democratic-Big Labor victory celebration was a moment in the third act of an opera with the fat lady ready to make her grand entrance.

Already there was growing discomfort among the troops by the late 1970s. You could find union leaders complaining that their members were drifting away from the solidarity of commitment to such mundane political chores as posting yard signs, driving voters to the polls, and many of the other housekeeping chores that invigorated a campaign. "We got 'em too much," one old-line United Rubber Workers leader once complained to me of the workers ("My f——g guys!") in his union. "They have cars and boats and live in good houses. They forget how they got there, and they vote Republican."

There were still crowds at the Barberton Labor Day parades that drew Vice President Walter Mondale, Senator Howard Metzenbaum, Senator John Glenn, congressmen, judges, councilmen, and their retinues—and even an occasional Republican. Afterward, the paraders showed up at Lake Anna for the customary anticlimactic speeches.

Fast forward: the *Plain Dealer's* report on the AFL-CIO Labor Day Parade in 2003 began this way:

"The labor unions of Northeast Ohio paraded through downtown Cleveland in a show of solidarity yesterday morning, but virtually nobody came out to watch."

Embedded in the crowds twenty-five years earlier were boosters from the United Rubber Workers, United Auto Workers, United Steel Workers, AFL-CIO, and a host of other unions. At the 1976 Democratic Convention, URW President Pete Bommarito held forth wherever there was a reporter and, of course, a TV camera. (By now newspaper reporters were becoming conscious of their subjects scanning over their shoulders for a possible camera.)

The Bomber, as Pete was called, mixed political hyperbole with the showy confidence that his opinion mattered to politicians. And, in fact, it did. They needed his union, his workers, and, of course, union money.

That was especially true in 1976 when all signs pointed to a razor-thin outcome between Carter and Ford in Ohio—a state always considered a bellwether for the national results. The Ohio AFL-CIO set in place a well-planned get-out-the-vote campaign that is generally regarded as the decisive stroke in Carter's behalf. At that, he carried Ohio's 25 electoral votes by merely 11,116 out of the more than 4.1 million cast. It was past ten o'clock the next morning before I could write the final lead on the *Beacon Journal* story that named Carter the winner in Ohio.

In the months leading up to the election, the routine was standard. Check the blowing winds with Bommarito or the late Bob Blakemore, an equally powerful county Democratic chairman who maintained party discipline and loyalty that translated into money and votes. The huge turnouts at the union halls for the rollicking dogs'n'suds gatherings lured candidates from around the state to boost themselves and the party's national ticket. Akron was Democratic country and to ignore it could mean political death by neglect.

The unions also provided colorful characters who would look strangely overdressed (and too tightly fitted at the belt line) in white shirts and ties and would be out of place in today's fashionable political scenery. They were all-in-the-family loyalists who brought home bread for years working on the grimy rubber lines or in the machine shops. Sometimes their language became too descriptive to print—but they had a sense of who they were, what they wanted, and to hell with political correctness. Francis "Pooch" Maile, Bommarito's right-hand political aide, often mispronounced his sources' names—Mispronounced? He wasn't even close, but after awhile you began to associate his names with real people. No matter. Maile had the wisdom of the street corners that enabled him to size up situations, good and bad. If your phone rang at midnight and there was a burst of clipped words that somehow made sense in the absence of certain connective syllables, Maile had something urgent on his mind. You listened and fibbed that he hadn't awakened you from a deep sleep. Not that he cared anyway.

But two things happened that changed the rules (that is, outcomes) of political fortunes. With the decline of the industrial unions, Ohio Democrats found themselves wanting for a cohesive political base. And with the rise of television, and its enormous costs, the old games of street politics, from union hall uprisings, bumper stickers, beer, and other paraphernalia, gave way to the slick salesmanship of TV ads that stretched credibility beyond the farthest recesses of the human mind. In today's slick TV theatre, Pooch Maile would never even have had a cameo role. Indeed, by the 1980s it became clear to me that Tip O'Neill's famous formulation was less and less relevant—"all politics" were no longer "local." TV ads created by anonymous fiction writers, miles from the scene of the crimes and produced elsewhere in equally vague offices that the average voter could never identify, began to set the tempos of campaigns, building up their candidates as TV celebrities as the costs grew exponentially.

The emergence of Ronald Reagan as the poster figure of conservatism shifted the political center of gravity to the right, a trend that was given additional momentum by the decline of Big Labor as a vibrant force in the Democratic camp. Liberalism, which had produced many of the social programs that the electorate insists on keeping to this day, lost its voice, partly through the soaring image of Reagan-style optimism and partly because the Democrats ran for cover without a vision of who they once were and what they intended to become.

But the tide turned in 1992 with President Bush's defeat by a brash Arkansan, Bill Clinton, who paid little heed to Bush's healthy approval ratings after the first Gulf War and moved the center of gravity back to the middle with the help of voters who turned to Ross Perot and shaved Bush's votes.

~

Today, the violent partisan assault on Clinton, with a $60 million special prosecutor's investigation that led to Clinton's impeachment in the House of Representatives, has locked in both sides to an ugly conflict well beyond the normal political differences. Nowhere do I find the former prevailing adage that politics is the art of compromise. Moreover, the rise of powerful influences from evangelical religious quarters—according to a *New York Times* poll, a third of the delegates to the 2004 GOP convention were born-agains or evangelicals—has contributed to no-retreat issues for the Republicans in Congress and the White House. And in their postelection bravura, Bush and the evangelicals didn't hesitate to lay down their own gauntlets. Boasted the president at a news conference:

"Let me put it this way. I earned capital in the campaign—political capital—and now I intend to spend it. It is my style." Still, a few analysts suggested he might deign to work with the Democrats by moderating his views on divisive moral issues.

Hold it right there: Richard Land, president of the Southern Baptist Convention's Ethics and Religious Liberty Commission, had some cautionary words for the president before he tried anything silly in his second term. *Newsday* recorded Land's warning: "As we say in Texas, he's [Bush] going to dance with the one who brung him."

The two-party system—once a debating society with margin for compromise—remains today a system of Hatfields and McCoys, which seems to displease even a few Republicans. Some observers trace the rising incivility as far back as 1978 when Newt Gingrich arrived in Congress and promptly started working on strict lines of demarcation between the two parties. A Republican senator confided to me in dismay that "you can't believe what's happening in Washington nowadays." U.S. Representative Ray La Hood, an Illinois Republican who has worked to reach common ground with the Democrats, was quoted by the *Associated Press* in June 2005 as saying: "It's as bad as I've seen it in my ten years in Congress—terrible." That's a long way from how Congressman Charley Carney, a Youngstown Democrat, once described to me his relationship with Republican Rhodes. "With Rhodes," Carney said triumphantly, drawing upon his own brand of political wisdom, "you could always cut a cake."

Today's cake, a veteran Republican operative explained to me, not entirely enthusiastically, can be described in one word: money. "It's all about money," he said.

Money and intense hatred from both sides of the aisle—a vengeful political combat that has released the grapes of wrath on most political issues and reflects a deeply divided congress by a deeply divided electorate, which gave Bush 51 percent of the vote. In November 2003, pollster Andrew Kohut reported the division was the greatest he had ever turned up in his polling. A year and a half earlier, columnist Paul Krugman wrote: "Many commentators still delude themselves with the comforting notion that all this partisanship is a temporary aberration. Sorry, guys: this is the way it's going to be, for the foreseeable future. Get used to it."

Krugman, an economics professor at Princeton, agreed with those who insist that the widening gap between the haves and have-nots has prompted the ugly partisan warfare. Others have argued that a sharp confrontational turn to the right by Republican leaders, led by Representative Tom DeLay of Texas, has discouraged "moderate" voices in the party from coming forward. The vitriol spilled over in a wave of mean-spirited—even for politics—attacks on Democrats by Senator Zell Miller, a Georgia in-name-only Democrat who abandoned reason and civility as the Republicans' keynote speaker at the 2004 convention, which earned him a job with Murdoch's Fox network. Longtime political columnist Richard Cohen described it as "as mad an eruption of hate as I have witnessed in politics." But no one should be surprised these days. After all, hard-line conservative Grover Norquist, head of Americans for Tax Reform and an influential hand in writing Gingrich's Contract with America in 1994, has been widely quoted on his disdain for political compromise, declaring: "Bipartisanship is another name for date rape."

The party's voice has changed considerably from the days when Akron's Ray Bliss gained a reputation as "Mr. Republican." A soft-spoken, highly successful, nonideological national chairman, Bliss once told me over lunch: "No one will ever know whether I am a liberal or a conservative. It doesn't matter. My job as chairman is to try to get the best Republican candidate, liberal, moderate, or conservative, to run for the job and win." Cautious, courteous, shy, but instinctively politically prescient, Bliss presided over the renaissance of the party that lost in a landslide in 1964 and then rose to Republican presidential victory in 1968.

The modern political dictionary has been expanded to include references to "politics of personal destruction," "politics of personality," and "gravitas." Reporters covering the Gore-Bush campaign dwelled on Bush's "likeability" rather than his qualifications and on what they decided to be Gore's less engaging personality. There's Kerry's elongated face and Bush's smirk. John Edwards was labeled the "Breck girl" (carefully coifed, prominently visible. Get it?). Arnold Schwarzenegger's macho references to the less muscular of the species as "girlie men" was hardly a slip of the tongue in a day of politicized biceps and commercially exploited sexuality. Reporters fussed over what the pols were wearing. What are their wives' coifs? Who are these guys, and what does their body language tell us about their leadership potential?

Oh, for God's sake. Is anybody really listening to what they're saying?

The centerpiece of unadulerated hate stifling honest debate was Dick Cheney's obscene attack—yep, the F-word that describes a physical impossibility—on Senator Patrick Leahy on the U.S. Senate floor, of all the presumably august places.

This would never have pleased Jack Knight (nor Ray Bliss).

Even in his day, you could find Knight complaining that political analysts spent more time on "horse races"—gauging a candidate's personality traits and his or her relative strength or weakness in the polls—than they did examining serious issues.

In the 2004 election's wake, nothing much had changed. The pundits continued to shout at each other for talent fees, and analysts debated whether Bush really had a mandate—not that it had any practical applications. The war grew bloodier. Bush continued to boast that the world was a safer place (except, alas, for the Iraqis whom we were said to have freed); the Democrats argued mightily among themselves whether they should be more like generic liberal Democrats or safe-journey Republicans to win back the White House, at times appearing to discount the fact that about fifty-six million Americans voted for Kerry, more than voted for Reagan). The emboldened religious right swarmed into new areas of conquest in textbooks, classrooms, legislatures, and the arts; and fired CEOs from scandalized Fannie Mae got princely bonuses. It was as though there had never really been a national election.

I've occasionally wondered whether there was really any room left in politics today for the gummy small-town chicken dinners, the union hall orations, and the vote appeals on the courthouse steps for the downtown office workers on blustery autumn afternoons. The late State Senator Oliver Ocasek of Akron, whose unforgivingly precise diction did not tolerate a single unvoiced syllable, once remarked that all politics could be reduced to a single necessity: "F-i-f-t-y-o-n-e-per-cent-of-the-vote." Although Ollie was a wise man with strong credentials as an educator, he would be hard-pressed to make his case today, when presidents are routinely installed in the Oval Office by a minority of the eligible voters.

Whenever I've had a silly notion to return to the playing field, I've had to warn myself that the rules of combat have changed so profoundly that if I were in need of one of their very quotable quotes I would never be able to find an Ollie Ocasek or Pete Bommarito in the extravagance of today's artful political productions. In fact, thumbing through one of my old telephone address books the other day, I didn't have the slightest idea whom I would even call.

Don't get me wrong. I don't regret a single second of tracking the pols for more than three decades. After eighteen-hour days living on stale cheese sandwiches, cold coffee, and taffy-like potato chips while trailing a candidate that we all knew had no chance of winning, I was always sustained by the thought the next day would produce something of more lasting value. And when it didn't, there was always the chance that we could find another way to amuse ourselves.

Actually, it was the personal touches that had nothing to do with the campaigns that often made the best after-hours chatter with my colleagues. There was Senator John Glenn, the astronaut and master of state-of-the-art technology, trying to figure out how a thermostat in a cold hotel room worked.

And Ronald Reagan, as expected, doing his Chicago Cubs broadcast schtick to me when I was trying to learn about his presidential plans.

Or then Governor Jimmy Carter, who I had to accompany to the restroom at a Blossom Music Center concert for a "walking" interview when he was in town with Governor Jack Gilligan.

Or Ray Bliss, a fastidious man, who carefully explained the importance of having the silverware in the proper order.

Or Senator Howard Metzenbaum trying to lead a group of senior citizens in a chorus of "Onward Christian Soldiers" when he didn't know the words. (He looked desperately at me, but I wasn't of much help.)

Or Mayor Dennis Kucinich, on the steps of city hall, "reviewing" every piece of the city's creaking mechanized equipment, with maybe the exception of a power lawn mower or two, that he had ordered to parade past him in response to his critics' complaints that the city was ill-prepared to handle snow removal.

Or Jim Rhodes arriving at a national presidential convention a day late to insist that conventions are for the birds and that to save time and money the delegates ought to mail in their votes.

Et cetera. Et cetera. Et cetera.

For some forty years. Just the thought of them today makes it all worthwhile for me, folks. I hope that will help you understand why somebody decided to reprint a representative selection of the et ceteras in these pages.

Meantime, although I have never considered myself a born pessimist, I have decided to heed *New York Times* columnist Paul Krugman's bleak outlook regarding America's seriocomic political theatre of the absurd:

Get used to it. It will probably only get worse.

Notes

An Age of Giants

1. See John H. Fenton, *Midwest Politics* (New York: Holt, Rinehart, and Winston, 1966); Thomas A. Flinn, "The Outline of Ohio Politics," *Western Politics Quarterly*, 13(3), 702–721, 1960; and "Continuity and Change in Ohio Politics," *Journal of Politics* 24(3), 521–544, 1962; Alexander P. Lamis and Mary Anne Sharkey, eds. in *Ohio Politics.* (Kent, OH: Kent State University Press, 1994).

Part I

1. Ralph Locher was mayor of Cleveland, 1962–1967.

2. The John Birch Society is a conservative group founded in 1958 and known for its staunch opposition to communism.

3. *The Reporter* was a national bimonthly public issues magazine, now out of print.

4. Curtis LeMay served as head of the Strategic Air Command (SAC) from 1948 to 1957. He later served as the vice presidential running mate of George Wallace on the 1968 American Independent Party ticket.

5. John J. Gilligan was elected to the U.S. House of Representative from the Cincinnati area in 1964 and was defeated for election in 1966 by Robert Taft Jr. He won the 1968 Democratic nomination for the U.S. Senate, but lost the general election to

Republican William Saxbe. He was then elected governor of Ohio in 1970 but was defeated by James Rhodes in 1974.

6. This essay is a satire that reflects the bitter confrontation that occurred at the Democratic National Convention in 1968 and compares the activities of Chicago Major Richard Daley to the tactics used in the Vietnam War.

7. Alabama Governor George Wallace ran for president in 1968 for the American Independent Party. One of the more successful third party candidates in American history, he drew almost 12 percent of the Ohio vote.

Part II

1. See "Aura of Invincibility Dies" in Section I.

2. Abe Zaidan was part of the team of reporters that assembled this story.

3. Abe Zaidan was part of the team of reporters that assembled this story.

4. Howard Metzenbaum defeated Robert Taft in 1976.

Part III

1. Proposition Thirteen, which rolled back property taxes in California, ignited a nationwide "tax revolt" in 1978.

Part IV

1. Ross Perot ultimately finished third in Ohio with some 21 percent of the vote.

2. This essay was written for this collection.

Part V

1. This concluding essay was written in 2005.

Index